AN INTRODUCTION TO
THIRD WORLD THEOLOGIES

The greatest change which has come about in Christian theology over the last generation has been the explosion of contextual theologies in different parts of the world. This book provides the first overview of the main trends and contributions to Christian thought from Third World theologies. It sets out the common context of these theologies in their experience of colonialism and Western missions, and suggests that they have forged new ways of doing theology which are quite distinct from the theological traditions of the Western world. With key contributions from experts in their fields on Latin America, India, East Asia, West and East Africa, Southern Africa and the Caribbean, this book situates Christian thought in the cultural and socio-political contexts of their respective regions, and demonstrates how Third World theologies are providing different perspectives on what it means to be a Christian in today's global world.

JOHN PARRATT is Professor of Third World Theologies at the University of Birmingham. He has taught and researched widely in Africa, India and the Pacific. His books include *Papuan Belief and Ritual* (1976), *Reinventing Christianity: African Theology Today* (1995), *A Reader in African Christian Theology* (1987, revised and expanded, 1997), *A Guide to Doing Theology* (1996) and *The Pleasing of the Gods, Meitei Lai Haraoba* (with S. Arambam Parratt, 1997).

AN INTRODUCTION TO THIRD WORLD THEOLOGIES

EDITED BY

JOHN PARRATT

University of Birmingham

PUBLISHED BY THE PRESS SYNDICATE OF THE UNIVERSITY OF CAMBRIDGE
The Pitt Building, Trumpington Street, Cambridge, United Kingdom

CAMBRIDGE UNIVERSITY PRESS
The Edinburgh Building, Cambridge, CB2 2RU, UK
40 West 20th Street, New York, NY 10011–4211, USA
477 Williamstown Road, Port Melbourne, VIC 3207, Australia
Ruiz de Alarcón 13, 28014 Madrid, Spain
Dock House, The Waterfront, Cape Town 8001, South Africa

http://www.cambridge.org

First published 2004

Printed in the United Kingdom at the University Press, Cambridge

Typeface Adobe Garamond 11/12.5 pt.   *System* LATEX 2ε   [TB]

A catalogue record for this book is available from the British Library

Library of Congress cataloguing in publication data
An introduction to Third World theologies / edited by John Parratt.
p.   cm.
Includes bibliographical references and index.
ISBN 0 521 79335 1 (hardback) – ISBN 0 521 79739 X (paperback)
1. Theology, Doctrinal – Developing countries.   I. Parratt, John.
BT30.D44A5   2004   230′.09172′4 – dc22   2003068836

ISBN 0 521 79335 1 hardback
ISBN 0 521 79739 X paperback

Contents

v

Contributors

JOSE MIGUEZ BONINO, former President of the Ecumenical Association of Third World Theologians, is Emeritus Professor of Systematic Theology and Ethics at the Facultad Evangelica de Teologia ISEDET in Buenos Aires, Argentina. Among his many books are *Doing Theology in a Revolutionary Age*, *Towards a Christian Political Ethics* and *Faces of Latin American Protestantism*.

KIRSTEEN KIM obtained her doctorate from the University of Birmingham, where she is currently an honorary lecturer and Tutor in Mission Studies at the United College of the Resurrection. She taught for several years at Union Biblical Seminary, Pune, and has also worked in Korea and the USA. She has authored numerous papers on Indian theology and missiology. Her most recent publication is *Mission in The Spirit: The Holy Spirit in Indian Christian Theologies*.

GEORGE MULRAIN is from Trinidad and is currently Connexional President of the Methodist Church in the Caribbean and the Americas (MCCA). He has been Lecturer in Missiology at the Selly Oak Colleges, Birmingham, and Senior Tutor at the United Theological College of the West Indies. He has worked and travelled extensively throughout the Caribbean region.

JOHN PARRATT is Professor of Third World Theologies at the University of Birmingham. He has taught and researched extensively in Africa, India and the Pacific. His publications include *Reinventing Christianity: African Theology Today* (1995) and *A Reader in African Christian Theology* (rev. edn 1997).

ISABEL APAWO PHIRI studied at the Universities of Malawi, Lancaster and Cape Town. She is currently Professor of African Theology at the University of Natal, Director of the Centre for Constructive Theology and Continental Coordinator of the Circle of African Women

Theologians. Her publications include *Women, Presbyterianism, and Patriarchy* (1997) and (as joint editor) *Her-Story: the Histories of Women of Faith in Africa* (2002).

DIANE STINTON is a Canadian, and completed her doctorate at the University of Edinburgh. She has been involved in theological education in Kenya since 1984 and is currently Senior Lecturer and Chair of Theological Research at Daystar University, Nairobi. Her book *Jesus of Africa: Contemporary Christology* is shortly to be published by Orbis.

EDMOND TANG is lecturer and Head of the Centre for East Asian Christianity at the University of Birmingham. He is China consultant for the British and Irish Churches, and has been editor of the *China Study Journal* since 1990. He is co-editor of *The Catholic Church in Modern China* (Maryknoll 1982) and author of numerous articles on Christianity in China and in Asia generally.

Introduction

John Parratt

The greatest single change that has come upon the Christian faith during the last century has been the demographic shift in its focus away from its traditional centres in Europe and North America. There it has been in deep decline for three centuries, and today professing Christians probably number no more than 15 per cent or so of the population. By contrast the growth of Christianity in the 'South' or 'Third World' has, within the last hundred years or so, witnessed a phenomenal growth. In the Pacific, Christianity is the religion of the large bulk of the population, while in sub-Saharan Africa reasonable estimates would indicate that more than 60 per cent would claim to be Christian. Even in the vast continent of Asia, where overall Christians would not number more than three per cent of the total population, there are concentrated areas of Christian presence. The Philippines is largely Christian while Korea has a substantial and influential Christian minority. In India the ancient heartland of the Syrian tradition, Kerala, is perhaps a quarter Christian, while in the northern states of Mizoram, Nagaland and Meghalaya, Christianity dominates. In Latin America, beginning from the fifteenth century when the cross of the Catholic priests accompanied the swords of the conquistadores, Christianity has overlaid the religion of the large proportion of the indigenous population. To all this must be added the resurgence of Christianity (along with other world religions) after the decline of communism in the former Eastern Europe and also in China. While simple data never tell the whole story, it is evident that Christianity can no longer be regarded as a 'Western' religion; it is a global one of which the Western church is only a small fraction.

Some evidence of the increasing importance of non-Western Christianity could be seen in the 1960s in the growing participation of Third World Christian leaders in world forums. At the Edinburgh Missionary conference of 1910 there were only three delegates born outside the Western world;

when its successor, the WCC, met in Delhi in 1961, the Third World presence comprised a substantial minority. In the same decade the impact of Third World bishops on the Second Vatican Council indicated the beginnings of a similar shift within the Roman Catholic Church. The ecclesiastical hegemony of the West can now no longer be taken for granted. If the demographic patterns of the past hundred years continue, Christianity will become only a residual faith of Caucasian peoples, while becoming the primary religious force in the southern continents, and a significant factor to be reckoned with in Asia.

Seen in the light of this radical 'moving of the centre' of the Christian faith it is remarkable that so little attention has been paid to the phenomenon of 'Third World theologies' in the theological discourse of Europe and North America. The irruption of the Theology of Liberation in Latin America did, it is true, create the beginnings of interest. Liberation Theology, however, presented less of a problem for it was initially conducted within the parameters of the Western intellectual tradition. But this did not prevent its being shunted out of mainstream theological discourse and confined to the ghetto of dangerously activist political theologies. Voices from elsewhere in the world, when granted a hearing at all, could be dismissed as exotics irrelevant to the 'real' task of theology.[1] In some ways the presence of Christianity in the 'South' itself represents a return to its geographical focus in the days before the rise of European christendom. Whatever the historical worth of the traditions that Mark founded the church in Egypt, or that Matthew visited India, there is no doubt that there was a Christian presence in these continents from very early times, and that Nestorian Christians had reached China before the capture of Jerusalem by the Muslims. In one sense, therefore, the growth of Christianity in Africa and Asia is simply its return to its orginal heartlands. The much larger scale of the Christian presence was, of course, due to what has been called 'the missionary movement from the West'. Beginning in earnest with the great voyages of discovery from around 1500, the expansion of the church to South America, Asia and Africa usually followed the European colonial enterprise. This association of the cross with sword and gun has left a continuing legacy which is yet to be completely overcome.

All theology is ultimately 'contextual', that is it arises from a specific historical context and it addresses that context. The questions which it

---

[1] It is perhaps significant that two of the widely acclaimed and widely used (and very bulky) theological 'readers', contain less than half-a-dozen contributions from contemporary Third World theologians between them: see A. McGrath (ed.), *The Christian Theology Reader*, 2nd edn (London 2001), and C. Gunton et al. (ed.), *The Practice of Theology* (London 2001). The latter categorises all things non-Western, along with feminist theology (!) as 'local theologies'.

asks, and the answers it seeks to give, are determined by its specific historical situation. This situation may be no more than the intellectual tradition out of which it arises, and it may seek for no more than intellectual explanation. On the other hand, few theologians in the past have been able, or indeed wanted, to abstract themselves completely from the events going on around them, and these events, especially the more dramatic ones, have shaped both the questions they have asked and the theological answers they have put forward. Augustine's *City of God* would never have been written without the sack of Rome by the Goths in 410, nor would Karl Barth's *Epistle to the Romans*, had the First World War not taken place. To understand the rise of Third World theologies we also need to take serious notice of the circumstances, historical, political and social, in which they arise.

THE COLONIAL LEGACY

However much countries of the Third World may differ, there are a number of important characteristics which they broadly share. The foremost of these is what might be called the *colonial legacy*. If we exclude Japan (which, while in no sense part of the Third World economically, certainly has some minorities which are so marginalised as to make them 'a third world within a first world') only two countries have escaped colonial occupation of all or part of their territories.[2] It is a remarkable fact that for a period a handful of European nations could dominate and control the destinies of most of the world's populations. That period was indeed mercifully a brief one. The colonisation of Latin America by the Spaniards and Portuguese gave way to independence movements by the colonial conquerors from their European homelands, though in the process created a foreign ruling elite which made the conditions of the indigenous people no better. In Africa the colonial period lasted only about a century, in some countries of Asia somewhat longer. But the effect of imperialism was out of all proportion to its length. As Peter Worseley has written:

Europe had accomplished a transformation which created the world as a social system. It was a world order founded on conquest and maintained by force. The 'new' order was no egalitarian 'family of nations': it was essentially asymmetrical. At the one pole stood industrialised Europe, at the other the disinherited. Paradoxically the world had been divided in the process of its unification, divided into separated spheres of influence, and divided into rich and poor. (Worseley 1978: 14)

---

[2] Even these two exceptions are more apparent than real. In Africa, Liberia, though never colonised (it was an enclave set up for freed slaves), has for periods of its history been to all intents and purposes under American tutelage; in Asia, Thailand, while retaining a semblance of independence, suffered brutal occupation by the Japanese in the Second World War.

Colonialism was thus a total system: it deprived the colonised of their own political structures, subjected their economies to the needs of the West, and destroyed large areas of cultural and social life. Though an external force of quite brief duration, it has shaped internal dynamics up until the present time. Though it has now run its course, its legacy is one that former colonised peoples still have to live with, and which determines to one degree or another the problems they face today. The carving up of the world between European powers (especially in the scramble for Africa) by drawing arbitrary borders, divided peoples against themselves by putting them into different new colonies. It imposed upon them new European languages and devalued their indigenous ones. Above all, however, the colonial era put into place an economic and political system which still dominates much of the world. The deleterious effects of this economic system were multiform, but determined very largely by the way in which resources could be used to enrich the colonial powers. The countries of the Third World became in effect vast plantation estates or sources of cheap raw materials. Conversely they were also seen as a markets for goods from the imperial countries. The effects of such policies were disastrous for the local economies. Little attempt was made to create a well-rounded economy, and a culture of dependence was set in place which stunted growth for long after independence had been achieved. To quote Worseley again: 'The most serious legacy of colonialism is in the economic sphere, in the form of backwardness, monocultural economies, foreign ownership of major resources, uneconomic "dwarf states", poverty, and an extremely low economic base' (Worseley 1978: 235). This is the more ironic when it is recalled that the larger percentage of the world's mineral resources and agricultural potential lies not in the rich Western world but in Asia, Africa and Latin America.

The factors which Worseley has identified remain important determinants of the Third World context today. They have been exacerbated by the problem of foreign debt created by the eagerness of Western banks to lend to Third World countries – to lend, at varying rates of interest, the surplus monies that became available after the oil boom of the 1980s. 'Development' proved a chimera for many countries, for many reasons. The incompetence of international 'experts' and the corruption of elite national politicians were probably the most debilitating. The situation of the former colonial world even today gives little ground for optimism. According to World Bank figures the gap between the richest 20 per cent of the population of the world and the poorest has more than doubled in the last thirty years. Eighty-five per cent of the world's income is consumed by the richest 20 per cent, and at the other end of the scale the poorest 20 per cent consume less than 1.5 per cent of its wealth. At the beginning of the twenty-first century some 40 per cent of the population of Asia and 50 per cent of sub-Saharan Africa are living in poverty, and some 37,000 children are dying each day of preventable or of poverty related diseases. Such conditions are exacerbated by low provision for health and education, by ecological spoliation, civil unrest and unstable governments. In such circumstances the question for Christian theology (as Gutierrez once put it) becomes one of how it is possible to speak of God to a world which is scarcely human. Before daring to speak about God at all it will have to analyse and reflect upon the social and political situation in which men and women exist.

ANTHROPOLOGICAL POVERTY

But there was also a second form of exploitation, no less damaging than the economic, which has concerned Third World theologians, and which they have termed *anthropological poverty*. What is being identified here is the denigration of integrity, humanness and culture. Perhaps the most obvious way this was done was the imposition of an alien language upon colonised peoples. As Ngugi wa Thiongo has eloquently pointed out, language speaks of personal and cultural identity (Ngugi 1993). Allied to this went the denigration of aspects of culture, and in particular of indigenous religions. If economic and political disruption resulted from Western imperialism, the demonisation of indigenous cultures was more likely to be the result of European Christian missions. This happened most dramatically with 'traditional' or folk cultures, from which the majority of Christian converts came. Popular Hindu 'idolatry' or African 'fetishism' became frequent themes, especially of Christian missionaries eager to gain support from their Western churches. In the process of description these forms of religiosity were demonised by the use of emotive and pejorative terminology. Little attempt was made to understand the kind of spirituality which gave rise to these religious forms. While colonial administrators were on the whole less likely to be concerned with value judgements on traditional religion, Christian missions usually pursued a policy of seeking to wipe the slate clean of 'paganism' so that the true faith could be written afresh on the mind of the native – a theory of 'displacement'. Bénézet Bujo has well captured this attitude when he describes how the Superiors of the Catholic Mission in the then Belgian Congo petitioned the government to take action against those elements of culture which it considered to be against good public order (by which they presumably meant their understanding of Christianity). These included offerings to spirits and ancestors, rites of passage – especially those surrounding birth, circumcision and female puberty, and marriage – and rituals for success in hunting and fishing (Bujo 1992: 44). Other elements of African religion were effectively secularised and thus trivialised: masks, which represented the deep sacrality of the presence of the ancestors, found their way into European museums, dances originally associated with rituals became mere tourist attractions. Deeply held religious beliefs were also dismissed as superstition, and little attempt was made to analyse the rationale behind the concepts of evil and causality. Even the most experienced of missionaries often quite misunderstood the belief systems of those to whom they sought to minister. There were indeed some remarkable exceptions, like the Belgian priest Placide Tempels, who as far back as 1945 published his analysis of Bantu thought forms in which he argued that they constituted a logical and coherent system (Tempels 1959). Parrinder's *African Traditional Religion* appeared in 1954, and soon African Christian theologians like Harry Sawyerr, Christian Baeta and E. Bolaji Idowu were rediscovering the real values of their religious traditions and seeking to bring them into dialogue with their Christian faith. The emergence of an African Christian theology had begun. But we are anticipating.

In those lands which had a long tradition of writing, with scriptures and learning which went back long before the Christian era, a casual dismissal of indigenous cultures by European missionaries was scarcely possible. While village Hinduism could be rejected contemptuously as simple idolatry, this was hardly possible with erudite and scholarly religious texts. Consequently a different tradition grew up, beginning with the translations of the Chinese classics by Catholic priests at the end of the fifteenth century, and continuing through the remarkable achievements of Carey and his followers in India. The textual study of non-Christian faiths came to the fore, not indeed for the missionaries as an end in itself, but as a means of demonstrating the supremacy of Christianity over ancient Asian faiths. A theory of 'fulfilment' took hold, which argued that all religions are fulfilled and superseded in Christianity. These earlier forays into how one deals with the impact of the Christian faith upon other religious cultures – however inadequate the replacement or fulfilment theories may have been – underline an ever present issue in doing Third World theology: that its context is a multi-religious one.

In those areas where Christianity has been to a large extent successful in overcoming traditional religiosities – in South America, sub-Saharan Africa, the Pacific, and tribal Asia – it has by no means eradicated them.

The underlying traditional worldview has remained as a sub-stratum which has to be taken very seriously, and a main task of Christian theology today has become one of struggling to give meaning to the ancient tradition within the new. In most parts of Asia, religious plurality raises a different problem, namely of how to exist as a Christian in a context which is determined by Muslim, Hindu, Buddhist or other religious or ideological values, and how to relate Christian theology meaningfully to a total culture which has no Christian (or indeed post-Christian) heritage. This is a context of doing theology which is unknown to the West. Despite the rapid secularisation of the Western world, and the more recent emergence of movements which claim to draw upon 'primal' pre-Christian survivals, Western theologians can by and large assume they have a thousand years of Christian civilisation (in one sense or another) behind them. Third World Christians in their own contexts have no such tradition on which to draw, and indeed may even find this tradition limiting rather than positive.

A NEW APPROACH TO CHRISTIAN THEOLOGY

What can we say about this newer – or better, resurrected – Christianity? Despite its modern origins from the missions of the mainstream Western churches, and in some areas its conservative tendencies, it primarily seeks to define itself in contradistinction to the churches and theology of the West. Bujo's assertion that African theology is a reaction to not being taken seriously by the Western church (1992: 49) is perhaps typical. In Africa this reaction may be seen in its most colourful form in the so-called African Independent Churches (more recently termed 'African Initiated Churches'), which have their own leaders and prophets, rituals (often quite elaborate) and theologies (usually unwritten) which seek some kind of modus vivendi with traditional cultures. Mainstream churches, that is, churches deriving from the work of Western missions, too have sometimes experimented with indigenous cultural forms. In terms of theology, it is probably true that a good deal of non-Western Christianity has still fairly uncritically absorbed without too much heart-searching traditional positions of the West (especially the more conservative ones). But a progressive trend in Third World theologies, that of questioning the form, content and categories of Western Christianity, has an impressive pedigree, which in India stretches back to the beginning of the era of Protestant missions in the sub-continent. Consequently, if we are to look for what is new in Third World theology, we would have to say it is a dynamic search for self-identity, an identity which takes seriously the traditions and cultures

in which it is located, but at the same time seeks to address the social world
in which Christians now live. What this in effect implies is that Third
World theologies have rejected the theological agendas which are set by the
West. The agenda must come from the context in which Christians live;
since Christians outside of Europe and North America must live their faith
in different historical, political, socio-economic and religious contexts, the
kinds of questions they are asking will be substantially different from those
in the Western tradition. As Desmond Tutu has remarked, Western theology has some splendid answers, but they are answers to questions that no
one elsewhere is asking! While no theology can help being in one way or
another contextual, making *explicit* the centrality of contextual issues does
represent a departure from the current Western mainstream, as does the
deliberate use of the social sciences to evaluate that context. Whereas the
Western tradition has generally proceeded (at least until fairly recently) by
marrying theology to philosophy, Third World theologians have preferred
a marriage with the social sciences. A further methodological question is
the point at which the theologian begins – should theology start with its
traditional sources (Bible, church tradition and so on), or by analysing
the context with the help of sociological tools? Most Third World theologians have preferred the latter starting point. Context has therefore become
primary for the theological task.

In 1972 the Theological Education Fund of the WCC launched its mandate *Ministry in Context* for which it coined the cumbrous term *contextualisation*. Contextualisation was understood as a critical assessment of the
peculiarity of the Third World contexts in which Christian theology has to
be worked out. While it did not ignore what it called *indigenisation*, that is
the response of the Gospel to traditional cultures, contextualisation went
beyond this. It sought to take into account 'the process of secularity, technology, and the struggle for human justice, which characterises the *historical
moment* of nations in the Third World' (TEF 1972: 19). The Taiwanese theologian largely responsible for this initiative, Shoki Coe, later elaborated
on this position (Coe 1980: 48ff.). Indigenisation, he believed, was a static
metaphor which was in danger of being past-oriented. Contextualisation,
on the other hand, 'seeks to press beyond for a more dynamic concept
which is also open to change and future oriented'. Thus 'the particular
historical moment, assessing the particularity of the context in the light of
the mission of the church' is the important factor. This could only be done
by involvement and participation, it 'involved not words but actions'. True
contextualisation is therefore in his view always prophetic. 'Arising out of
a genuine encounter between God's Word and His world (it) moves out

toward the purpose of challenging and changing the situation through rootedness in and commitment to a given historical situation.' Theology as a praxis which emerges from a response to a specific historical situation is a theme which also characterised the emergent Theology of Liberation around about the same period. A possible objection to contextualised theology, Coe agreed, is that it could become a 'chameleon theology', changing its colour according to its context. However he argued that it is precisely by taking the concrete situation seriously that contextual theology becomes truly catholic. For Coe, true catholicity is not the same thing as what he calls 'colourless uniformity', but rather a manifold and diverse theology which responds to a different context, just as 'the Incarnate Word did on our behalf, once and for all'. The theological ground for contextuality is therefore the fact that the Son of God was incarnated within a specific human history and culture, through which grace has been made available to all.

Other writers have preferred different terminology. On the African continent 'indigenisation' was quickly replaced by terms such as *adaptionism* (or *adaptationism*) which implied the use of African thought forms in Christian theology and of African rituals in the liturgy. *Incarnationism* later found more favour with Catholics, while some missiologists coined the term *translation*. While these terms have been sharply defined by some writers, Third World theologians tend to use them with a fluidity which defies rigid definition. Ironically all are terms which derive from European languages and are to some extent Western, and therefore alien, categories. The coining of categories of theological methodology from non-Western languages is as yet fairly undeveloped, but will need to develop if Third World theologians are fully to break out of First World parameters of doing theology.

A NEW THEOLOGICAL EPISTEMOLOGY

The context is both the framework and part of the source material for doing theology. Theology however also implies a way of looking at the world, bringing to the task something of one's own historical and cultural experience. As Franz Rosenzweig once remarked, 'We all see reality through our own eyes, but it would be foolish to think we can pluck out our eyes in order to see straight.' If creating theology is in part a matter of perspective it should not be surprising if Third World perspectives often differ drastically from those of the West. The primary factors which have helped shape what might be called a Third World epistemology have already been discussed – the impact of colonialism and Western missions and the situation of religious plurality. Much Third World theology has taken the form of reaction against Western Christianity. To escape from the 'colonisation of the mind' self-definition and affirmation of identity is necessary over against the colonising other. It is perhaps significant to note in this respect that a number of the prominent members of movements for political independence both in sub-Saharan Africa and in India were Christian. The question for theology also became one of 'how should our theology be different?' This took different forms indeed, but the assumption was always the same, namely that the kind of Christian thinking which had been inherited from Western missions was altogether inappropriate for the needs of the non-Western world. As far back as the beginning of the twentieth century the Bengali Christian and political activist Bhavani Charan Banerji (better known by the name he later assumed, Brahmabandhav Upadhyaya 'friend of God') was protesting that the very foreignness of Christianity kept Indians from embracing it. 'It is the foreign clothes of the Catholic faith,' he wrote, 'that have prevented our countrymen from perceiving its universal nature . . . When the Catholic Church in India will be dressed in Hindu garments, then will our countrymen perceive that she elevates man to the Universal Kingdom of truth by stooping down to adapt herself to her racial peculiarities' (quoted in Boyd 1975: 83). His solution to this problem was to replace the Graeco-Roman categories in which the Gospel had been handed down by those of Hindu philosophy, on the grounds that just as Greek thought was a vehicle for the truths of the Gospel in Europe so 'the truths of the Hindu philosopher must be "baptised" and used as stepping stones to the catholic faith' (Boyd 1975: 64). Banerji believed that the validity of the religious experience of Hinduism could not be denied. But he was inclined to regard this as 'culture' rather than a religion in opposition to Christ. Thus it was possible for him to be a 'Hindu Catholic' since 'by birth we are Hindus and shall remain Hindus till death'. Conversion to Christ therefore does not deny personal identity or tradition, and conversely that (Hindu) tradition provides the religious categories, the 'field', within which Christian faith is understood. Banerji stands within a tradition of Indian thinkers who straddle the boundaries between Hinduism and Christianity. He thus typifies what has become a distinctively Asian contribution to Third World theologies, that of rethinking Christian faith within the parameters of religious pluralism.

Indian thinking about the meaning of Christ was already nearly a hundred years old by the time the Latin Americans dropped the second bombshell of the twentieth century on the playground of the theologians. For the Theology of Liberation, as it came to be called, self-definition was put in terms of Marxist dialectic, of the rich and the poor, the oppressors and the oppressed. The reason, as Assmann put it, that 'the time had come to stop importing ready-made theologies from Europe and the United States and to start working out (our) own', was primarily because such foreign theological imports did not speak to the real situation in South America. That situation was one of structural injustice which had brought about the grinding poverty and oppression. Theology was therefore an 'option for the poor', and the church's mission had to be defined in terms of social revolution, for the struggle for a just society was itself part of saving history. While European theology might agonise over Bonhoeffer's question of how theology could speak to a world come of age, for Latin America theology's question was (in Gutierrez's words) 'how are we to tell people who are scarcely human that God is love and that God's love makes us one family'. The people of God's especial care here are not so much the church but the oppressed.

It would be tempting to make a generalisation and argue that each of the three continents which have produced the most written theology in the Third World has contributed its own unique perspective: Latin America, the emphasis on liberation in the socio-political and economic dimension, Africa, the integrity of indigenous cultures and religions, and Asia, the need to do theology in a religiously plural context. In very broad terms this is probably true, and the development of EATWOT (the Ecumenical Association of Third World Theologians) to some extent bears this out. It is evident from the EATWOT's development that while the Latin Americans began by seeking to export their liberation insights, almost as a solution to all the world's problems, contact with African and Asian theologies soon caused them to acknowledge the importance of the dimensions of culture and religious plurality. While emphases differ from continent to continent, and from theologian to theologian, it would be true to say that liberation is now being redefined to take in culture and religious pluralism alongside social and political analysis.

It could perhaps be argued that what brings much of the Third World together is a sense of pain, what (as Edmond Tang points out) the Koreans would call *han*, a sort of righteous indignation at the wrongs perpetrated upon their world. What brings the Third World together as Christian theologians is, I suggest, something more than this. It is the sense that God also shares in that *han*, that God, as the Bengali poet Tagore beautifully has it, is a God whose 'robe is covered with dust',[3] who somehow shares in the marginalisation of non-people, and in the pain of the oppressed: but further, a God who is active in doing something about it in the process of human liberation.

This volume is intended as an introduction for readers (with or without formal theological training in the Western sense) who are approaching Third World theologies for the first time. The term 'Third World' is not used here, of course in any pejorative sense. Probably deriving originally from the 'third estate' in revolutionary France, that is the people, as opposed to the power blocks of the nobility and the church, the term 'Third World' was espoused as a self-definition by the non-aligned nations at Bandung in 1965 in order to set themselves apart from the power blocks of the democracies of the West and communist Eastern block. Its use today of the non-Western underdeveloped world has become a useful shorthand to designate those countries which suffer severe economic, social and political problems caused in one degree or another by their historical colonisation by Western colonial powers. The term is admittedly inexact in that it includes countries which are desperately poor even by the standards of the Third World itself, as well as others, especially on the Pacific rim, which now compete very favourably with Western industrialised nations. Nevertheless it remains a useful designation. It is one which theologians from these countries have also embraced in the Ecumenical Association of Third World theologians which has increasingly become a focus for non-Western theological thought.

But, as Mulrain points out, to be part of the Third World is not to be third rate in theology. Consequently the contributors have sought, within the limited parameters of their chapters, to show what is different in Christian thought in their regions, and what is genuinely innovative. They have also suggested how these insights might be relevant for the wider task of doing theology world-wide. In this respect we hope that this introductory volume may make a modest contribution to 'south to south' dialogue, and that it may help in awakening (where appropriate) colleagues in the West from their dogmatic slumbers and geographical insularity! This volume is not

[3] It was not a Western theologian but a Japanese, who in the aftermath of the Second World War and Hiroshima, first argued that the essence of theology is the 'pain of God' (Kitamori 1965). The quotation from Rabindranth Tagore is from his *Gitanjali*.

meant as an exercise in historical theology. While it has been necessary in most of the chapters to adopt some kind of historical framework, the guiding principle has been that of contextuality, that is the rooting of theological thought firmly in those issues, whether socio-political, cultural or religious, which have shaped the way theology has developed in each geographical context. At the same time most contributors have sought to give some space to aspects of theological expression such as Christian art and worship, but above all oral and popular theology, which are more generally neglected in Western writing.

Of course it has not been possible to be comprehensive, either within the individual chapters or the book as a whole. Regionally we have focused on those areas where Christian believers have been most numerous (South America, Africa, the Caribbean) and those countries in Asia where, despite being a minority, Christian thinkers have most vigorously pursued innovative agendas and have had a substantial impact upon society as a whole (India, China, Japan, Korea). This obviously ignores huge geographical areas, some of which will certainly have great influence upon Christianity in the twenty-first century. In terms of sheer numbers the most important of these is the Pacific. Since the arrival of the first missionaries in Tahiti in 1797, the islands of Oceania were christianised with spectacular success. While oral theology (in the sense used by Stinton and Mulrain) flourishes, this has not as yet been matched by a similar written output. In the ongoing task of exploring creative theologies for Oceania the insights gained from African theology, which emerged from a similar background of traditional primal religions, will no doubt be important. By contrast, the largely Christian Philippines, from its location on the Pacific rim, has produced significant work, both Protestant and Catholic (Tano 1981).

Neither have we been able to deal with the interaction with the Buddhist world. An earlier collection (England 1981)[4] indicated that political as well as inter-religious issues were already on the agenda in some Buddhist dominated countries. However it is in Sri Lanka where the Christian–Buddhist dialogue is most developed, especially in the work of Roman Catholic theologians like Aloysius Pieris and Tissa Balasuriya. The former's *Toward an Asian Theology of Liberation* was perhaps the earliest to argue that Asian poverty is not simply economic, but that the social and the religio-cultural realities are closely interwoven. For Pieris the poor are the proper subjects of theology, and the 'Third World' is a synonym for God's people. He

[4] For other useful surveys on Asian theology generally see F. J. Balasundaram, *Contemporary Asian Theology* (Bangalore 1998); S. Batumalai, *An Introduction to Asian Theology* (New Delhi 1998); and R. S. Sugirtharajah, *Asian Faces of Jesus* (London 1993).

understands the great Eastern religious traditions also to have a message of liberation and therefore sees them as collaborators with, rather than rivals of, Christianity. Balasuriya's most influential book *The Eucharist and Human Liberation* argues that the real meaning of the eucharist is in taking the option for the poor against the dominant, both within the church and outside it, and in building a more just and egalitarian society.

In most parts of south-east Asia, however, Christians come less from the mainstream populations than from the great 'tribal belt' stretching from north-east India through Burma, Thailand and Laos. Writing from these areas (partly due no doubt to political constraints) has been relatively small.

Writing from within the Muslim countries in the Third World has also been sparse, and is unlikely to see much development in an era marked by the appearance of a more aggressive strain of that faith. Exceptional is Indonesia, the most populous Muslim state in the world, which has produced its fair share of Christian thinkers. Marianne Katoppo's contribution is especially significant. Her short book, *Compassionate and Free* (1979), ranks as a seminal contribution to the development of women's theology in the Third World. It movingly explores the dilemma of Asian women, while at the same time exposing the positive feminist imagery in early Christian sources.[5]

Ironically it was in what is now the Muslim Middle East where the most significant 'alternative tradition' to the hellenistic way of doing theology, which has been dominant in the Western world for so long, had its roots. The Syriac tradition, whose most able exponent was the fourth-century monastic Ephrem, poses a direct challenge to a theological method which in the West has for so long regarded itself as normative. As Sebastian Brock points out, 'Ephrem provides a refreshing counterbalance to an excessively cerebral tradition of conducting theological inquiry, while for Asian and African Christians Ephrem is the one great Church Father and theologian whose writings will be readily accessible' (Brock 1992: 15). Ephrem's tradition is alive and well among minority Christians in the Middle East and south India, and persists both in Orthodox and popular theology in Ethiopia. In other theologies emanating from the Third World, Ephrem's approach has been echoed, if seldom directly referred to. The irruption of Christian theology in the Third World during the last half century or so may perhaps best be understood not as taking a completely new direction,

---

[5] For a useful collection of Asian feminist theology see Virginia Fabella and Sun Ai Lee Park, *We Dare to Dream* (Maryknoll 1989); also, more generally, J. S. Pobee (ed.), *Culture, Women, and Theology* (Delhi 1994); R. R. Ruether, *Women Healing Earth* (Maryknoll 1996); and U. King, *Feminist Theology from the Third World* (London 1994).

but as the re-emergence of the ancient tradition of Syriac counter-theology. This sets aside the hellenistic theology of dominance, and its obsession with philosophical definitions and systems, and of Jesus as *logos*; rather it finds its expression in orality, poetry and symbol, and its basis in social and spiritual poverty, and in the human Jesus who is one with us.[6]

REFERENCES AND FURTHER READING

Balasuriya, T. 1977. *The Eucharist and Human Liberation*. Colombo
Boyd, R. 1975. *An Introduction to Indian Christian Theology*. New Delhi (rev. edn)
Brock, S. 1992. *The Luminous Eye: The Spiritual World Vision of Saint Ephrem*. Kalamazoo
Bujo, B. 1992. *African Theology in its Social Context*. Maryknoll
Coe, S. 1980. 'Contextualisation as the Way Toward Reform' in Elwood, J. (ed.) *Asian Christian Theology: Emerging Themes*. Maryknoll
England, J. 1981. *Living Theology in Asia*. London
Katoppo, M. 1979. *Compassionate and Free*. Geneva
Kitamori, K. E. T. 1965. *The Theology of the Pain of God*. Richmond (original Japanese edn 1946)
Ngugi wa Thiongo. 1993. *Moving the Centre: The Struggle for Cultural Freedom*. London
Pieris, A. 1988. *Toward an Asian Theology of Liberation*. Maryknoll and Edinburgh
Tano, R. 1981. *Theology in the Philippines Setting*. Quezon City
Taylor, D. G. K. 2000. 'Christian Regional Diversity' in P. F. Esler, *The Early Christian World*. London
Tempels, P. 1959. *Bantu Philosophy*. Paris (orig. French edn 1945)
Theological Education Fund (WCC) 1972. *Ministry in Context: The Third Mandate Programme of the Theological Education Fund, 1970–77*. TEF, London
Worseley, P. 1978. *The Third World*. London

[6] As David Taylor puts it in his discussion of the Syriac tradition: 'It is time Christians world-wide acknowledge that whilst European Christianity represents one theologically rich offshoot of the early church, it does not have the monopoly of interpretation of the divine self-revelation. In time of great change we may have much to learn from other branches of Christianity that have successfully preserved and taught their faith through long centuries and to diverse cultures' (Taylor 2000: 342–3).

2

Latin America

Jose Miguez Bonino

To characterise Latin America – or any other area of the world – as 'Third World' is to relate it to the history of its incorporation into the 'First World' area of influence. This process has had different times, conditions and characteristics. For Latin America, it starts at the end of the fifteenth century from Spain and Portugal and takes the form of the appropriation of the land and the subjection of the indigenous populations of the south of what is now called North America, some of the Caribbean islands and the totality of Central and South America. In order to understand the 'theologies' that have developed in these lands we would need to take into account the conditions – religious, cultural, social, economic, political – of these lands before the 'appropriation', the corresponding characteristics of the 'appropriator', and of the process of 'appropriation' and then follow the developments that have brought us to the present. Although it is quite evident that this is not possible within the limits of this chapter, we need at least to enumerate some of these factors. In order to try to design this sort of *vademecum* I suggest we distinguish four periods: (1) invasion, control and colonisation (1492–1808); (2) emancipation and nation building (1808–1960); (3) the crisis of the development project (1961–72); and (4) 'the national security doctrine' and the conditions of globalisation (1973 onwards). The characterisations I have used try to be descriptive but, as any others that could be used, they do carry a certain interpretation which should be one of the areas of study and discussion when we try to interpret the theological understandings developed in the Latin American 'Third World'.

INVASION, CONTROL AND COLONISATION (1492–1808)

Latin America was invaded – 'discovered' was the way the invaders interpreted their experience – and controlled, in a process that took little more than fifty years to cover almost the totality of the land and the inhabitants.

The invasion led to appropriation and 'colonisation', that is, the various forms used for trying to organise the political, social, economic and cultural–religious life of both the colonisers and the colonised people.

Spain had, at the time of the 'discovery' under the 'Catholic Kings', just completed the full possession of its own territory by expelling (in 1492) both the last remnants of the Muslim occupation that had lasted almost seven hundred years, and the Jewish community which had developed in Spain a cultural, industrial and commercial treasure which, to a large extent, they had to leave behind in their forced pilgrimage to other European countries. The 'discovery' of the 'new world', which Columbus thinking he had traversed the globe moving west baptised as 'Indies' (and therefore their inhabitants as 'Indians'), completed the glory of Spain – the country 'where the sun never sets'. But it also gave reality to the dream of having reached the land of the Golden Fleece (the gold, silver and all kinds of wealth of which, in fact, they began to take possession, although not as easily as they had thought). This sense of being God's special country, the bastion and bulwark of a triumphant Christendom, was confirmed by the relation to the Pope, who gave the Spanish Crown the right of the 'Royal *Patronato*', the rights of the State to name incumbents of ecclesiastical posts.

How does one combine this last 'glorious Crusade' of Spain's divine mission, the quest for glory – the military enterprise – and the thirst for gold? Hernán Cortés, one of the early and most famous 'conquistadores', puts it in three brief paragraphs (as quoted by Ginés de Sepúlveda in his *Crónica Indiana*):

Many times I have played in my thoughts with such difficulties [the war with the Aztec people] and I must confess that sometimes I felt quite restless in my thoughts. But, looking at it from other angles, there are many things that give me courage and satisfaction. In the first place, the dignity and holiness of our cause, because we fight for the cause of Christ when we fight against idol worshippers who, as such, are enemies of Christ since they worship demons instead of the God of kindness and omnipotence, and we wage war both to punish those who persist in their idolatry and to open to those who have accepted the authority of Christians and of our King . . . But other thoughts come also to my mind: that is, the benefits that we can obtain if we come out victorious, because there are many other reasons for fighting these wars . . . There are some who fight for land and things, others for power and glory . . . And many times find satisfaction for their ambitions when, having defeated their enemies, they control the lands and the cities . . . But it is not only one of these causes but all of them at the same time that move and constrain us to continue this war.

Some questions arise: is this combination of causes possible? Can the conqueror evangelise? We begin by asking: who are this people baptised as 'Indians'? We should properly speak in the plural. While it is possible to speak of 'one race' – an immigration from Asia to the Alaska Peninsula, as the most accepted theory would indicate – it is not possible to speak of one 'Indian' population, because there are numerous self-contained, independent and even totally non-communicated indigenous histories. These histories, moreover, are at very different stages of development, and consequently the result of the encounter with the Spanish conquest is highly diverse.

For the sake of clarity I will speak of only four different types among the ten to fifteen million indigenous people (there is no full agreement about the numbers) that populated America at the time of the discovery:

(1) Primitive groups in different places and varying mainly according to environment: Patagonia, Chaco, Brazil, California, etc.: hunters, fishermen, gatherers, some nomadic, others sedentary (for long periods), with different languages and practically no tribal organisation. In religious terms, most of them had the idea of a 'Highest God' (or, in Patagonia 'The Most Ancient') who had no relation to nature, except for myths of creation, but whose religion had mainly to do with demons and spirits of nature and few ceremonies related to the life cycle. These groups had no relations with the whites until the second half of the seventeenth century. Many of them were pushed out of their usual territories or exterminated.

(2) Agricultural groups, the first to be met by Spanish *conquistadores* around the Caribbean Sea (Venezuela, Colombia, part of Central America, Florida, the Amazonia). These sedentary groups, who cultivated corn, beans, potato, cotton, tobacco and built dams and irrigation systems, were organised into tribes and clans with names of animals or plants considered as totems, had a pantheon which included, besides the Supreme Being, the solar god, the earth goddess, civilising heroes (founders of groups and givers of instruments), warrior gods, spirits and demons. The priests represented among these peoples a very important role because of their relation to agriculture and social organisation. Most of these groups were conquered and subjugated. They were mostly used as the basis for rural work in the systems of servitude – *encomienda* and *repartimiento*.[1]

---

[1] Lit. 'commission' and distribution': the granting to colonists a distribution and control of land and of Indians to work for them.

(3) Groups of intermediate culture, a more complex political organisation, with aristocracy and slaves, state and dynastic tendencies, industries like tapestry and pottery, as the chibchas in Andean Colombia. These cultures, which represented the superimposition of an aristocratic tendency on an agricultural situation, are reflected in the religious life in which the Supreme Being is more directly related to the worship of the Sun and the civilising heroes to which the dynasty traces their ancestry. In some cases there are human sacrifices and priesthood as a class which mediates for agriculture and exercises authority.

(4) Finally, we have the more developed civilisations represented by the Aztec in Mexico, the Incas in Peru and the Maya in Yucatán which, besides the political and religious characteristics of the previous group, had developed a complex hierarchical imperial system, an advanced cultural and production organisation and a military force which had conquered other groups and incorporated them to the empires. It is particularly the relation of the Spanish conquest to these last two categories which constitutes the most important root of the colonial social, economic and religious system.

In the encounter between the two societies and civilisations, the Spanish and the indigenous, there were, as Cortéz had realised, two distinguishable tasks: conquest and evangelisation. For him the quest for glory, wealth and evangelisation are amalgamated in one. The 'Indians' had to be defeated, controlled and dominated in order to be evangelised. Their demonic idols and cults had to be eradicated. We can call this the 'rigorist' conception of evangelisation. But not all the Catholic missionaries (mostly from the religious orders in the beginning) who came with the conquerors shared this view. Some Franciscans, like Toribio de Benavente (Motolinia) or Sahagun, while they were convinced that the Indian religion had to be replaced by the Christian faith, tried to dig into the indigenous culture, understand it and find a way to evangelise 'from within' it. Others, particularly from the Dominican order, took on directly the defence of the indigenous people against the genocide that the invaders were committing. 'I am a voice in the wilderness', Montesinos would preach from the pulpit in Hispaniola, 'you [the conquistadores and colonisers] are in mortal sin . . . for the cruelty and tyranny you use in dealing with this innocent people . . . by what right or justice do you keep these Indians in such cruel and horrible servitude? . . . are these not men? . . . Have they not rational souls, are you not bound to love them as you love yourselves?'

Another Dominican, Bartolomé de Las Casas, missionary and 'encomendero' at the same time, was converted by Montesinos' preaching, and his own experience as 'encomendero' and has become the symbol of 'the other way of evangelising'. He attacks the system in two directions. On the one hand, condemning domination – particularly as reflected in the slavery of the 'encomienda' or the 'repartimiento' – and on the other defending 'the only method of attracting men to the true faith'. The language of his book about *The Destruction of the Indies* is violent and, perhaps, even demagogic. But the central arguments were clear and effective. The Spaniards had committed a threefold crime: (1) they had invaded a foreign land and established a 'tyranny' (the very term Spaniards used to refer to the Moslem conquest of Spain), and therefore their possession is illegitimate; (2) they had established a servitude, as 'slavery', and this is 'unjust'; (3) through these violations of a people's land and human freedom they had betrayed Spain's missionary vocation as a Christian country. This last argument leads to the second level of discussion, developed in *Del Unico Modo de Atraer a Todos los Pueblos a la Verdadera Religion* (1537): (1) the 'Indians' are human beings and, as such, they have all the same inalienable rights; (2) besides, they are rational beings and consequently they can be led to faith by the use of reason; thus, (3) evangelisation cannot be advanced by domination but only through conviction: and finally, (4) 'the teacher has to present himself as an example of what he says, so that he teaches more through his works than through his own words'. Unfortunately, as we know, this was not the direction taken by the Spanish State and Church in the following centuries. The power of 'the secular priests' more directly under the control of the Crown (over against the relative freedom of the 'orders') and of the Inquisition which established itself powerfully from Mexico and Peru over all the continent from the second half of the sixteenth century, smothered all attempts to soften the theological and institutional rigidity of the system. On the other hand, the very interesting attempt of the Jesuits to create a new model of evangelisation through the development of relatively independent but very disciplined communities (a much debated question among historians) was cancelled out in the second half of the eighteenth century by their expulsion from Spain, Portugal and the American colonies in 1767.

Thus, a second question appears: can a colonial Church generate a truly contextual Christianity? The answer to this question continues to be a debated issue. Was Latin American Christianity merely a transplant of the Spanish Catholicism of the time? Or a genuinely Latin American Christianity that had 'synthesised' the local cultures and religions and the Christian faith of Spain? Or was it simply the co-existence of a formal

Catholicism under which the indigenous religions remained as they were? We cannot enter here into an analysis of the complex debate that continues (and can easily be followed in the readings included in the bibliography). But perhaps a brief reference to a particular case can help to flesh out the issue.

As I write these lines, Pope John Paul II is in Mexico performing the canonisation of Juan Diego. The story runs like this: on the morning of 9 December 1531, a poor Indian boy heard, as he was passing along a low hill called Tepeyac, a song, a voice that called him:

Juanito, littlest of my sons . . . know the Mother of the true God in whom we live . . . I greatly desire that a temple be built me here, that in it I may manifest and give to all my love . . . go to the palace of the bishop of Mexico and tell him that I have sent you . . . that here on this spot a temple be erected to me . . .

The rest of the story is well known. The incumbent bishop, Juan de Zumar-raga, a committed defender of the rights of the indigenous people, doubted and dismissed Juan Diego. The vision continued to appear, the message went back three times to the bishop, the last with a sign, and finally the temple was built and has played a central role in Mexican faith and history. But, as important as the fact in itself is the discussion that has grown since the very beginning. Was it true? Is Juan Diego a real historical person or simply a construction? Is it by coincidence that the place of the temple may have been an old sanctuary of the indigenous religion? Is this a symbol of a Latin American legitimate incorporation of the Christian faith or was it another case of a 'syncretism' in which the Christian faith is simply 'used' to legitimate the 'pagan' religion? Is the canonisation of Juan Diego an affirmation of the dignity of the indigenous people? Or is it the use of popular feeling for the strengthening of the Roman Catholic faith? The debate will go on and shows the complexity of the historical process of the incorporation of a new people, a new society, new traditions, new ways of understanding and honouring the *mysterium tremendum et fascinosum* in the encounter of peoples, cultures, religions.

EMANCIPATION AND NATION BUILDING (1808–1960)

It has been said that Latin America entered, after the conquest, 'a colonial sleep' that lasted for more than two centuries. This is only partly true: there were latent contradictions that would explode early in the nineteenth century, first as the struggles for independence (roughly 1808–50) and then

as the conflict between 'conservative' and 'modernising' elites to define
the 'kind of nations' that should emerge with independence (1850–1945)
and the kind of 'globalisation' that would follow the Second World War
(1945–60).

The process of independence results from two sets of factors. On the one
hand, the decline of the Iberian empire: the weaknesses of the Borbonic
monarchy, the defeat in the war with Britain, and the Napoleonic conquest
which followed, the increasing power of the British colonial and economic
empire beginning in the eighteenth century, and the consolidation of the
USA, still in process. On the other hand, in Latin America itself a new
economic and social situation had appeared: the economic expansion had
created regional markets and small local industries. A new 'criollo' (Latin
Americans born from Iberian parents) class appeared which looked for
standards of living and an exercise of power commensurate with their new
importance. The obstacle was Spanish monopoly. The situation was ready
for an 'ideology' of opposition to Spain: liberalism provided it – criticism of
the slowness and inefficiency of the Spanish administration and the control
of thought exercised through the Inquisition. The Napoleonic occupation
of Spain provided the opportunity for the emancipation movements. The
circumstances varied from area to area but by 1850 practically all the Latin
American countries had reached emancipation.

Emancipation, however, produced internal conflicts which we must take
into account if we intend to understand the religious situation. During the
first half of the century, the social sector in power was politically 'conservative', controlled by the 'traditional families' for which emancipation
meant appropriating the control hitherto exercised by the Spanish Crown.
Economically, they continued a trade of primary products; culturally, a
pre-Enlightenment worldview; and religiously, the exclusive rights of the
Roman Catholic Church and the transfer of the 'Patronato' to the new
authorities.

A new period began, with differences from country to country, in the
second half of the century with the triumph of the 'liberal' elites. Ide-
ologically, they introduced democratic institutions – the universal vote,
democratic constitutional governments (in many cases inspired by the
US Constitution). Culturally, they were led by the ideas of the French
Revolution, the Rights of Man and later, the positivist Comtian philosophy
and its aggressive laicism. In order to modernise society, they gave education
a central role and adopted some of the new ideas and methods of the United
States' modern education system. They wanted to introduce a dynamic
economy, increasing production and initiation of industrialisation. In order

to carry out these projects, they put into practice a policy of immigration, mainly from Europe, as a way of generating a dynamic middle class.

The 'religious field' changed at different points during these two periods. During the emancipation struggles the control of Spanish Catholicism in Latin America broke down because both the majority of the local hierarchy in Latin America and the Holy See in Rome sided with Spain until the 1830s, while sectors of the priesthood embraced the cause of independence, and the popular piety moved almost independently of control and leadership of the institutional Church. When the situation settled down and the Holy See accepted the independence of the new countries, began to negotiate with the new national authorities, and sent her representatives and reordered her dioceses, it was a new Catholicism that appeared: the post-tridentine Roman Catholicism with its centralised ecclesiastical order, its baroque piety, its conservative political alignment to the Vienna Congress of 1814, and the anti-modernist policies of Pius IX. This, not without some internal struggles and opposition, was the dominant theology in Catholic seminaries and clergy until the mid twentieth century. Meanwhile, the popular piety, sometimes influenced (particularly in the urban areas) by a baroque Italian style, ran parallel to or mixed with the 'official Church' which, with some exceptions, had inherited the 'Patronato' or established itself as 'state Church' in the new countries. Although the Inquisition had disappeared there was no religious tolerance, and much less freedom, in most Latin American countries until the 'enlightened' elites took power in the second half of the nineteenth century.

THE PROTESTANT MISSIONS

It is at this point that we should introduce Protestantism. There is, to be sure, a 'Protestant pre-history' represented by francophone Swiss presence in Rio de Janeiro (1555–60), Dutch Reformed in North Brazil (1630–54), German Lutherans in Venezuela (1528–46), Huguenots in Florida (1564–5) and (if we can put them in the same category) the Erasmian and similar dissident currents in the sixteenth and seventeenth centuries. But the control of the Inquisition and, in some cases internal conflicts, totally neutralised non-Catholic religious influences until the mid nineteenth century. On the other hand, the missionary movements of the eighteenth and even nineteenth centuries in the Protestant European 'mainline churches' saw Latin America as a Roman Catholic area and therefore outside the 'missionary field'. For this (and probably also other reasons) it was excluded from the Edinburgh International Missionary Conference of 1910, although a significant number of members at the Conference, particularly from Great Britain and the USA, concerned with missionary work in Latin America, met during the Conference and began a movement that resulted in the Cincinatti (Ohio) agreements of 1911 (concerning the areas of Latin America in which the different churches would concentrate their missionary service), the Foreign Mission Conference in New York in 1913, and subsequently established itself permanently in the inclusive Panama Congress of 1916. We are basically speaking of four streams in which Protestantism entered Latin America in the second half of the nineteenth and the first of the twentieth century:

(1) what have been called 'transplant' churches related mostly to immigrations from Germany, Holland, France and the Scandinavian countries which retained their language, organisation and ties with the mother churches until the late twentieth century and, with few exceptions, did not attempt any direct missionary activity outside their own communities (although one could claim that their very presence was a challenge to the 'one religion' tradition);

(2) the 'mainline' churches from Britain and the USA – Baptist, Methodist, Presbyterians, Congregational, Episcopal and, later on, Christian Church (Disciples of Christ) – which concentrated their action in evangelism, education and social service;

(3) the 'holiness' churches – Nazarene, Pilgrims, Salvation Army, Christian Missionary Alliance, and others like Plymouth Brethren, Seventh-Day Adventists – with a strong evangelistic emphasis and an early, not yet political, fundamentalism; and

(4) since 1910 the Pentecostal movement, which in the course of the second half of the twentieth century has become probably the most numerous, dynamic and visible Protestant presence.[2]

How are we to characterise the theology which, granted some denominational differences, inspired the Protestant evangelisation and its social and cultural presence in Latin America in the second half of the nineteenth and the early twentieth centuries, and how may we assess its role in the historical development of the emerging countries? Let me risk the following possible hypothesis. In a moment in which Latin America began to slowly emerge from its colonial history and was stumbling to find its integration to the modern world, Protestantism sounded a call to change, to transformation, centred in the religious field, but with repercussions in the understanding

---

[2] A more detailed characterisation will be found in my *Faces of Latin American Protestantism* and the histories indicated in the bibliography.

of life and society. The validation of this hypothesis has to be pursued in several directions.

(1) The dominant emphasis of the Protestant proclamation in Latin America has undoubtedly been the call to personal conversion, conceived in terms of the theology and practice of the Anglo-American 'evangelical awakening'. Over against the background of traditional Roman Catholicism, Protestant preaching underlined the need for a personal encounter with Jesus Christ, a living experience of forgiveness and change and the evidence of a new life. Expressions such as 'a new person', 'a new life', 'a different person', 'a new birth' constantly reappear in the testimonies of the early Latin American Protestants. One can immediately see three directions in which this experience relates to the transition to a modern society. The first is 'personalisation': the person is called to 'individualise' him or herself. It frequently means 'losing their friends', 'being cut off from their family', and entering a voluntary community, built from personal independent decisions. The present and the eternal life of the person is for the first time 'in his/her hands'. He/she is the owner of their destiny. Although they may not see it in these terms, we are clearly in the presence of 'the free person' of modern society. The second aspect is 'subjectivity'. In the traditional religion to which a Latin American was used, religious categories are projected on to a supernatural screen. Rain, sickness, love, enmity are related to supernatural causes: saints, spirits, otherworldly powers which have to be magically controlled through religious ceremonies. The supernatural realm does not disappear in Protestant preaching, but is perceived and met in a different way, projected on the screen of subjectivity. Again, the terms that constantly reappear in testimonies and preaching are 'peace', 'joy', 'certainty'. The cosmic struggle has been transposed to consciousness. One could say that, in the religious field and at a popular level, we have moved to a 'Cartesian' world.[3] A third characteristic has been frequently underlined: the moral universe opened by conversion. It is the sphere of the internalising of duty, the sense of responsibility and the virtues of early capitalism: industriousness, honesty, moderation, self control, frugality. It is the moral universe of achievement, of personal effort, of the quest to better oneself morally. In other words, the psycho-social and ethical realisation

---

[3] In new forms of Pentecostalism, like the Spiritual War or the *IgrejaUniversal do Reino de Deus*, developed in the last years, the supernatural seems to be returning, although in a different, perhaps one could call 'post-modern' form. For 'Spiritual War' see Peter Wagner, *Espíritus territoriales*, Miami, Charisma, 1995 and E. Voth, S. Laura and M. Breneman, *La Guerra espiritual: ¿realidad o ficción?*, Buenos Aires (Kairos 2002). For the Universal Church of the Kingdom of God, L. Silveira Campos, *Teatro, Templo e Mercado*, Petropolis (Brazil, Editorial Vozes, 1999) and Anders Ruuth, 'Igreja Universal del Reino de Dios', en *Estudos de Religião*, XII, no. 20, Jan/Feb. 2001, pp. 81–131.

takes the characteristics of the modern man and woman as distinct from those of traditional society. This process is, to be sure, happening in other ways in the larger society. Protestantism contributes to it within the limits of the religious field and to the extent of their limited number.

(2) The Protestant theology of this period has also to be characterised as polemical. The emphasis on personal conversion is related to radical, and sometimes virulent, polemics against Roman Catholicism. Latin American controversialists resort to all the classical arguments developed in Europe since the Reformation. Sometimes the opposition is characterised as 'faith' (Protestantism) over against 'religion' (Catholicism). But behind these classical arguments one can discern a more fundamental rejection: religion as something transmitted and inherited with culture, as a compound of observances, ritual, ceremony mediated by institutions, sacraments, priesthood. Faith, on the other hand, is seen as immediate, personal and spontaneous participation. Frequently one hears the opposition: 'a living faith' over against 'a dead religion'. Conversion, therefore, is a liberation from a socio-religious structure as much as an openness to subjectivity.

A second polemical line moves the opposition to the doctrinal level: the authority of the Bible, justification by faith alone, the unique mediation of Jesus Christ. That is, the classical themes of the Protestant polemics against justification by works, mass, tradition, veneration of images, Mariology. However, it is interesting to look at the way these issues are read. While the theological arguments are taken from the classical European controversies, they move here to show how 'Rome' uses 'false doctrine' to 'enslave', 'keep in ignorance', 'dominate the conscience' of the people. The theological argument becomes a political weapon.

(3) This interpretation of theology leads to the third – and perhaps the more typical – dimension of the controversy: the socio-cultural. Catholicism is seen as the result and the bearer of a feudal world, 'the dark middle ages', social and political oppression, scholasticism, obscurantism, cultural backwardness, the outdated Hispanic order which has to disappear to open the place for a new democratic, liberal, enlightened and dynamic modern order. In this sense, Protestantism inserts itself within the larger revolt against the 'segneurial' system, a revolt that characterises the 'modernity' which the 'progressive' elites of Latin America struggled to introduce in the continent. While this association is consciously, theologically and ethically, but also critically defended by the Protestant leadership, it operates as a form of piety, a 'sung' and 'prayed' theology, as feeling and attitude in the local congregations, made up mostly of peasants, workers and emerging middle-class people.

THE CRISIS OF THE DEVELOPMENT PROJECT (1960–72)

By 1930 the liberal modernising project could be seen as partly successful. As the decade advanced, however, cracks began to appear. The First
World War (1914–18) had stimulated the creation of substitution industries
and given some impulse to the economy, but the recovery of Europe and
the fantastic progress of the USA soon stopped an incipient industrialisation that, deprived of heavy industry and with small internal markets,
could not grow on its own. A certain use of technology in agriculture, the
exhaustion of some mineral resources and the emigration of poor moun-
tain and forest populations to the urban centres, suddenly created a mass
of poor people struggling for a place. The world economic crisis of the
early 1930s hit also the Latin countries. The enlightened democracies of
the liberal project were unable to respond. Some nationalist groups tried
populist answers, sometimes stimulated by the initial successes of fascism
in Europe. But the attempt to launch an independent national development was already impossible: the USA control of Latin American economy
was too great and, when it failed, particularly in Central American and
Caribbean countries, the US marines were ready to intervene. The Second
World War provided a certain breathing space but, after the war, when
the new economic order with its institutions – the Bretton Woods system,
World Bank, International Monetary Fund, GATT and later the GC – was
in place, there was no more room for autonomous nationalist adventures.
Under the aegis of the USA, 'development plans' were implemented. But
the objective conditions of world economy, the interests of the international enterprises which participated in the programs, and the corruption
of the national governments diverting loans and investment to their own
personal or group benefit, worked havoc with these plans. By the mid 1960s
it was becoming clear that the dream of development of the fifties and early
sixties had failed.

Similar things were happening in other areas of 'the Third World', and a
group of economists in North Africa, India, Latin America was developing
a theory called 'the theory of dependence' – a critical application of some
Marxist analyses to an understanding of the relation between the economic
growth of the 'first world' as resulting in a process of 'underdevelopment' in
the 'dependent' countries. The attempts to create 'Third World' coalitions
were seen as a way out of the crisis for the Latin American countries. Revolutionary liberation movements with socialist projects began to develop
in almost every Latin American country. Very few of them were 'orthodox
Marxists'. In fact, with a few exceptions, the Communist parties were very

small and non-influential. Rather, it was a form of populist socialism with nationalist tendencies. The early successes of the Cuban Revolution had a strong repercussion and, although the Cuban regime was not seen as a model, the idea of a socialist alternative was quite attractive. In some cases, these movements resorted to guerrilla or insurrection models; in others, the change was sought through popular movements and electoral processes. Both alternatives, however, in the framework of the Cold War and the reaction of national armies tied to privileged economic interests at home and abroad, had no chance of success. The response was repression. This resulted in the late seventies and eighties in violent military regimes and the violation of all human rights in most southern countries (Brazil, Chile, Uruguay, Argentina, Bolivia) or imposed 'elected' governments (most of Central America). This is the background against which we can project the developments in the Catholic and Protestant churches after the Second World War.

(1) The social and political crisis of the modernising model posed an acute dilemma for a young generation of Protestants, the children and grandchildren of the early converts, many of whom were now arriving at the universities and being caught in the turmoil of that time. It was a challenge to their faith: were not their churches allies that provided religious legitimisation to American imperialism and colonialism, in close connection with power groups of Latin America which had led their countries to dependence, injustice and frustration? Perhaps even more deeply: was it not the gospel itself that produced the social resignation, the passive acceptance of exploitation and class oppression? They had not lost their faith, but they revolted against a church and a message that they saw as being in complicity with the worst forces of destruction and injustice in their societies. The ecumenical movement came at this point to their rescue. The Student Christian Movement related to the World Student Christian Federation had began to gather Protestant students in Latin America since the 1950s: it offered a strong biblical theology together with an invitation to social and political commitment. The World Council of Churches had also an increasing presence. Barth's theology and Bonhoeffer's testimony made a strong impact. And these young Latin American Protestants, eager to find a way to respond with integrity to the call of Jesus Christ and their love for their people found in this theology, at the same time as a radical criticism of the liberal bourgeois ideology, a passionate concern for justice and freedom and a sympathy for socialist alternatives. Moreover, the anti-Catholic spirit of earlier Protestants had lost its force with this younger generation. They saw in their young Catholic friends the same concern,

the same critical questions about the role of their Church in society and the presence of a new theology – at the time the 'New Theology' of Dutch, French and some German Catholic theologians. Thus, some movements of ecumenical origin like the SCM (Student Christian Movement), ISAL (Church and Society in Latin America), MISUR (Urban and Industrial Mission) enlarged their membership by including Catholics and began to assume a role in relation to the political discussion and struggle in Latin American society.

(2) On the other hand, a different, and to some extent an opposite development, had taken place in other sectors of Latin American Protestantism, mostly the churches that are usually called 'evangelical' in the Anglo-Saxon world: the fundamentalist reaction. Protestant fundamentalism is a complex and changing phenomenon. Several historians have called attention to what Moberg has termed 'the great reversal' which, in the early decades of the twentieth century, moved the evangelical churches from a concern for 'revival *and* social reform' to an alternative of 'revival *versus* social reform'. Particularly, a movement that had been counter-cultural 'in the defence of faith' turned, during and since the First World War into 'the defence of Christian America' against 'the Kaiser', and later the 'Communist Soviet Union' which took the place of the Pope and the Muslims as the representatives of the 'Antichrist'. Fundamentalism has deeply affected Latin American Protestantism since the 1950s, but became particularly strong and aggressive in 'the anti-communist phase' in the 1960s, seventies and eighties. International fundamentalism (mostly as expressed by the US 'Christian right') was strongly present in Latin American countries, partly in national and Latin American associations of fundamentalist churches but also in the significant presence of new missionaries who came to Latin America after the closing of missionary admission to some Asian and African countries. Some churches officially adopted this position but its influence was felt throughout Protestantism, both at the theological and, in some cases even more strongly, at the ideological and political level. Until very recently the fundamentalism/ecumenism option has been a dividing line between churches and groups, across which there has been no communication until the end of the 1980s.

As we have already indicated, important changes were taking place in Latin American Catholicism. The new vision of the religious situation was, perhaps, already present in the Buenos Aires Eucharistic Congress of 1930, presided by the then Cardinal Pacelli, soon to become Pius XII. Already in 1941 a Chilean theologian, the Jesuit Alberto Hurtado had raised a serious question in a book called *Is Chile a Catholic Country?* Almost fifteen years later, a Latin American Congress of *Acción Católica* in Chimbote (Peru) in 1954, took up the question at a Latin American level and made a critical analysis of the degree and quality of people's Catholicism in this alleged Catholic territory. Their assessment was disturbing: 'practised Catholicism' was very limited (15 per cent to 25 per cent active participants are the data brought by different countries) and even these minorities frequently had a doctrinally and ethically poor religious practice. Two decades later, when the Vatican asked all Latin American bishops for their 'proposals' (votes) for the approaching Council, they underlined an urgent need: Latin America is for Catholicism 'a land of mission'. The missionary question has appeared as a goal of CELAM (the Latin American Episcopal Council) since its creation in 1955. Does this mean that 'Mission' had replaced 'Christendom', and consequently a fundamental theological reversal had taken place? My answer is 'yes and no'. The Rio meeting of 1955 reasoned in these terms: Catholicism is threatened by its enemies – socialists, secularists, Freemasons, Protestants – who dispute a territory that, by tradition and presence, belongs to the Roman Catholic Church. Hence, mission meant 'reconquest' (a very important term in Spanish and Latin American history). To reconquer meant the creation of a new Christendom. But, in another sense, the question itself implicitly evoked a real 'break': it was not a question of 'protecting' an already achieved evangelisation but of evangelising a lost, or never really possessed, or only partially or precariously gained, space.

This question generated a pastoral and theological process that culminated in the post-Vatican II Latin American Episcopal Conference of Medellín (Colombia) of 1968. It is not difficult to detect its theological background, with the influence of 'the new theology' that, in different forms, had already reached some Latin American theologians, and which was strongly represented in the Council by the French, Belgian, Dutch, and German bishops and theologians: a theology which accepted pluralism, religious liberty, a new and more ecumenical view of the role of the Church in social questions, a recognition of the historical conditioning of the religious field and the 'modern' concern for the individual and subjectivity. It was, in other words, what the Uruguayan Jesuit theologian Juan Luis Segundo would call a Church of 'adult Christians' instead of the permanent 'minority' of a subject. But Medellín cannot be defined merely in terms of the 'exogenous' factors. Rather, these new theological instruments were re-interpreted in this twofold connection: as a new way of understanding mission and in the awareness of the economic condition, a theology 'for the poor' and 'from' the poor. The cry of the poor is both a sociological and a political reality. Latin America is not merely a 'situation', nor an unfortunate 'condition': it is a structural condition that can and should be analysed and confronted sociologically and politically and a call from God who has made 'an option for the poor' and invites his Church to participate in it.

This is the root of a 'theology of liberation' and, perhaps more importantly, a 'pastoral of liberation'. This is the point of encounter between Latin American Protestant 'ecumenical' and Latin American Catholic 'post-conciliar' theology. SODEPAX, the Roman Catholic/WCC joint committee on Society, Development and Peace heard, in their meeting of 1969, two Latin American young theologians, the Peruvian Roman Catholic priest Gustavo Gutiérrez and the Brazilian Presbyterian minister Rubem Alves. Both presentations were, in fact, the core of two books that would appear shortly afterwards: *Teologia de la Liberacion: perspectivas* (1971), by Gutierrez and *Cristianismo: ¿opio o liberacion?* (1971) by Alves. They represented a new 'way of doing theology' that was emerging with different characteristics but a common concern in many areas of the Third World. For Latin America, it would be the first 'contextual' theology after Bartolomé de La Casas and his colleagues of the sixteenth century. It would be called 'Theology of Liberation'.

Theology has always been contextual: implicitly or explicitly, consciously or unconsciously, deliberately or against the will of the theologian. What happens, however, when that condition is taken up consciously, explicitly and deliberately? Is it really, by virtue of this recognition, 'a new way of doing theology'? Without trying to adjudicate this question theoretically, I will briefly summarise what has happened in the course of three decades, from 1960 to 1990.[4]

(1) Who is the theologian?

In Latin America, the 'professional theologian' has been an almost unknown species. Most of the well-known 'theologians' are priests or ministers, sisters,

---

[4] To date 'Liberation Theology' is already a controversial issue. The initial dating of the late 1960s seems to be more easily argued in the concurrence of Catholic and Protestant/ecumenical young theologians. But can we speak of LT after the crisis of the late seventies and eighties when the Vatican reprehended and sanctioned some of the most recognised liberation theologians, when repression 'disbanded' or executed theologians, both Catholic and Protestant and when theologians, in any case, seem to change, correct or disown some of the sociological and political positions they had supported? The answer depends on the understanding of what is the heart and source of a 'liberation theology'. My own response looks for continuity and change in two directions: The central theological 'locus' around which LT develops, 'the centrality of the poor', 'God's preferential option for the poor' is not only still present but has become ever more critical and decisive. On the other hand, the new conditions prevalent since the late seventies demand a more complex set of tools of analysis, both in terms of economy, sociology, anthropology and cultural analysis.

actively fulfilling pastoral functions, or lay people, mainly journalists, teachers, faculty, doing interdisciplinary work. But the question – 'who is the theologian?' – goes further than that. If the theological renewal was a response to the 'cry of the poor', are these merely the object, or the beneficiaries, of theology or are they, in some way, protagonists? There is, I think, a twofold answer to this question. In the first place, the professional theologian (pastor, teacher, and so on) conceives her or his task as being closely related to the life of the community: he/she tries to understand what is happening in the worship, the life, the suffering of the community and put it in the context of the Scripture and the tradition, and then to test it by bringing it back to the community. In this sense, the theologian tries to articulate the cry of the poor and see whether the poor recognise in this interpretation the echo of their voice. But there is another aspect, for which we have to refer to the specific ecclesial phenomenon called 'basic ecclesial communities' (CEBs/BECs), that is, intentional clusters of people, almost always of poor conditions, who gather regularly for prayer, celebration, mutual support and action in the larger community that surrounds them. In two aspects of these communities there is an explicit 'theology by/from the poor'. One is the reading and discussion of the Scripture, a central feature of the meeting of the BECs. The other is the 'new hymnody', the songs created by the community and their spontaneous musicians and poets. In a number of books, some testimonies of this primarily theological material are now available.

A second aspect in which this deliberate contextuality affects the theologian is the consciousness of her/his social location in reality. We all 'have been placed' by birth, education, socialisation in a given country, at a given time, in a given social class, and so on. One must begin by recognising this influence on what we think, we feel, we do. But we can also 'place ourselves' by choice: this is what is called 'the option for the poor'. This option has material aspects: some decide to leave everything and assume the condition of the poor, some settle among the poor, some choose a certain lifestyle which approximates them to the poor, some 'commute' between the two worlds. We are all aware that this does not make us poor in the full sense of the experience. There is no total 'kenosis' possible for human beings. But there are choices that have to be made, analysed, corrected. And these choices imply a perspective, now explicit and avowed, from which we look at Scripture, the history of the Church, the functioning of society. We claim that there are things in all these areas which are seen from this perspective that could not be seen from another – the one that unconsciously has been that of the bulk of the theological profession, at least for some two hundred years.

(2) *The hermeneutical circle*

The expression was introduced by Juan Luis Segundo and is already well known. I only want to call attention to one of the points he makes. He points out that, when 'a relocation in reality' as that we have mentioned is deep and embracing enough, we begin to discover an inconsistency between 'received' interpretations of Scripture and tradition and the reality in which we live. This leads to the 'suspicion' as to whether that interpretation may have been shaped by another reality. James Cone has called attention to the fact that, while for a white European Christian, Moses is the 'giver of the Law' and David 'the King', for the black slaves in America, Moses was 'the liberator' who led the people across the sea and the desert and David was the 'singer'. A brief visit to modern exegesis of the biblical teaching about rich and poor is perhaps all that is needed to realise what are we talking about. A new perspective obscures some things, but it illuminates others. And since the perspective of the rich has been illuminated enough, perhaps the change can be healthy, since there is no way in which humans can stand in two locations at the same time!

Given this fact, how can we avoid becoming totally determined by the perspective? How can the text be respected in its autonomy and at the same time read as a critique of our chosen perspective? This is a difficult question for which we have not any perfect answer. One protection is found in the critical work, the different hermeneutical tools that have been forged in biblical studies, to which we shall refer later.

(3) *How do we understand the poor?*

I have already mentioned Gutierrez' reference to the understanding of poverty and the poor in structural terms as a social class. It reflects the beginnings of Liberation Theology and it remains a fundamental consideration which has to be constantly actualised as economic and social conditions change in the continent. But we have always been aware that such considerations could not exhaust an understanding of 'the poor'. Through failures and experience, other disciplines came to join the effort for understanding. Concretely, the poor are also a culture, or rather 'cultures', which have to be understood through cultural anthropology. The poor belong to ethnic groups (Indian, mestizo, black) which have developed their own cultures. Poverty affects in different ways different sectors of society, such as women and children. That is: there is not an homogenous context but a diversified one that has to be understood in its diversity. This can be now seen in recent theological production. The five hundred years anniversary in 1992 has been an excellent opportunity for this diversity to become visible and be honoured and celebrated, but also to organise and express itself. Recent publications begin to witness to that change.

(4) *Theological* loci

Which theological topics have claimed priority in Latin American theology? Sometimes people think that 'Liberation' – understood from a socio-political point of departure – has been the exclusive concern of Latin American theologians, their 'specialisation'. As a matter of fact, it is not so! 'Liberation' is a perspective rather than a topic. It is possible to speak of God from the location of the struggles for liberation, as many biblical writings attest, and it is possible to speak of God (and so eloquently) from the perspective of the slave-owner. And this can be said of almost any possible theological 'locus'. However, it is also true that some 'loci' have claimed a priority attention. Clearly, Christology has been, from the beginning, a central issue. In Latin America, where Christ has been either the 'heavenly King' or the 'powerless victim', the discovery of the Jesus of the Gospels was a spiritual and a theological experience: poor people are amazed, excited, challenged and encouraged as they read the Gospel stories in which they can easily identify themselves and find a new relation to the grace and the power of the one whose name they knew but whose life they totally ignored.

A second central locus has been ecclesiology. The experience of 'being Church' within *the* 'base communities' calls into question many aspects of what Christians had been taught, and had experienced in the institutional Church. How should we put together these two contradictory experiences? This is a question to which Leonardo Boff has given central attention in books like *Ecclesiogenesis* or the much debated *Church, Charisma and Power*. In a somewhat different way, Juan Luis Segundo has seen the Church as a committed 'minority' which does not intend to include everybody but is a 'sign' of the new humanity which is the goal towards which God is working, a view very much influenced by Teilhard de Chardin.

Even classical *loci* like the doctrine of the Trinity can be read from a new perspective which develops dimensions which had not been usually explored. Thus Segundo and later Leonardo Boff have recovered the Eastern Orthodox emphasis on the 'triune' God to challenge the 'imperial' divine, isolated image of God and see 'God as community', where apparently purely academic doctrines like *perichoresis* or even *enhypostasis* and *synergism* can gain a new and very concrete meaning for the understanding of the Christian faith and praxis. Very important issues such as the place and role of women, race relations and the understanding of indigenous religion can be approached in a new way from a deeper and more encompassing theology.

In recent decades, biblical studies have gained a central place in the theological production, as both a historico-critical and a semiotic exegesis and hermeneutics of Scriptures have opened the possibility of approaching issues of economics, peace and violence, power and justice in a new way. The works of Severino Croatto, Pablo Richard, Milton Schwantes, Alicia Winters, Elsa Tamez and Nancy Cardoso, among many others and journals like *RIBLA* (*Revista de Investigacion Biblica Latinoamericana*) have opened new perspectives on an academically responsible and critical discussion of urgent issues.

Worship, celebration, a new life, a new attitude in relation to society and to 'others' come together in what we call 'spirituality' – a way of standing 'before God and with the brother and sister' as Bonhoeffer would say. This was part of the foundational experience of Liberation Theology. But it was implicit. As the conditions of life deteriorate and suffering and active patience become a fundamental part of the struggle for liberation, the consciousness of the need to make explicit that 'spirituality' makes itself felt. Gutierrez' books, *The Power of the Poor in History* and particularly *On Job: God Talk and the Suffering of the Innocent* (a meditation on the book of Job) are good examples of this theological concern. John Sobrino, Segundo Galilea, Julio de Santa Ana, Jaci Maraschin, Elsa Tamez, and others have contributed to this reflection.

THE TRIUMPH OF GLOBALISATION: FROM 1973

The choice of 1973 as the point of departure of a new period is, like many of these historical 'datelines', somewhat arbitrary and debatable. We have earlier referred to the failure of the 'plans for development', the movements of rebellion in the quest for a new social, political and economic organisation. The response of both the USA government and the dominant economic sectors of Latin American countries, we said then, was repression, violent military regimes and the violation of all human rights. By the 1980s the liberation movements, the critical intellectual leadership in the universities, political parties, and culture in general had been killed, gone into exile or isolated. How did Christian churches fare during the period and what was their role in the new 'safe', 'security', 'controlled' democracies that emerged? How would theological thinking respond to the new conditions? This is today a question which Christian churches, organisations, theologians and groups are trying to understand and respond to. Here we can only sketch some lines in this direction.

The reaction of churches to the brutal repression was by no means unanimous, neither between different confessions nor within the particular churches. There are places where Catholic, Pentecostal and Evangelical churches overtly sided and supported the military regimes and policies, acclaiming them as God's instrument for the defeat of revolution and communism. Others claimed to be neutral, to ignore, to deny or to discount the brutal repression, disappearances and mass executions. On the other hand, many well-known religious leaders, bishops, ministers, theologians and lay men and women of different churches and confessions took the defence of human life as the central focus for a theological interpretation, in the denunciation of the violation of all human rights and of other possible forms of protection of the victims. Some, like Archbishop Romero in El Salvador, Bishop Angelleli in Argentina, ecumenical leader Professor Mauricio López, and many other known and unknown priests, pastors and church men and women lost their lives in this struggle. On the theological level, the issues of God's concern for human life, of justice and law, punishment and forgiveness became central, both during the persecutions and afterwards in the attempts to return to a democratic order.

Before we return to the consideration of the present theological developments, however, we want to trace back one, if not the most significant Christian presence in Latin America at this time: the Pentecostal movement. If we do it at this point it is because their growth in numbers, visibility and weight in the social life in Latin America has developed more strongly in the last three decades, although not exactly in the same periods in different countries.

PENTECOSTALISM IN LATIN AMERICA

Modern Pentecostalism appears at the beginning of the twentieth century in the USA. By 1910 it was already present in Chile and Brazil. Although it is initiated by Pentecostals from abroad (mainly USA but also Sweden), in some cases by missionaries, but also frequently by lay members of Pentecostal churches, it soon became a 'people's religion' and grew in poor areas, among miners, dock workers, shanty towns, migrants from the countryside to the cities and native and black populations. More than any other Church except Catholicism, it became a 'church of the people'.[5] The debate about the social role Pentecostalism has played in Latin America has moved in different directions: for some, Pentecostalism was 'a refuge for the masses' that created a space for people displaced from their rural world and thrown into the urban world; others, on the contrary saw it as an instrument of integration into modernity. More recently, anthropologists and the Pentecostal leadership have insisted that Pentecostalism cannot be reduced to sociological interpretations which do not take account of the specific 'religious' dimension. Moreover, Pentecostalism is a diversified phenomenon which, in the course of time, has developed, or is seen as related to, new expressions like the 'spiritual war' movement and religio-political-cultural expressions like the 'Universal Church of the Kingdom of God' in Brazil. At this point I will only refer to the theological directions in the more classical Pentecostalism.

The first thing that has to be said is that, although there is a great variety, both in terms of the Pentecostal churches that came from abroad, as in those that have emerged in Latin America, we can say that the fundamental Pentecostal 'reading' of their common evangelical tradition is, on the whole, almost the same, namely: (a) salvation by the grace of God and through the vicarious sacrifice of Jesus Christ received by faith: here the personal experience of this salvation is the central emphasis; (b) the baptism of/in the Holy Spirit, interpreted as a second experience and related to sanctification: there are differences concerning the importance of the gift of tongues as sealing the baptism and as to whether we should receive immediate or progressive sanctification; but in any case it means empowerment as a promise to all believers, generally received in the community of faith, with prayer and laying on of hands; (c) an apocalyptic eschatology, almost always premillenarian, defined as resurrection, second coming, millennial kingdom, final judgement and the hope for the eternal Kingdom. Of course, the classical Protestant doctrines – the inspiration of Scriptures, the doctrine of God, Christology – are accepted and some particular differences in relation to miracles and so on, are found in different Pentecostal traditions. However, what Donald Dayton has called 'the foursquare model' – 'Christ as Savior, Sanctifier, Healer and King' – represents the common Pentecostal tradition.

The main question, however, is raised by some Latin American Pentecostal theologians who insist that these classical theological formulations are

---

[5] There is a large and growing literature concerning Pentecostalism in Latin America, coming from sociologists and anthropologists, both Latin Americans and foreigners since the 1960s, and theological approaches from the Pentecostal ranks themselves in the last decade.

reinterpreted (mostly implicitly) and 'experienced' by Pentecostal believers and congregations in relation to their conditions. 'When a Pentecostal says', remarks the Chilean Pentecostal theologian Juan Sepúlveda, 'that "this world offers nothing, it only offers perdition" [lostness and damnation] . . . he/she is not stating a dogmatic affirmation but is rather giving voice to his/her own experience: misery, unemployment, illness, alcoholism', or, when they speak of 'the power of the Spirit' they are not making a general statement but referring to their own experience of 'multiple manifestations . . . from angelic tongues to simple joy, including dance and visions, to the certainty of the nearness and living presence of a forgiving and accepting God'. Bernardo Campos, a Peruvian Pentecostal theologian, claims that the 'Pentecostality' which has always been present in Christianity finds expression in terms of the local culture, creating forms of Pentecostalism, for instance, that correspond to the indigenous traditions, in his country, of the *Quechua* and *Aymara* people. Whether Pentecostalism will continue to grow at the same speed or whether, as some observers have noted, there are points of 'saturation', it is clear that the Pentecostal presence, moving into new areas of social life, will continue to be a significant factor in Latin American Christianity.

PROSPECTS

We need, however, to return to the total picture of theological developments during the last decades. For reasons of space, but also because we move, both in the religious and in the social, economic, political and cultural areas into an unexplored and changing space, I will simply make some general comments on possible theological developments in the near future.

(1) In terms of the conditions, we have to note that we are moving into (a) a religious field which is enlarged, pluralised and dynamised by new religious movements, the growth of charismatic and Pentecostal churches, the visible and dynamic manifestations of old religious (i.e. pre-Colombian) spiritualities and diverse syncretistic popular creations – popular, indigenous, Afro-American – which had been hidden, ignored or persecuted; and finally, by conflicts and theological and ideological tensions in more traditional churches, including Roman Catholicism; (b) a cultural field enriched by the new awareness of ethnic, regional, gender identities and at the same time conditioned by the globalisation of massive means of communication and the imposition of cultural models of diverse origin; (c) a political and social situation almost totally conditioned by the 'neo-liberal' economic model, the immediate results of which, whatever the idyllic images of the

perfect future may be, have meant so far the concentration of economic power, the growing precariousness of work, the growth of unemployment and the social, health and educational vulnerability of large sectors of the population, the growth of marginality, delinquency and anomy, the scepticism towards political action in our condition of purely formal democracies, and the appearance of social movements of different types whose role and weight in society we cannot yet evaluate with any clarity.

Is it possible to move beyond these remarks on 'the conditions of production' of a responsible Latin American theology as we move into the third millennium? We can at least open a discussion on some areas:

(a) In the last ten years we have experienced in the Protestant/Evangelical churches a growing encounter, cooperation and coincidence around social, ethical and spiritual concerns that grow from the everyday experience of their members. The very seriousness of the issues our people are facing – poverty, uncertainty, despair – challenges our Christian responsibility and we are all led to try to find together ways of responding to 'the cry of the people'. This has led the different Protestant associations, theological schools, local congregations to think, pray and act together and, in critical situations, to offer a public testimony of the social demands of the faith. Spontaneous ecumenical groups, from classical, evangelical and Pentecostal people, have begun to think together and common programmes of social help, of political reflection appear frequently and sometimes they create, without leaving their communities, significant centres of thought and action.

(b) There are theological battles to be fought, at least in two interrelated fronts: (i) there is in the public area of society, politics and ideologies a struggle for life, human dignity and hope against 'the ideological weapons of death' – the idolatry of the market, the post-modern rejection of any 'great story' which may give meaning to human life and history. This struggle belongs to the political and ideological area but it challenges our theological responsibility concerning concrete plans and policies of marginalisation, the degradation of life, the destruction of nature, and even 'holy wars' that pretend religious and theological legitimation as expressions of freedom and instruments of justice: (ii) in the sphere of the churches which, alarmed by the uncertainty of a religious field which becomes 'unmanageable', or intimidated and at the same time seduced by triumphant and apparently irresistible 'models', dig themselves in and close on themselves to ensure 'order' and continuity and/or adopt 'prosperity theologies' or 'theological realisms' that serve as accompanying music to the system.

(c) There are pastoral tasks of support and encouragement of the impoverished, marginalised and increasingly anomic and despairing masses of people which the 'model' produces. There is a fundamental difference between accompanying the struggle of the poor who feel called to a project of transformation, and trying to generate even small signs of hope in marginal, chronically unemployed, undernourished children, teenagers or young adults who see no possible horizon of hope. There is here a task of theological understanding of these situations, and of discernment and interpretation of the small and timid signs that begin to appear in the solidarity movements and particular claims and vindications which may look limited and partial, but which are expressions and seeds of a claim for human dignity and initiatives that 'point' to a re-conception of politics as a building up of power on the basis of honesty, truth and service.

(d) There are theological tasks in the encounter, dialogue and cooperation between the different 'subjects' which the new configuration of the religious field has placed on the scene. This is a yet unknown exercise for theology in our continent, still conditioned by the dream – generated by power – of a massively Christian, or even Catholic society, in which other religious expressions could be 'tolerated' but do not deserve any further thought. As one of the still uneasy and somewhat confused and unprepared theologians thrown into these questions, I suggest some two or three possible contributions for this encounter: (i) Christian theology has the responsibility of offering a coherent, unequivocal and public defence, not only of tolerance but of total freedom and juridical equality of all religious communities and expressions, rejecting all disqualifying expressions and characterisations and denouncing the mechanisms of repression; (ii) an encounter, dialogue and authentic cooperation which are only possible if they are built on a recognition of our own and the other's identities: therefore, all attempts to 'infiltrate' the identity of the other and claim oneself as part of it or the attempt to incorporate the other into our own are simply expressions of the same religious imperialism for which we should be ashamed; (iii) identities, however, are not immutable entities but social constructions built along the centuries of our continent (including those before the European conquest), the product of encounter, struggle, living together, in which diverse elements have been incorporated, myths and foundational stories have been reinterpreted, and languages have fused. To recognise this history and to find in it motifs and nuclei of conversation and common values does not mean denying our own identity but recognising the 'space' of the 'other' as 'a tangential space' (Foucault), 'an epiphanic space' (Westhelle) which appears at the border of my own identity; (iv) this dialogue, encounter and cooperation from our own identity is always a mutual challenge and claim: to reject it does not mean respect for the other but a secret and perhaps unconscious contempt. In this sense, evangelisation is not an alternative to dialogue or cooperation but an inseparable dimension of it – to 'evangelise' from equality and powerlessness is to place oneself at the service of the other and to run the risk of being 'converted', or the possibility that, in the dynamics of a common history, and not as an artificial 'synthesis' produced in a theological laboratory, a new common identity may emerge.

REFERENCES AND FURTHER READING

This is only an initial bibliography in which I have privileged books in English except in cases in which there is only Spanish or Portuguese bibliography. Further bibliographic references will be found in the books here alluded to.

BIBLIOGRAPHIES AND JOURNALS

John H. Sinclair. 1967. *Protestantism in Latin America: A Bibliographical Guide*. The Hispanic American Institute, Austin, Texas

Bibliografía Teológica Comentada del area latinoamericana (BTC) Latin American Bibliography published by ISEDET – Instituto Superior Evangélico de Educación Teológica (published annually since 1973 – now discontinued)

Revista de interpretación bíblica latinoamericana (RIBLA). Spanish and Portuguese, Apartado 390-2070, Sabanilla, San José, Costa Rica. Published from 1988

Cristianismo y Sociedad. Apartado 20-656, México, DF 01000, México since 1962

Encuentro y Diálogo. Journal of the Asociación de Seminarios e Instituciones Teológicas; Buenos Aires, Argentina

Signos de Vida. A publication of the Latin American Council of Churches, CLAI. Quito, Ecuador: Inglaterra 937 y Mariana de Jesús, Quito, Ecuador Tel and Fax 593-2 553-996 and 529-933

Cuadernos de Teología. Buenos Aires, Instituto Superior Evangélico de Estudios Teológicos: Camacuá 252, 1406 Buenos Aires, Argentina

Xilotl. Seminario Evangélico, Managua, Nicaragua. Ediciones Nicarao, Managua, Nicaragua

LATIN AMERICAN HISTORY

Bethel, L. (ed.) *The Cambridge History of Latin America* (11 vols.). Cambridge

Herring, H. 1967. *A History of Latin America*. (4th edn) New York

Skidmore, T. E. and P. H. Smith. 1989. *Modern Latin America*. Oxford

Albornoz, N. S. (ed.) 1985. *Historia de América Latina*. (3 vols.). Madrid

LATIN AMERICAN CHURCH HISTORY

Prien, H-J. 1978. *Die Geschichte des Christentums in Lateinamerika.* Göttingen
   1985. *La historia del Cristianismo en América Latina.* Salamanca
Bastian, J. P. 1990. *Historia del Protestantismo en América Latina.* Mexico
Dussel, E. 1981. *A History of the Church in Latin America.* Grand Rapids, Mich.
Goodpasture, H. MacK. 1989. *Cross and Sword: An Eyewitness History of Christianity
   in Latin America.* Maryknoll

INVASION, CONTROL AND COLONISATION (1492–1808)

Pagán, L. N. R. 1992. *Evangelización y Violencia.* San Juan, Puerto Rico
Gutiérrez, G. 1993. *In Search of the Poor of Jesus Christ.* Maryknoll
Adorno, Rolena and Guamán Poma. 2000. *Writing and Resistanse in Colonial Peru.*
   Austin, Texas
Mires, F. 1987. *La colonización de las almas.* San José, Costa Rica

INDEPENDENCE AND 'NATION BUILDING' (1808–1960)

Committee of Cooperation in Latin America. 1917. *Christian Work in Latin
   America: The Panama Congress, 1916* 3 vols. New York
Inman, S. G. 1917. *Christian Cooperation in Latin America.* New York
Rycroft, S. 1958. *Religion and Faith in Latin America.* Philadelphia
Browning, W. E. 1924. *Roman Christianity in Latin America.* New York/London
Considine, J. (ed.) 1964. *The Church in the New Latin America.* Indiana
Bonino, J. Miguez. 1997. *Faces of Latin American Protestantism.* Grand Rapids

THE CRISIS OF THE DEVELOPMENT PROJECT
(1961–1972)

McGovern, A. F. 1989. *Liberation Theology and its Critics.* Maryknoll
Gibellini, R. (ed.) 1979. *Frontiers of Theology in Latin America.* Maryknoll
Costas, O. E. 1976. *Theology of the Crossroads in Contemporary Latin America.*
   Amsterdam
Hennelly, A. T. 1979. *Theologies in Conflict.* Maryknoll
Gutiérrez, G. 1973. *A Theology of Liberation.* Maryknoll
Segundo, J. L. 1973–4. *A Theology for Artisans of a New Humanity.* Maryknoll
   1976. *The Liberation of Theology.* Maryknoll
Bonino, J. Miguez. 1975. *Doing Theology in a Revolutionary Situation.* Philadelphia

THE TRIUMPH OF GLOBALISATION PROCESS
(1973–2000)

Comblin, J. 1998. *Called for Freedom: The Changing Context of Liberation Theology.*
   Maryknoll

Schipani D. (ed.) 2002. *The Promise of Hope.* Amsterdam

Cesar, W. and Richard Shaull. 2001. *Pentecostalismo e futuro das Igrejas Cristas.* Petropolis

Gutiérrez, G. 1999. *The Density of the Present.* Maryknoll

Bonino, J. Miguez. 2001. *Poder del Evangelio y poder político.* Buenos Aires

Sung, Jung Mo. 1998. *Desejo, mercado e religiâo.* Petrópolis

Sigmund, P. E. (ed.) 1999. *Religious Freedom and Evangelization in Latin America.* Maryknoll

3

India

Kirsteen Kim

Distinctively Indian Christian theologies began to emerge in international discussion nearly two hundred years ago. The late 1960s and 1970s saw the publication of several volumes analysing the life and work of pioneers by Robin Boyd (1969), Kaj Baago (1969), M. M. Thomas (1970) and Stanley Samartha (1974). These were used as texts for seminary courses on Indian Christian theology, which in turn stimulated further theological endeavours to understand Indian religions and society and respond in a way that was 'biblically sound, spiritually satisfying, theologically credible, and pastorally helpful' (Samartha 1991: ix) in the Indian context. This chapter begins by considering Indian realities and then identifying and describing three distinct tracks of response. Indian re-readings of Christology and the theology of the Holy Spirit (pneumatology) will help to focus these, highlighting the 'Indianness' of the emerging theologies and their challenge to traditional modes of theologising.

INDIAN REALITIES: RELIGIONS AND SOCIETY

India is not only a nation but a subcontinent with a diverse mixture of communities facing complex social and economic challenges. Indian realities are sometimes represented by the shorthand: 'religions and society' or 'religions and poverty' (Abraham 1990, 3–27). These and their interrelationship produce the three main questions with which Indian theologians grapple: the position of the Christian faith in the plural – particularly the multifaith – context; the relationship of Christianity to the dominant tradition of Hinduism; and the Christian response to socio-economic oppression.

India is the homeland of Hindu religion and culture in its many forms, and the related faiths of Jainism, Buddhism and Sikhism. Hinduism forms a complex religious culture which has been compared to a *banyan* tree: it is a family of religions, 'microcosmically polycentric, macrocosmically one'. The various manifestations of Hinduism are held together by a number of features that overlap in its making but none of which define it. Some of these are the Vedas – the ancient scriptures; *brahminism* – the way of the priestly caste who are trained to preserve and maintain Hindu religion; belief in the rule of *karma* (acquired merit or demerit) and rebirth; the caste system; and the ancient language of Sanskrit. Hinduism's diversity is linked to its inclusivity: its readiness to absorb other religious traditions into its spreading tree (Lipner 1994, 1–21). The majority of the Indian population come within the Hindu canopy but there is also a substantial Muslim minority and a long-established Zoroastrian (Parsi) community.

Christianity, which represents between two and three per cent of the population, has been present on the Indian sub-continent since at least the second century when the Mar Thoma Syrian (Orthodox) Church was established. According to tradition, the Apostle Thomas came to India, landing in Malabar in 52 AD. The Mar Thoma community has a distinctive and continuous history and has preserved the ancient Syriac liturgy. The first Roman Catholics to arrive, in the sixteenth century, tried to bring the indigenous Christians under the authority of Rome, while missionaries laboured to evangelise believers in other faiths. The Jesuit Robert de Nobili, though anxious to refute Hindu religion, adopted the lifestyle of a *sannyasi* (Hindu contemplative) and studied Sanskrit in order to convert *brahmins*. From the early eighteenth century Protestant missionaries such as Ziegenbalg and Plütschau of the Danish-Halle Mission, East India Company chaplain Henry Martyn, and the Baptist William Carey began their work by translating the Bible and thus defined a basic Christian theological vocabulary. Carey and later missionaries increasingly promoted education in an English medium as *preparatio evangelica*. This exposed Indian leaders not only to Christian teaching and practice but also to British culture and technology with its accompanying rationalism (Boyd 1975, 7–18). The captivity of the Christian gospel to Western culture and its association with British imperialism were the chief challenges faced by Indian Christian theology as it emerged in the nineteenth century.

Though Hindus are a large majority in modern India, the leaders of the independence movement, Mohandas K. Gandhi, Jawaharlal Nehru, and others who shaped the Constitution did so with acute awareness of the subcontinent's multi-religiosity. They established India as a secular state, not in the sense of 'a state which is separate from religion' but in the sense of 'a state which aids all religions impartially' (Smith 1963). The importance of peace between religions was underlined when negotiations with the Muslim community could not be reached and, amidst much bloodshed, in 1947 colonial India was partitioned into India and Pakistan. Despite the impact of modernity, religion remains a major factor defining community identity in India. Conversion from one religion to another is not only a religious but also a sensitive political issue because significant numbers of conversions will upset the balance of power between communities. Furthermore, since for many to be Indian is to be Hindu, conversion to another religion is seen as disloyalty to the nation and it is the main stumbling block in Hindu–Christian relations (Kim 2002).

Hindus, whose religion is inclusive of many diverse traditions and prides itself on tolerance, have found it difficult to understand the Christian emphasis on conversion which appears arrogant and exclusive. Furthermore they have been angered by 'mass conversions' of whole caste groups in the nineteenth and twentieth centuries (as documented by Pickett 1933) for what Hindus see as socio-economic rather than spiritual reasons. The use of Western resources for Christian evangelism has also led Hindus to suspect a continuing plot even post-Independence to destabilise India and undermine Hindu power (Shourie 1994). At Christian insistence, the right to 'propagate' religion was enshrined in the Indian constitution but since 1947 several states have taken steps to control and effectively block individuals or groups from changing their community allegiance, except by 'home-coming' (*shuddhi*) to Hinduism. There is a strong movement of *Hindutva*, or Hinduisation, which has recently achieved central political power in India, and threatens minority groups in an increasingly overt way. At the time of writing harassment and violence against non-Hindus is increasingly reported.

India looks set to overtake China as the most populous nation on earth and, although in this vast population there are many extremely wealthy people, some 312 million (according to World Bank figures) live below the official poverty line. India's poverty may be laid at the door of its colonial history and the present global economic system as well as internal systems of inequality, most notably the caste system and gender discrimination. British commercial interests and later rule of India exploited Indian resources and made the Indian economy dependent on that of the West. From the early twentieth century, the Indian National Congress asserted *swadeshi* (self-reliance) and *swaraj* (self-rule) and, under the leadership of Mohandas K. Gandhi, waged the successful campaign of *satyagraha* or non-violent action for social and political reform which built up the nation both politically and morally and paved the way for Independence in 1947. In the post-Independence period, India attempted a non-aligned status, while following a broadly socialist economic path, and achieved considerable improvements in living standards of its people. However the one-sided nature of global economic power, particularly since 1989, led to a move toward a capitalist system. While there has been considerable economic and manufacturing growth, income disparity has also increased.

Through the ancient caste system, which continues to be supported by certain forms of Hinduism, discrimination on grounds of birth blocks the social mobility of many. '*Dalit*' (meaning broken or downtrodden) is the self-designation of Indians who are outside the caste system and were formally known as 'untouchables'. They are regarded as 'polluted' by birth and by occupations such as sweeping and carrying night soil. *Dalits* are not a homogeneous group but are divided into many different communities. They represent about fifteen per cent of the Indian population and are overwhelmingly found in the rural areas, where they are usually landless and excluded from access to even the most basic amenities, such as village wells. *Dalit* women are 'the *dalits* of the *dalits*', thrice alienated by class, caste and gender (Manorama 1992). The famous *dalit* leader B. R. Ambedkar championed their cause during the nationalist movement and in newly independent India. But despite a system of preferential support unparalleled in any other country, the situation of *dalits* as a whole has not substantially improved and deeply ingrained cultural and religious barriers to their integration continue to blight the life of *dalit* communities. Since the 1970s *dalits* have faced increasing violence from caste Hindus and have come together to campaign actively for their human rights (Webster 1992). There are also tribal communities – about five to seven per cent of the total population – who also receive certain social benefits. They are also known as 'forest dwellers' (*vanvasi*) and 'first settlers' (*adivasi*) showing that they generally live in isolated areas and are thought to be aboriginal people of the subcontinent.

Women in India are in an ambiguous position. On the one hand, India is one of the few countries in the world where the number of females is less than the number of males due to selective abortion, female infanticide, deprivation and abuse. On the other hand, woman is deified as goddess and earth mother. In Vedantic religion the feminine principle, *shakti* is God's consort and nature is understood as her embodiment. This represents a Sanskritisation of an earlier, pre-Aryan tradition of a goddess or feminine concept of divine power, which has left a forceful image of woman and motherhood in India, represented in the traditions of Kali. Indian women have been prominent both nationally and internationally and India has a vibrant feminist movement that has raised awareness of problems of the dowry system, lack of education, discrimination, ill-treatment and lack of representation (despite government quota systems) which contribute to their oppression. Drawing on *shakti* traditions, Indian feminists are also at the forefront of environmental movements in India and have challenged concepts of development that reproduce Western patriarchal structures and marginalise women's knowledge and activities (Shiva 1988).

INDIAN THEOLOGICAL RESPONSES: INCULTURATION, LIBERATION AND DIALOGUE

The Indian realities above – the fact of plurality, Hindu religio-cultural traditions, and colonial and caste oppression – give rise to three missiological responses, which form the main strands of Indian Christian theology: dialogue, inculturation and liberation (Indian Theological Association 1991). Inculturation and liberation are recognised as two distinctive models of the way in which the gospel relates dynamically to (different aspects of) the context in which it is set (Bosch 1991, 432–57). Inculturation theologies are attempts to express the gospel with respect to the religio-cultural setting and often use the tools of cultural anthropology and comparative religion, whereas liberation theologies are revolutionary theologies using the tools of sociology to challenge social injustice. Theologians of dialogue are most aware of the pluralist nature of Indian society and of the social and political need for a harmonious relationship between communities. Late elder statesman of Indian Christian theology, M. M. Thomas explains that, in chronological order, renascent Hinduism during British rule led Indian Christians to articulate their faith in a Hindu way (inculturation). Christians then came involved in nationalist movements for Independence and this brought the gospel into contact with secularism and socialism (liberation). Given the pluralistic Indian context, Indian Christians of both camps were bound to formulate theologies of dialogue with other faiths and ideologies (Thomas 1997; Chandran 1993).

The first to raise the question of an Indian understanding of Christ and an indigenous Christianity were leaders of the Hindu cultural renaissance in the nineteenth century, many of whom found the figure of Jesus Christ and the ethical teaching of Christianity extremely attractive but saw no reason to join the church or accept Christian doctrines about Jesus. In debate with Western missionaries in the early nineteenth century, Ram Mohan Roy used Jesus' moral teaching to reform Hinduism but rejected the doctrines of the incarnation and atonement. Keshub Chunder Sen, reacting against Roy by taking a mystical approach, described Jesus as the incarnation of the eternal *logos* and made the seminal suggestion that the Christian Trinity could be interpreted within Hinduism in terms of the Vedantic definition of

Brahman (God) as *sat-chit-ananda* (truth-consciousness-bliss), Jesus Christ being the incarnation of *chit*. Hindu converts to Christianity tried from within to relate their new faith to their Hindu identity and sought to create an indigenous expression of church. Krishna Mohan Banerjee argued that Christianity should be regarded as the fulfilment of Hinduism and coined the term 'Hindu-Christian' to express the indigenous Christianity he sought to lead.

Brahmabandhav Upadhyaya, a *brahmin* who became a Roman Catholic, popularised the work of Sen and Banerjee and, using the dualistic understanding of body and soul propounded in the philosophy of Thomas Aquinas, attempted to reconcile Hinduism and Catholicism. He argued that it was possible to remain culturally a Hindu while embracing Christianity as a religion: to be a Hindu by birth and a Catholic by rebirth. He went on to build Christian doctrine on the foundation of Indian rather than Greek philosophy, laying the groundwork for indigenous expression of Christian faith. In view of its Thomistic framework, his work is regarded as 'straightforward fulfilment theology at its most brilliant' rather than an attempt 'to reconstruct Christian insights in the indigenous fires of a Sanskritic crucible' (Lipner 1999, 178), nevertheless Upadhyaya is regarded today as the pioneer of Indian Christian theology. One of his plans was for an order of Indian Christian *sannyasis* based around an *ashram* (hermitage) but he was refused permission by the Vatican. More than fifty years later, and inspired by this vision, the first Catholic *ashram*s were founded, initially as an Indian form of monastic life (see, for example, Griffiths 1966). In the wake of the Second Vatican Council the *ashram* ideal developed into 'an open community of *guru* and disciples engaged primarily in contemplative pursuit of *Brahmavidya* (knowledge of God)' (Vandana 1982, 3–4). The Catholic *ashram* movement is chiefly motivated to bring peace between religions and *ashram*s have been centres of inculturation and inter-religious dialogue in India.

In a society with multiple cultural and religious traditions, inculturation cannot proceed without answering the prior question of which culture is most appropriate for interpreting the Christian gospel. Upadhyaya particularly developed the expression of Christian doctrine in terms of what was regarded as the highest of Hindu philosophy: *advaita* or non-dualism, as classically described by the philosopher Sankara in the seventh century. Sankara taught the oneness of the Divine (*Brahman*), who is Spirit, and the human spirit or self (*atman*). In his philosophy, the knowledge (*jnana*) that 'all is Brahman' is realised through a way (*marga*) of renunciation and self-transcendence through development of the interior life. Sankara regarded

monism as the highest form of religion, below which is theism or quali-
fied non-dualism, and below that are various forms of polytheism. In the
mind of the *advaitin* therefore, Christian belief in a personal God stands
in need of enlightenment. It was for this reason that Upadhyaya attempted
to show that, even in *advaitic* philosophy, *Brahman* is 'related within' – as
Sat-Chit-Ananda – and this self-knowledge (*Chit*) is the origin of the *logos*
of Christian theology.

Attention to the *advaitic* tradition of Hinduism was to dominate Indian
Christian theology until recently but other pioneers, such as A. J. Appasamy,
bishop of the Church of South India, preferred the *bhakti* tradition of
Hindu mysticism. *Bhakti* is a form of devotion that finds its inspiration
in the *Bhagavadgita* and its philosophical foundation in the 'personalist'
or 'theistic' approach of the eleventh-century philosopher Ramanuja.
Appasamy understood *bhakti* as 'love' in an ethical as well as an emotional sense and emphasised that biblical love meant 'the communion of
the human soul with a personal God' rather than the identity of the two.
Appasamy stressed *bhakti marga* over *jnana marga* in Hinduism because he
paralleled *advaitic* Hinduism with gnosticism. He wished to counter tendencies to pantheism by using Ramanuja's philosophy and the Johannine
logos to show that God was present within the cosmos but not identical to
it, as the soul is related to the body. He also criticised what he saw as *advaitic*
neglect of history and ignorance of morality: 'The Fourth Evangelist is thoroughly aware of the importance and supreme value of knowledge [*jnana*]
and yet he prefers to lay all his emphasis on love [*bhakti*]' (1928; 1931).
The choice of *bhakti* has more popular appeal than *advaitic* approaches
because it does not impose requirements of asceticism and because it lends
itself to use in corporate worship. Appasamy saw Christian *bhakti marga*
exemplified in the life of Sundar Singh, a Sikh convert who took up the
wandering life of a *sadhu* (wandering holy man) and interpreted New Testament teaching in everyday language and symbols, offering Indians 'the
Water of Life in an Indian cup' (Dayanandan 1994).

The pre-Aryan *shakti* tradition is attractive to those who reject the hegemony of Vedic Hinduism and seek to subvert it. Pandipeddi Chenchiah,
a judge and convert from Hinduism, is regarded as 'India's most radical
Christian theologian' (Boyd 1975, 144). He was a leader of the 'Rethinking Christianity' group, based in Madras (now renamed Chennai), which
in 1938 produced a book of that name that challenged the Indian church
to new depths of indigeneity (Job et al. 1938). Chenchiah attacked both
absolutist claims of Christianity and also absolutist interpretations of
advaitic philosophy by making the process of human history ultimate and

the Absolute the construction of the human mind. So Chenchiah reversed *advaita* mysticism by advocating the affirmation of creation and of activity rather than withdrawal from the world, on the grounds that the universal Spirit or *Brahman* is manifested in the power of *shakti*, which comes upon the world from outside not within and empowers a process of evolution of creation toward a better humanity – a concept that he derived from the philosophy of Aurobindo Ghose (Thangasamy 1966). Appasamy, who was also associated with the 'Rethinking Group' though not a contributor to the original book, disagreed with Chenchiah's approach believing it was more Western than Indian, it was incompatible with orthodox Christian doctrine, and complaining that it ignored the church (Francis 1992, 70–81). For his part, Chenchiah rejected Appasamy's *bhakti marga* because he saw it as a way of retreat as opposed to a dynamic way forward (Boyd 1975, 157).

As the above examples make clear, Indian Christian theology takes many different shapes depending on the particular tradition which is chosen for its indigenous expression and there has been considerable discussion as to which is most appropriate. For many theologians, however, this discussion is secondary to the aim of actualising the gospel in India in social terms. In view of the injustices of colonial control in late nineteenth-century India, renascent Hinduism issued in Indian nationalism. Upadhyaya himself moved from an inculturation approach to a struggle for liberation when his attempts to express the gospel in an Indian way were thwarted by the Vatican. He became a freedom fighter in his native Bengal and died while under arrest for sedition. Under the leadership of Gandhi the nationalist movement used non-violent methods and in 1947 achieved national independence under an ideology of social humanism. In this climate many Christian theologians felt the need to prove their allegiance to the nation and their Indianness. In the freedom struggle, leaders such as K. T. Paul of the YMCA urged Christians to transcend communal interests in recognition of the full humanity of each person, which Jesus Christ came to establish. Christians pressed for a secular constitution and refused separate communal representation in the *Lok Sabha* (Parliament).

Due to the colonial legacy, the church in India was tainted with a 'smell of foreignness' (Samartha 1981, 131–2) and its 'political parentage' (Job et al. 1938, 81–100) made it unwelcome in many quarters. The desire to develop an indigenous church, free from Western domination, has been one of the chief motivations for Indian theologies. This was, in part, achieved when Indian Christians came together in 1947 to form the Church of South India and later the Church of North India, which were intended for witness to and service of the nation. However, the solution to the problem of the church in India is more than Indianising Western patterns, uniting churches, and liberating them from foreign control. It raises deeper issues about the nature and importance of the Christian church given that institutions do not play a part in traditional Indian religious thinking. There are also questions of whether or not the church can be distinguished from the Christian community and how it can rise above the problem of 'communalism' (sectarianism).

In an attempt to address this issue and show their commitment to building the new Indian nation, Christians developed theologies of economic development and social justice, especially through the Christian Institute for the Study of Religion and Society (CISRS). Paul David Devanandan, its first director, saw the influence of the Christian gospel within Hinduism as contributing to a transformation in which cultural and spiritual resources for national self-awakening and nation-building were emerging. He understood the Christian mission as bearing witness to the new humanity in Jesus Christ and actively participating in the struggle for a new society in dialogue with Neo-Hindus and secularists (1961; 1964). He was succeeded as director of CISRS by M. M. Thomas, who was committed to the Nehruvian vision of India as a socialist and secular society and saw the contemporary 'Asian revolution' as evidence of God at work (1966). Thomas followed Chenchiah in making the new creation wrought in Christ the starting point for theology and he was most interested in interpreting the gospel for modern, secular India rather than in traditional, religious terms. He was critical of mystical approaches, both *advaita* and *bhakti*, which neglected God's involvement in history and came to advocate constructive social action as the main expression of Christian faith. In Hindu terms, Thomas espoused the path of action, *karma marga*, in preference to *jnana marga* or *bhakti marga* (Boyd 1975, 311–17). Thomas insisted that humanisation must be inherent in the Christian understanding of salvation and that spirituality and metaphysics should be put to serve the regeneration of human life. He developed a vision of the church in India not as a communal entity but as a 'Christ-centred secular fellowship', that is, 'an open fellowship able to witness, in all religious and secular communities, to Christ as the bearer of both true human life and salvation' (1971).

Whereas before Independence the focus had been on liberation from British rule, after it the internal oppression of lower castes and outcast groups gained greater attention. Theologies of humanisation were used to justify Christian involvement in development projects and political campaigns for justice for *dalits* (e.g. Rayan 1975). In the 1970s, under the influence of Latin American theology, especially among Catholic theologians the language of humanism gave way to the language of liberation and the Christian option for the poor and oppressed. While acknowledging a debt to Marxist analysis, Indian liberation theologians soon recognised its limitations in dealing with the caste system. They also challenged the historical and rational framework of Latin American liberation theology and led the way among Third World theologians in developing a spirituality of liberation which draws on indigenous cultural traditions and experience (Rayan 1983). There are a number of paths of liberation theology in India: theologians such as Xavier Irudayaraj have attempted to reinterpret the realisation of the self in *advaitic* philosophy to mean a conversion to the self in others; T. K. John, among others, has shown how the *Bhagavadgita* has been re-read at decisive moments in Indian history to motivate people to unselfish action (*nishkamakarma*) for the sake of the welfare of all (*lokasamgraha*); Walter Fernandes has identified popular expressions of *bhakti* – as opposed to classical, Sanskritised forms – as liberating to the 'underclasses'; and Sebastian Kappan has used his study of transformative movements in Indian history, such as Buddhism, to argue that it is the role of the church to reinforce them to prevent them succumbing to caste Hinduism (Wilfred 1992).

There is a diversity of India's religious life outside the 'elitist' traditions (Das 1987), which liberation theologians have shown a willingness to appropriate and use as indigenous spiritual resources for socio-political liberation. However, if they do not engage with the beliefs which these symbols represent, they are open to the accusation that they are using them to further their own end of 'a single universal culture of socialism' and therefore violating the spiritual values of the poor (Scott 1998). Alongside expressions of solidarity, Indian theologies of liberation also include the voices of the oppressed themselves. Those who converted to Christianity in mass movements now make up a large majority of the church in India as a whole but are poorly represented in its leadership. These Christian *dalits* suffer doubly because they do not qualify for government benefits intended to counter discrimination on the grounds that Christianity does not (officially) acknowledge caste. Thus the *dalit* Christian struggle is not only with Hindu society but also with the Christian community in which caste discrimination is by no means eradicated. Using the tools of liberation theology but applying them to caste rather than class, theologians of outcast groups have developed a theology from below, of the *dalits* rather than for them (Prabhakar 1988) to counter what V. Devasahayam has described as their 'pollution, poverty and powerlessness' (1997). A. P. Nirmal began *dalit* theology when he sought to affirm *dalit* identity forged in the *pathos* of the *dalit* servitude (Nirmal 1988). It is vehemently anti-*brahmin* and therefore

seeks to move Christian theology out of its 'Sanskritic captivity' and recover
the alternative pre-Aryan oral tradition of the *dalits* as a resource for theologising (Parratt 1994). Tribal identities are generally stronger than those
of *dalit* communities because of their distinct languages, religions, social
relations (particularly gender relations) and identifiable homeland, which
provide a framework for their theologising (Thanzauva 1997).

The liberation strand of Indian Christian theology also includes feminist
theology and ecotheology. Vandana Mataji has meditated on Saraswati, the
consort of *Brahman* in Vedic tradition, whom she describes as 'the source,
sustenance and ultimate goal of all creatures', 'the light of pure knowledge' and 'the all-white, pure one' and on Mary, the Mother of Jesus. She
concludes by identifying the heart of both Catholic and Hindu spiritual
traditions as 'feminine' and has actively promoted women's education and
leadership in the Catholic Church (1991). The predominantly rural nature
of Indian society and Christian involvement in development issues contributes to growing ecological awareness among Indian Christians (e.g.
Marak 1998). Astrid Lobo Gajiwala explains how, in rural Indian society,
women are most in contact with the natural environment: 'Women and
young girls balancing pots of water on their heads or hugging them on a
hip; women laden with bundles of fire wood or fodder; women engaged
in the backbreaking tasks of planting, weeding and harvesting.' Therefore,
they are most active in shaping it and also most immediately affected by
its deterioration (1998). Aruna Gnanadason has been a spokesperson for
women's rights in India and in the World Council of Churches. She has
used the *shakti* tradition and the close association between the female and
nature to motivate feminist theology's commitment to the liberation of
both women and creation (1993).

An attitude of dialogue is presupposed in both the inculturation and
liberation approaches to theologising – dialogue with Hindu culture and
with Indian social realities – though the term has been more applied to
religions than to ideologies. The relationship between Christianity and the
religious traditions of India was at first understood as one of fulfilment.
Building on the work of Upadhyaya, the 'Calcutta School' of Catholic
theologians sought to introduce Christians to Hinduism as 'the light of the
East'. This significantly influenced the positive approach of *Nostra Aetate*,
the declaration produced by the Second Vatican Council on the relation
of the Church to non-Christian religions (Gispert-Sauch 1997). In the
light of this, Dom Henri le Saux, a French Benedictine better known as
Abhishiktananda, took up the life of a *sannyasi* and used Hindu methods
of meditation to enter fully into the *advaitic* experience described in the

Upanishads, the mystical union with God which takes place 'in the cave of the heart'. In dialogue with Hindus, he concluded that Hinduism and Christianity converge and have their source in this 'ultimate encounter' and, in his later work, moved from a fulfilment theory of religions to suggesting their essential equivalence. For Abhishiktananda the aim was to go 'beyond religions', beyond all names (*nama*) and forms (*rupa*), to the common spiritual experience of all humankind, which each religion imperfectly expresses (1974; Gispert-Sauch 1997, 465).

Abhishiktananda has a strong following and his teaching has recently been graphically illustrated in Vandana Mataji's *Shabda Shakti Sangam*, which is an anthology of writings on various aspects of Christianity and Hinduism to which eighty scholars and mystics of both Christian and Hindu traditions have been persuaded to contribute. These include such internationally known figures as: Raimundo Panikkar and Stanley Samartha. The 'upside-down book' begins on one cover with Hinduism and on the other with Christianity, and these meet in the middle. Two individuals who have attempted to bring them together are discussed on either side of the centre: Abhishiktananda and Swami Vivekananda, who spoke so persuasively at the World's Parliament of Religions in 1893 about the harmony of all religions. Their pictures are joined by a painting by Jyoti Sahi which combines a crucifix and a dancing Shiva by means of streams of water. Christianity and Hinduism are portrayed as mirror images of each other that meet at the looking glass of a common spiritual experience but have different – yet parallel – religious structures. The implication is that the seeker can start from either side of the mirror but the aim is the confluence point, the heart of each, which is also the point at which they merge into one (1995). Panikkar has followed Abhishiktananda's ideas through in the realms of systematic theology, also moving from a fulfilment theology of religions to a theocentric or pluralist approach. He described *Brahman* as 'the unknown Christ of Hinduism' but his theology also implies that Christ is the unknown *Brahman* of Christianity because of his insistence that in human experience God must always be encountered as 'Trinity', that is all religions, by definition, recognise the ontological mediator between the absolute and the relative. Panikkar affirms the transcendent nature of Christ and, on the basis of this, looks toward the 'universalisation of Christianity', which he sees as a step toward 'the development of all religions, toward unity' (1973; 1981).

Protestant theologians also developed the idea of fulfilment, classically expressed in J. N. Farquhar, *The Crown of Hinduism* (1913). At the Tambaram (Madras) meeting of the International Missionary Council in

1938, Hendrik Kraemer attacked fulfilment theologies believing they led to
theological relativism and, applying the theology of Karl Barth, asserted the
discontinuity between the revelation in Christ and all religions (1938). In a
review of Kraemer's book, Chenchiah also rejected fulfilment theory but on
the rather different grounds that its 'facile presumption that in Hinduism
we have a search for salvation without satisfaction and that Christianity
satisfies the longing' was 'untrue to the fact'. At the same time Chenchiah
upheld fulfilment in the sense that, as a convert, he saw himself as indebted
to Hinduism as well as Christianity. While disagreeing with Kraemer's negative assessment of other religions, he shared his radical understanding of
the Christian message and regarded the Christian as doubly emancipated
from the traditions of both Hinduism and Christianity. In Chenchiah's
view, 'Christianity neither condemns nor accepts other religions' but is
related to them like 'a new creation to the old'. However, unlike Kraemer,
Chenchiah expected that the Spirit of Christ would transform Hinduism
from within (Job et al. 1938). Similarly, and reacting against Panikkar by
emphasising the explicit nature of the Hindu response, Thomas went on
to identify 'the acknowledged Christ of the Indian renaissance' specifically
in the message of leaders of renascent Hinduism (1970).

Inter-faith dialogue as it is understood in the World Council of Churches
was directly derived from the Indian multi-religious model under the guid-
ance of Stanley Samartha, first director of the WCC's unit on this topic,
whose initial experience of dialogue was gained at CISRS under Devanandan and Thomas. Samartha particularly appreciated that Devanandan was
non-exclusive and against imposing narrow limits on God's activity (1996,
17–23). With Thomas, Samartha understood theology as 'a spiritual source
of constructive and discriminating participation' in the struggle of the people (1974, 8). Thomas and Samartha shared a concern for 'the dialogue
between Christ and India' and Samartha also published a study of Hindu
responses to Jesus Christ. However, whereas Thomas' primary engagement was with secular Indian society, Samartha's was with Indian religions.
Rejecting 'the effort to discover the *hidden* Christ within Hinduism itself'
of Panikkar as subjective, neglectful of history, and open to serious misunderstanding by Hindus because Hinduism is not 'Christianity in disguise',
Samartha described the 'Unbound Christ' encountered beyond the boundaries of Christianity. He saw the enduring attraction of Jesus Christ in India
resulting in an 'unbaptised koinonia' outside the church so that though
'Christianity belongs to Christ, Christ does not belong to Christianity.'

The theology of dialogue that Samartha promoted placed discussion of
other faiths in the context of religious pluralism and human communities. It

was aimed at enabling different religious communities to live in peace with one another. Samartha stressed that dialogue takes place 'in community' because discussion does not centre on 'other faiths' as religious systems but on their adherents, whom Samartha called 'our neighbours of other faiths'. Thus he stressed the experiential nature of dialogue and was concerned not so much with 'systems of thought' as with 'living faiths'. In Samartha's view, though seeking truth is the aim of dialogue, truth can only be an issue when mutual respect of one another's convictions has first been reached; that is, a pluralist approach in which no one tradition can claim a monopoly on truth is a prerequisite for dialogue. However, he was at pains to point out that this does not mean that the partners in dialogue suspend their respective religious commitments since dialogue is a combination of 'commitment with openness' (1971).

The question of the focus of dialogue in India – whether with traditional Hinduism or with modernising forces, with religions or with poverty – has been a source of considerable tension between theologians in India. This is heightened by tensions in Indian society. Inculturationists have interacted mainly with high-caste Hindus and their philosophy, whereas liberationists have supported the lower or outcaste groups (Gispert-Sauch 1997, 460–1). Paul Knitter, distinguishing the two in terms of their understanding of church – *ashram* or base community – has observed in some detail the debate between the two groups in the Catholic Church, which came to a head in the early 1990s (1995, 163–6). Liberationists accused inculturationists of pandering to the elite and of collusion with an oppressive system. They advocated the revolutionary overthrow of traditional Hindu society and its replacement with a socialist model. Inculturationists responded that theologians of liberation followed an imported theology or ideology and that in their haste to achieve freedom, liberationists were insensitive to the long and venerable religious traditions of India. They argued that liberation could be achieved by peaceful and spiritual means beginning with the individual soul. Sebastian Painadath, among others, has sought a way forward by stressing the unity in Hindu thought between the three *margas: jnana, bhakti* and *karma* (1993) but essentially the argument is about whether peace or justice is the priority in Christian mission. A similar debate between inculturation and liberation has taken place within Protestant circles between those loyal to Vedantic traditions and *dalit* theologians (Boyd 2002).

In the present climate of rising Hindu nationalism both inculturation and liberation approaches have come under attack. Attempts to present the Christian gospel in a Hindu way, particularly the *ashram* movement, arouse the suspicions of Hindus that they are a duplicitous attempt to win more converts. Hindu writer Sita Ram Goel has described the leaders of Catholic *ashram*s as 'swindlers' and accuses them of the 'spiritual genocide of Hindu dharma'. He compares their methods to a Hindu donning a friar's habit and preaching Hinduism in the Italian countryside (1994). Liberation theologians have also been criticised as the contemporary successors of missionaries who encouraged 'rice Christians' because of their justification of motives of social advancement for Christian conversion. Promotion of a social gospel is seen as encouraging conversion for what Hindus see as 'ulterior motives'. In this debate, Indian Christians who are the products of mass conversion movements see the motives of their ancestors impugned by both Hindus and Christians (Kim 2002). F. Hrangkhuma's recent work challenges this perception of converts of mass movements as objects of mission by letting them tell their stories of the search for liberation and identity which led to their conversions (1998).

Theologians of dialogue have tended to stress the continuity between religions rather than the differences in the interests of peace between communities. *Dalit* theologians, on the other hand, do not want peace at the expense of justice. They may altogether refuse to dialogue with *brahminic* Hindus unless they reject *Hindutva*, which they regard as a fascist movement incompatible with *dalit* human rights (Razu 2001). While Samartha defended his theology by arguing that he used only the 'unitive vision' of *advaita* and not the whole edifice of *brahminic* Hinduism (1991, 92–111), his justification for dialogue appeared to buy into a Hindu understanding that all religions are equally valid paths to the Ultimate Mystery (of God), and therefore the Christian responsibility to evangelise and the phenomenon of conversion were down-played. Israel Selvanayagam, while greatly appreciating Samartha's legacy, has developed a more robust understanding of inter-faith dialogue in the light of recent debates and of dialogue with Hindu nationalists. Selvanayagam says of Christians in India: 'as converts, mostly from the Hindu or pre-Hindu religious traditions, their existence as a religious minority cannot be justified unless they take the unique position of being evangelical and dialogical'. He urges Christians to take more seriously the evangelistic passion of the Apostle Paul and the biblical message that the Christian message is for all people, while also engaging in dialogue (2000, 338–53).

Indian proponents of inter-faith dialogue, who are mainly ecumenicals of Protestant or Catholic traditions, tend to see religious plurality as a blessing which enriches understanding of God. Whereas many of their fellow Protestants and Catholics see other religions negatively as a threat

to the normativeness and finality of Jesus Christ and dialogue as having
a tendency to compromise the distinctiveness of Christianity by mixing
it with other religions. They wish to stress the uniqueness of Christian
tradition and universal claims of Jesus Christ, working for and expecting
conversion to Christianity, with the attendant change of religious community. They tend to regard ecumenical use of dialogue with other religions
as a substitute for proclamation of Christian revelation, which they see as a
primary aim of mission (Ramachandra 1996). In the war of words between
the two camps, those who designate themselves 'pluralists' label the others
'exclusivists', accusing them of narrow-mindedness and of perpetuating a
colonial model of mission. The 'exclusivists', on the other hand accuse
'pluralists' of abandoning their commitment to Jesus Christ and 'surren-
dering some of the essentials of biblical Christian faith' (Samartha 1996,
146–66). In his response to such criticisms of his work by Sunand Sumithra
and Ken Gnanakan, Samartha failed to recognise that Sumithra's concern
for Christian holiness is not because of lack of awareness of the beliefs
of other faiths but out of a desire to stress Christianity's distinctiveness
among other religions (Sumithra 1992, 79–97). Nor did he appreciate that
in describing the 'pluralistic predicament', Gnanakan is actively searching
for a theology of religions which both upholds the biblical text and also
points evangelicals to a greater openness to recognising the work of God
outside the boundaries of the Christian church (Gnanakan 1992, 149–71).
The relationship between 'commitment and openness' is an ongoing issue
for Christian theology in the complex community relations of India.

Having identified three main strands of Christian theology in India,
we will now look at the outworking of these approaches in two areas of
theology: Christology and pneumatology. But first it is worth noting that
what is known as 'Indian Christian theology' has been articulated and
developed through the writings of highly educated theologians, often in
the medium of English. Without questioning its validity as an indigenous
expression of Christian faith in India, it should be pointed out that it is not
necessarily representative of the grass-roots theologies of Indian Christians,
which emerge in vernacular languages through oral traditions and practices.
There are many indigenous Christian movements in India which do not
produce theological writing but nevertheless express their Christian faith in
Indian ways (Hedlund 2000). An important example is the rapidly growing
Pentecostal movement in India, many of whose members are defectors from
'mainline' churches (Kavunkal 1998). Michael Bergunder estimates that
20 per cent of South Indian Protestants are Pentecostals and argues that
this is an indigenous version of Christianity, a view which he substantiates

by showing the strong parallels between it and traditional Indian popular religion in the areas of miracle healing and exorcism (Bergunder 2001). The impact of Pentecostalism on academic English-medium Indian Christian theology is yet to be realised.

The gospel account which has appealed most to Indian theologians is that of John. Appasamy explained this predilection for the Fourth Gospel as due to its mystical nature that is in keeping with Indian thought and he produced studies of the themes of love and life in John (1928; 1931). Samartha quotes most often from the Fourth Gospel to justify dialogue. Abhishiktananda referred to it as 'the Johannine Upanishad' because he recognised an affinity with Hindu scriptures in style and content. He inspired Vandana to produce an acclaimed commentary in an Indian style on the theme of water in John (1989). She describes John's Gospel as 'particularly suitable to the Hindu psyche' because of its emphasis on the interior spiritual life and its use of symbolism (1992, 223). However, those who wish to make more of a distinction between the Christian gospel and Hindu traditions point out that the Fourth Gospel also preserves an historical tradition (Samartha 1996, 12). Precisely because the Gospel of John is much admired in India for 'its atmosphere of mysticism and its contemplative horizon', Rayan wishes to show that '[i]ts contemplation fixes on . . . Jesus' love for and service of the people' and use it to inspire action for human liberation (Rayan 1978, 213). The meaning of the word 'sign' in the Gospel – concrete historical action or mystical truth – is crucial to the interpretation of John in India.

In the Indian context, the interpretation of the significance of Jesus Christ has not been the monopoly of Christians. We have already mentioned notable Hindus who have given influential interpretations which vary between the ethical and the mystical. P. C. Mazoomdar, a disciple of Sen, claimed Christ for India when he described 'the oriental Christ' as 'the incarnation of unbounded love and grace', in contrast with the Western Christ, 'the incarnation of theology, formalism, ethical and physical force' (1883, 46). Mazoomdar inspired Upadhyaya and others to view Christ not as the historical Jewish Jesus but as the *Sat Guru* (True Teacher), or the indwelling teacher of the heart in Hindu tradition. *Guru* is the most common representation of Jesus Christ in Indian art and, by presenting him in this way, theologies of inculturation have been able to minimise discontinuity between Hindu and Christian traditions. On the other hand, since to accept Christ as the inner *Guru* of one's choice, *Ishta Devata*, is an option within Hinduism, Christian *advaitic* interpreters have been challenged to explain the uniqueness or distinctiveness of Christ. By explaining God the Son or the *logos* as the *Chit* of the Hindu Trinity, Upadhyaya insisted that Christ was not less than *Brahman* and upheld uniqueness and the credal confession of the union of two natures in Christ.

Christ as *Guru* is central to the *ashram* strand of the inculturation approach since an *ashram* is centred around a *guru*, and there has been great interest, especially among Catholic theologians, in the *advaitic* spiritual experience to which the *guru* leads the disciple, the unmediated self-realisation. Whereas Upadhyaya and earlier theologians tended to present the experience of Jesus himself of union with the Father as a fulfilment of the Hindu experience, Abhishiktananda came to the conclusion that the two were one and the same: that the '*Abba* experience' of Jesus described in the Fourth Gospel is 'the advaitic experience' (1976; 1984). This identification is questioned by others, who point out that 'the distinction between Jesus and the Father as an irreducible component of Jesus' experience is altogether certain in the biblical record' (Dupuis 1997, 272–4). The implication of Abhishiktananda's view for Vandana's Christology is that Jesus Christ is only one entry point to a way of life which is about principles of 'love or oneness' rather than about the historical Jesus. What is unique about Jesus is not his *guru*-ship but his heart, which is the womb of the universe, the source of the life-giving Spirit (1989, 64–6).

Other theologians who have used *advaitic* philosophy have done so in a more critical way. Stanley Samartha, who has published two books of Christology, is anxious not to 'identify Christ with the Brahman', as he believes Panikkar does, because he is afraid the historical contribution of Christianity will be lost. He stresses the Christian doctrines of salvation, the cross and the resurrection because he believes they have a distinctive and positive contribution to the Indian context by furnishing the historical dimension to faith, that is 'the connection of Being with life', which he believes an *advaitic* framework lacks (1974, 185–98). On the other hand, he argues positively that the use of *advaita* frees Jesus Christ from the grip of Barthian and Kraemerian exclusivist claims of lordship and uniqueness for Jesus Christ, which he regards as having unacceptable political consequences in a plural religious context, and allows for varied ways of responding to 'the unbound Christ' from within and without Christian faith. This leads him to reject classical (Chalcedonian) creeds of the 'substance' of Jesus Christ as irrelevant and unhelpful in the Indian context. Critically examining the biblical record, Samartha finds that Jesus Christ himself was theocentric and concludes that 'the notion that Jesus Christ is ontologically the same as

God', which he labels 'christomonism', is contrary to the New Testament. His 'revised Christology' moves from a position of the 'normative exclusiveness' of Christ to 'relational distinctiveness'. That is, Jesus Christ remains 'central to Christian faith' but what he sees as the 'inflated claims' made for him are inappropriate except (possibly) within the Christian community (1991, 89–91, 132–41). Samartha's Christology is unacceptable to many Christians because of his apparent dilution of Christian doctrine and selective approach to scripture. However Samartha repeatedly states that he does not wish to deny that Jesus Christ has a distinctive relation to God and to the world. His objection to Chalcedon is that the Greek dualistic concepts in which the status of Christ is expressed are inappropriate to the Indian and post-colonial context. He claims his use of *advaita* and his concept of the unbound Christ is intended to represent a high Christology, intelligible to Indians, that makes Christ universally accessible and active (1996, 146–66).

As a corollary of choosing the *bhakti* tradition in preference to *advaita*, Appasamy represented Jesus Christ as *Avatar* in preference to *Guru*. *Avatar* (literally 'descent') in Vaishnava tradition is a temporary incarnation of God to restore the world in a time when evil is dominant. Rama and Krishna are *avatars* of Vishnu. Upadhyaya rejected the use of the *avatar* concept for interpreting Christ because it represents a lower order of divinity than *Brahman* and because multiple incarnations are allowed for. Appasamy, however, believed that such a widespread concept with obvious parallels to Christian ideas of incarnation, which was already being used by Christians, was helpful as long as it was made clear that in Christian belief Jesus Christ is the one and only *Avatar* (1935). Like Appasamy, Vengal Chakkarai took as his starting point for Indian Christian theology the *bhakti* experience of Jesus Christ. But whereas Appasamy focused on the loving relationship with Christ and paid little attention to the cross, Chakkarai laid great emphasis on the actual death and resurrection of the human Jesus and its objective effects. That is, he begins theology from below, with what he called 'the Christhood of God' rather than 'the Deity of Christ'. In Chakkarai's Christology, by his kenosis or complete self-abnegation, Jesus chose the Cross. In his crucifixion human sin was burned up and a channel was opened of the Holy Spirit (*shakti*) to humanity. So Chakkarai described Jesus as the one permanent *Avatar* who remains forever the God-Man in human history by the Holy Spirit (1932a; 1932b).

Like Appasamy and Chakkarai, Chenchiah also began his theology with the experience of Jesus Christ. His interest was in 'the Raw Fact of Christ', the historic human being whose permanent entry into human life, and particularly his resurrection, signalled the beginning of a new creation. Chenchiah resists any equation of Christ with *Brahman* and also rejects *avatar* as a category to describe Jesus Christ. He understood Jesus as a new species, a God-Man, and his followers as reborn as part of an evolutionary process toward a new race. Historical readings of the *Bhagavadgita* as an incentive for decisive action as well as Chenchiah's portrayal of Jesus as one who breaks into history laid a Christological foundation for Indian theologies in which Christ is portrayed as Revolutionary or Liberator rather than ascetic. In *Jesus and Freedom* (1997), Sebastian Kappen presented Jesus as a passionate freedom fighter who confronted and challenged his contemporaries in the prophetic language of images, symbols, pictures and parables rather than engaging in philosophical or esoteric dialogue. George Soares-Prabhu drew attention to Jesus' teaching in the villages, which he described as a non-elitist, praxis-oriented pedagogy with revolutionary and liberative authority, raising critical questions and demanding response. Samuel Rayan pointed out how Jesus was 'friend of the outcast' standing 'outside the gate, sharing the insult' with the marginalised and despised. He 'unmasked the myth of pure ancestry' and called all people to commitment to share the bread of life, not primarily in a ritual and eucharistic sense but in the sense of creating an egalitarian, socialist society where all are fed (Wilfred 1992).

The *Guru* and the Revolutionary in Indian Christian theology can appear as poles apart and yet there is a colossal figure in recent history who often appears in the minds of proponents of both views: Gandhi. The manner in which Gandhi combined political involvement with spiritual detachment makes him an icon and a Christ-figure for theologians of both inculturation and liberation, who indeed bridges the two in his concern for an Indian liberation. However, Gandhi is not universally admired. *Dalit* theologians, for example, generally reject Gandhi as a model because of his failure to accord *dalits* proper political representation, despite his public protestations of support for them (Parratt 1994; Webster 1992). Nirmal began *dalit* Christology by describing Jesus not as friend of *dalits* but as a *dalit* himself. The *dalitness* of Jesus was shown by his ancestors, which included Tamar and Rahab; he was referred to disparagingly as a 'carpenter's son'; and he identified with *dalits* – publicans, prostitutes, lepers and Samaritans. As Son of Man, Jesus was rejected, mocked and despised by those of the dominant religion. He cleansed the temple and allowed the *dalits* of his day – the Gentiles – access to it. He suffered brokenness (*dalitness*) when he died on the cross (1988). For Prabhakar, the identification of Jesus with the Suffering Servant shows that 'the God of the Dalits . . . does not create others to do servile work, but does servile work Himself'. He sees *dalits* as suffering with God to bring about the redemption of humanity. The cross and resurrection of Jesus vindicated them, gave them dignity, and empowered them to fight against suffering. In *dalit* Christology, Jesus Christ is Saviour and Liberator whose resurrection made his particular historical sacrifice available to all (Prabhakar 1997). It is not the concern of *dalit* theology to work out a philosophical framework to explain this but to proclaim it in liberative action.

THE SPIRIT IN INDIA: *ADVAITA*, *ANTARYAMIN* AND *SHAKTI*

As the above examples show, in dialogue with the religious traditions of India and in awareness of the material poverty of its people, Indian theologians have tended to concern themselves with the role of Jesus Christ in mediating the presence and salvation of God rather than with the traditional Western Christological interest in justifying the claims about the person and nature of Christ. Indian Christology tends therefore to be 'Spirit Christology' rather than '*logos* Christology', that is, it gives preference to the function rather than the ontological status of Jesus Christ. It begins from the work of God in the world through God's Spirit since the creation, which Jesus Christ was chosen to fulfil. That is, Spirit Christology amounts to a recognition that 'Jesus is not only the giver but also the *receiver* of the Spirit' (Heron 1983, 127). The New Testament record would seem to give grounds for Spirit Christology as one of the earliest traditions, which was combined with *logos* Christology in the development of the Trinity (Dunn 1998, 74–9).

In a pluralistic context, Spirit Christology is preferable to the earlier 'cosmic Christ' theologies which justified and affirmed the presence and activity of God outside the boundaries of the church or Christendom but were criticised as patronising to those of other religions or ideologies, by describing them as 'anonymous Christians' or in other ways appearing to co-opt them into Christian faith. It shifts the question of uniqueness and universality in India from Christ to the Spirit. Among Protestants, Spirit Christology tends to be presented as an Indian framework for theology as opposed to the Greek one of *logos* but this makes it difficult for those who wish to retain their allegiance to the historic creeds and a common Christian confession. The difference between these approaches is illustrated by the respective interpretations by Samartha and Lesslie Newbigin, former Bishop of the Church of South India, of John 16.13, in which it is said that the Spirit will lead 'into all truth'. Samartha is confident that the truth to which the Holy Spirit leads includes the truth of other religions (1994,

47–8), whereas Newbigin argues that, since all truth is found in him, 'the Holy Spirit does not lead past, or beyond, or away from Jesus' (1982, 216–17). Samartha often refers to God as Mystery in order to say that God is greater than human understanding and though Jesus is the Revealer of God, there is room for other revelations. Whereas Newbigin stresses the fullness of the revelation in Jesus Christ which has made known what was unknown (Newbigin 1995).

In 1988 Cardinal Jozef Tomko, Prefect (or Head) of the Catholic Church's Congregation for the Evangelisation of Peoples directed a strongly worded attack against the Christology of Catholic theologians of inter-religious dialogue, particularly from the Indian subcontinent, for their alleged view that 'the mystery of God is not exhausted in the revelation in Jesus Christ but is also revealed in other religions' (Mojzes and Swindler 1990). Pope John Paul II in the encyclical *Redemptoris Missio* (1990) apparently shared Tomko's concerns in that the encyclical resisted what it described as a sep-aration of the work of the Spirit from Christ or the church. *Redemptoris Missio* was interpreted in India and elsewhere as an attack on Indian the-ologies (Burrows 1993). Since then Indian Catholic theologians and their supporters have defended themselves and largely succeeded in establish-ing the legitimacy of Spirit Christology as long as it is understood that it is complementary to traditional Christology not an alternative (Dupuis 1997).

Spirit Christology is another way of saying that there is more to theology than Christology. It understands the event of Jesus Christ from the per-spective of the presence and activity of the Holy Spirit of God in the world since creation. So it is that in Indian Christian theologies the doctrine of the Holy Spirit appears as prior to other doctrines and the doctrine of the Holy Spirit is, in many ways, 'the corner-stone of Indian Christian theology'. In Indian tradition *Brahman* or God is understood as the supreme or universal Spirit so Jesus Christ is seen in the light of the Spirit and pneumatology often underlies the formulation of other doctrines. Felix Wilfred explains to critics of Indian theology that, in keeping with Eastern religions in general, Asian Christian theologies recognise particularly 'the inexhaustible aspect of the divine mystery which St John expresses laconically: "God is spirit" (Jn 4.24)' (1998). This distinctive starting point for theology leads to a ten-dency 'to blur the distinctions between the persons of the Trinity . . . and especially to view all of God's dealings with us today as the work of the Spirit' (Boyd 1975, 242).

Boyd pointed out that the concept of the Holy Spirit may be rendered in Sanskrit by several different words, each reflecting a different tradition and carrying different connotations (1975, 241). The word *atman* (spirit, soul, self) and its cognates – including *Paramatman* (Supreme Spirit) and *antaratman* (inner spirit) – comes from *advaitic* or classical Hinduism. Describing the Spirit as *atman* draws attention to the interior dimension, the spirit within, and its union with the universal Spirit, *Brahman*. Gispert-Sauch (1999) finds the expression 'ground of being' a better translation of the concept of *atman* than 'soul' or 'self'. Abhishiktananda described the Holy Spirit as '"the *advaita* of God", the mystery of the non-duality of the Father and the Son' (1984, 184). In this vein, Vandana (1993) presents *ashramic* spirituality as a holistic approach to life, leading to and flowing from a realisation of oneness with the One Spirit and hence a connectedness with the universe and with 'spiritual' people regardless of gender, caste and religion. This image of the Spirit as the unifying principle of the Godhead and therefore of the universe lies behind Samartha's theology of dialogue and his insistence on the relevance of *advaita*. The Spirit or *advaita* provides the 'unitive vision' that holds Indian communities together and allows for the 'traffic across the borders' that is dialogue. Samartha describes dialogue itself as not so much a method or technique but 'a mood, a spirit, an attitude of love and respect' for 'our neighbours of other faiths'. That is, dialogue takes place in the 'milieu' of the Spirit (1981, 100 and 75).

Another word used for the Holy Spirit is *Antaryamin* – 'Indwelling One', a term from the *bhakti* tradition. Appasamy used this concept to interpret the doctrine of the Holy Spirit in terms of 'abiding' in John's Gospel, understanding this to refer to the inner life of the believer, particularly in its moral dimensions (Francis 1992, 22–42). In fact, Appasamy uses *antaryamin* to refer to the indwelling of all the persons of the Trinity, as do other famous *bhaktas* such as Narayan Vaman Tilak, the Maharashtrian poet (Jacob 1979). It seems the closeness of the *bhakti* relationship with the divine needs no mediation and therefore no explicit theology of the Holy Spirit, though the language is highly spiritual. This is clearly evident in Chakkarai who regards the Holy Spirit as the continuing presence of the resurrected Jesus, the permanent *Avatar*, and concludes that 'the Holy Spirit is Jesus himself taking his abode within us'. Chakkarai's theology starts from the reality of the experience of the Spirit, of 'faith-union' with Christ and he accuses Western theologians of obscuring this fact with creeds and formulations (1932a, 116–31). For the *bhakta*, the union with the Christ is not the result of renunciation and a process of self-realisation but an immediate experience in the midst of life from which loving devotion flows (Neill 1974). This is what gives *bhakti* its popular appeal. It is a revival or pentecostal-charismatic type of spirituality and many indigenous Christian movements of India, such as those described by Hrangkhuma (1998), could be described as *bhakti* movements.

Believing that the Bible affirmed the presence of God in creation from the beginning, Appasamy identified the meeting place of the communities of India as a spiritual one and this paved the way for the dialogue with religion and society initiated by Devanandan. In Appasamy's view, the Christian experience of the Holy Spirit was an intensification of the general presence of the Spirit that preceded it. He therefore disagreed strongly with Chenchiah who emphasised the 'new cosmic energy' of the Holy Spirit released in 'an outburst or inrush into history' by the resurrection of Jesus Christ, as if it had not been present before. Chenchiah believed this would lead to the establishment of a new universe by a process of unconscious change in which the Spirit, like a gas, was infused into history (Francis 1992, 70–81). Like Appasamy, Chenchiah found the immanence of the Spirit in the Fourth Gospel in keeping with 'the intellectual and spiritual leanings of India' but he differed in that he based his theology of the Spirit on a dynamic conception of *shakti*, which is used by Christians to refer to the power of the Spirit, rather than the more static *antaryamin*. 'Rethinking Christianity' in terms of *shakti*, Chenchiah insisted that the uniqueness of Christianity could not depend on its institutions or doctrines but only in its transcendence over other faiths as the religion of new birth by the Holy Spirit (Job et al. 1938, 47–62, Appendix).

The tension between the presence of the universal Spirit and the activity of the unpredictable Spirit of creation is another way in which the inculturation–liberation debate is expressed in India. We have seen above how the dynamic, transforming power of *shakti* has been used in liberation theologies. Thomas recounts how Hindu reformers struggled within classical Hinduism to transform a static concept of the world as the unfolding of the Universal Spirit into a purposive one in which the Spirit is 'the dynamic of cosmic evolution'. Though they succeeded in so doing, they still tended to lack a 'realistic appreciation of the depth of evil which the Spirit of God has to contend with', as described in the New Testament by the language of Satan and evil spirits (Thomas 1990). The language of non-*brahminic shakti* contains within it the 'spirituality for combat' that Thomas is searching for. Rayan, in his highly developed liberation pneumatology, sees 'the Holy Spirit, the Spirit of God and of Jesus Christ' as the 'heart of the Christian gospel'. Furthermore, he portrays the Spirit as a 'breath of fire', who comes 'to enable us to re-create our earth, not to put us to sleep' and is present 'not in ethereal euphoria, but in committed historical action' (1979, vii). Like Thomas, he advocates 'spiritual warfare' to overcome the forces of violence and oppression in society but Rayan's theology of 'mission in the Spirit' is also a comprehensive approach to the whole of life in which action and contemplation are combined (John 1991). The image of *shakti* lies behind the understanding of the earth as a theological and a liturgical reality which has made Rayan a leading voice in ecotheology in ecumenical circles (1994). His awareness of the Spirit's activity in the world as Liberator and presence as Creator brings together action for human welfare with aesthetic and mystical concerns.

India not only has an awareness of God as Spirit, it is also a land of many spiritualities, of which *advaitic* Hinduism, *bhakti* devotion and *shaktism* are three major types. 'Spirituality' is a very difficult term to define but it is used by Indian theologians to distinguish religious approaches or attitudes from religions themselves and thus it crosses the boundaries of religious communities. As we have seen above, the term need not apply only to 'passive self-interiority or transcendentalism' – though it is most used by this camp – but also to active response to the world that issues from a relationship with the Divine (Selvanayagam 1998). Nevertheless, the awareness of God as Spirit explains why Asian (as illustrated by Indian) theology gives much more importance than Western theology to the categories of interiority, experience and mystery. In other words, there is a close relationship between theology and spirituality and between the mode of theologising and the religio-cultural traditions of India (Wilfred 1998).

Though Indian theology may be very rational, Indian theologians of many persuasions insist that theology should be interpreted more broadly than systematic formulation of doctrine. Theology is enriched by the use of symbol and myth and expressed in varied cultural forms; in other words, it is an art-form as well as a science (Samartha 1991, 89–91; Rayan 1979b). In the visual arts, there are a number of prominent Indian Christian practitioners. Sahi is the most well known and is appreciated across a wide theological spectrum. He has reflected deeply on his work and the significance of art as a mediator of the gospel and a form of theologising. A Catholic with a Protestant and Reformed Hindu background, he aims to bridge inculturation and liberation through his work by expressing the 'theology of Indian Christian culture' through its diverse traditions (Sahi 1986). The heritage of *bhakti* leads many theologians to express themselves in poetry and song. Thomas Thangaraj advocates a 'singable theology' as a way of changing the heart as well as educating the mind (1992) and, similarly, Rayan describes the Spirit as a poet who 'sees and senses symbolism, relationships, and meanings . . .' and points them out in order to inspire action for liberation (1979a, 110).

Dance is also an immensely popular art-form in India and so Vandana creatively interprets the role of the Spirit in John's gospel as the 'dance of the waters', moving gracefully in and between contemporary movements in India under the direction of the Master Choreographer (1989, 9–24). In India, theology is not only propositional but also sometimes mystical, analogical and creative in its imagery (Wilfred 1998).

The forms of Indian theology reflect the diversity of Indian religious and social life. Yet despite the diversity, there is a shared Indianness about all the theologies mentioned here because they are expressed in a shared cultural language and arise out of a common historical experience. The struggles among Indian Christian theologians relate closely to tensions within Hinduism and Indian society and the solutions they propose draw from the same wells of indigenous thought and practice. And yet these theologies of the Indian context have many points of contact with other theologies arising in quite different places as well as insights to share, particularly on issues of religions, oppression and the nature of God as Spirit. Indian reflections offer a rich contribution to the global conversation of theologies.

REFERENCES AND FURTHER READING

Abhishiktananda, Swami. 1976. *Hindu–Christian Meeting Point – Within the Cave of the Heart*. Delhi
　1984. *Saccidananda: A Christian Approach to Advaitic Experience*. Delhi
Abraham, K. C. (ed.) 1990. *Third World Theologies: Commonalities and Divergences*. Maryknoll
Appasamy, A. J. 1928. *Christianity as Bhakti Marga: A Study of the Johannine Doctrine of Love*. Madras
　1931. *What is Moksa? A Study in the Johannine Doctrine of Life*. Madras
　1935. *Christ in the Indian Church: Some Thoughts on Christian Faith and Practice*. Madras
　1958. *Sundar Singh: A Biography*. London
Indian Theological Association, 1991. 'Towards a Theology of Religions: An Indian Christian Perspective'. Statement of the Twelfth Meeting of the ITA, 1988 in Kunchria Pathil (ed.), *Religious Pluralism: An Indian Perspective*, pp. 324–37. Delhi
Baago, Kaj. 1969. *Pioneers of Indigenous Christianity*. Bangalore
Bergunder, Michael. 2001. 'Miracle Healing and Exorcism: The South Indian Pentecostal Movement in the Context of Popular Hinduism', *International Review of Mission* 90/356–7, 103–12
Bosch, David J. 1991. *Transforming Mission: Paradigm Shifts in Theology of Mission*. Maryknoll

Boyd, Robin H. S. 1969. *An Introduction to Indian Christian Theology.* Delhi
  1975. *An Introduction to Indian Christian Theology,* revised edition. Delhi
  2002. 'Beyond Captivity?' in Israel Selvanayagam (ed.) *Moving Forms of Theology: Faith Talk's Changing Contexts,* pp. 121–5. Delhi
Burrows, William R. 1993. *Redemption and Dialogue: Reading Redemptoris Missio and Dialogue and Proclamation.* Maryknoll
Chakkarai, Vengal. 1932a. *Jesus the Avatar.* Madras, reproduced in P. T. Thomas (ed.) 1981. *Vengal Chakkarai,* vol. I, pp. 42–198. Madras
  1932b. *The Cross and Indian Thought.* Madras, reproduced in P. T. Thomas (ed.) 1981. *Vengal Chakkarai,* vol. I, pp. 199–383. Madras
Chandran, J. Russell. 1993. 'Methods and Ways of Doing Theology' in R. S. Sugirtharajah and Cecil Hargreaves (eds.) *Readings in Indian Christian Theology,* vol.1, pp. 4–13. Delhi
Das, Somen (ed.) 1987. *Christian Faith and Multiform Culture in India.* Bangalore
Devanandan, P. D. 1961. *Christian Concern in Hinduism.* Bangalore
  1964. *Preparation for Dialogue.* Bangalore
Devasahayam, V. (ed.) 1997. *Frontiers of Dalit Theology.* Delhi/Madras
Dunn, James D. G. 1998. *The Christ and the Spirit: Collected Essays,* vol. 2. Edinburgh
Dupuis, Jacques. 1997. *Toward a Christian Theology of Religious Pluralism.* Maryknoll
Farquhar, J. N. 1913. *The Crown of Hinduism.* Oxford
Francis, T. Dayanandan (ed.) 1994. (3rd edn) *The Christian Bhakti of A.J. Appasamy: A Collection of His Writings.* Madras
Gajiwala, Astrid Lobo. 1998. 'Making a Path to the Womb: Eco-Feminism and Its Implications' in Joseph Mattam and Jacob Kavunkal (eds.) *Ecological Concerns – An Indian Theological Response,* pp. 54–67. Bangalore
Gispert-Sauch, George. 1997. 'Asian Theology' in David F. Ford (ed.) *The Modern Theologians: An Introduction to Christian Theology in the Twentieth Century,* pp. 455–76. Oxford
  1999. 'Atman', *Vidyajyoti Journal of Theological Reflection* 63/1, 80.
Gnanadason, Aruna. 1989. 'Women and Spirituality in Asia' in *In God's Image,* pp. 15–18
  1993. 'Towards a Feminist Eco-Theology for India' in Prasanna Kumari (ed.) *A Reader in Feminist Theology,* pp. 95–105. Madras
Gnanakan, Ken R. 1992. *The Pluralistic Predicament.* Bangalore
Goel, Sita Ram. 1994. *Catholic Ashrams: Sannyasins or Swindlers?* Delhi
Griffiths, Bede. 1966. *Christ in India: Essays Towards a Hindu-Christian Dialogue.* New York
Hedlund, Roger E. (ed.) 2000. *Christianity is Indian: The Emergence of an Indigenous Community.* Delhi
Heron, Alasdair I. C. 1983. *The Holy Spirit: The Holy Spirit in the Bible, in the History of Christian Thought, and in Recent Theology.* London
Hrangkhuma, F. (ed.) 1998. *Christianity in India: Search for Liberation and Identity.* Delhi/Pune

Jacob, Plamthodathil S. 1979. *The Experiential Response of N. V. Tilak*. Madras

Job, G. V., P. Chenchiah, V. Chakkarai, D. M. Devasahayam, S. Jesudason, Eddy Asirvatham and A. N. Sudarisanam. 1938. *Rethinking Christianity in India*. Madras

John, T. K. (ed.) 1991. *Bread and Breath: Essays in Honour of Samuel Rayan SJ*. Anand

Kappen, Sebastian. 1977. *Jesus and Freedom*. Maryknoll

Kavunkal, Jacob. 1998. 'Neo-Pentecostalism: A Missionary Reading', *Vidyajyoti Journal of Theological Reflection* 62/6, 407–22

Kim, Sebastian C. H. 2002. *In Search of Identity: Debates on Religious Conversion in India*. Delhi

Knitter, Paul F. 1995. *One Earth Many Religions: Multifaith Dialogue and Global Responsibility*. Maryknoll

Kraemer, Hendrik. 1938. *The Christian Message in a Non-Christian World*. London

Lipner, Julius. 1994. *Hindus: Their Religious Beliefs and Practices*. London

    1999. *Brahmabandhab Upadhyay: The Life and Thought of a Revolutionary*. Delhi

Manorama, Ruth. 1992. 'Dalit Women: The Thrice Alienated' in T. Dayanandan Francis and Franklyn J. Balasundaram (eds.) *Asian Expressions of Christian Commitment*, pp. 194–98. Madras

Mansingh, Surjit. 1998. *Historical Dictionary of India*. Delhi

Marak, Krickwin C. and Atul Aghamkar (eds.) 1998. *Ecological Challenge and Christian Mission*. Delhi

Mazoomdar, P. C. 1883. *The Oriental Christ*. Boston

Mojzes, Paul and Leonard Swindler (eds.) 1990. *Christian Mission and Interreligious Dialogue*. Lampeter

Neill, Stephen. 1974. *Bhakti: Hindu and Christian*. Madras

Newbigin, Lesslie. 1982. *The Light Has Come: An Exposition of the Fourth Gospel*. Edinburgh

    1995. *The Open Secret: An Introduction to the Theology of Mission*. Grand Rapids

Nirmal, Arvind P. 1988. 'Towards a Christian Dalit Theology' in Arvind P. Nirmal (ed.) *A Reader in Dalit Theology*, pp. 53–70. Madras

Painadath, Sebastian. 1993. 'Towards an Indian Christian Spirituality in the Context of Religious Pluralism' in Dominic Veliath (ed.) *Towards an Indian Christian Spirituality in a Pluralistic Context*, pp. 3–14. Bangalore

Panikkar, Raimundo. 1973. *The Trinity and the Religious Experience of Man: Icon-Person-Mystery*. New York/London

    1981. *The Unknown Christ of Hinduism: Towards an Ecumenical Christophany*. London

Parratt, John. 1994. 'Recent Writing on Dalit Theology – A Bibliographical Essay' *International Review of Mission* 83/329, pp. 329–37

Pickett, J. Waskom. 1933. *Christian Mass Movements in India*. New York

Prabhakar, M. E. 1988. 'The Search for a Dalit Theology' in Arvind P. Nirmal (ed.) *A Reader in Dalit Theology*, pp. 41–52. Madras

    1997. 'Christology in Dalit Perspective' in V. Devasahayam (ed.) *Frontiers of Dalit Theology*, pp. 402–32. Delhi/Madras

Ramachandra, Vinoth. 1996. *The Recovery of Mission: Beyond the Pluralist Paradigm.* Carlisle

Rayan, Samuel. 1975. 'Evangelization and Development' in Gerald H. Anderson and Thomas F. Stransky (eds.) *Evangelization.* Mission Trends No. 2, pp. 87–105. Grand Rapids

1978. 'Jesus and the Poor in the Fourth Gospel', *Bible Bhashyam* 4/3, pp. 213–28

1979a. *Breath of Fire – The Holy Spirit: Heart of the Christian Gospel.* London

1979b. 'Theology as Art', *Religion and Society* 26/2, 77–90

1983. 'Theological Priorities in India Today' in Virginia Fabella and Sergio Torres (eds.) *Irruption of the Third World – Challenge to Theology*, pp. 30–41. Maryknoll

1994. 'The Earth is the Lord's' in David C. Hallman (ed.) *Ecotheology: Voices from South and North*, pp. 130–148. Geneva/Maryknoll

Razu, I. John Mohan (ed.) 2001. *Struggle for Human Rights: Towards a New Humanity. Theological and Ethical Perspectives.* Nagpur

Sahi, Jyoti. 1986. *Stepping Stones: Reflections on the Theology of Indian Christian Culture.* Bangalore

Samartha, Stanley J. 1974. *The Hindu Response to the Unbound Christ: Towards A Christology in India.* Bangalore

1981. *Courage for Dialogue: Ecumenical Issues in Inter-Religious Relationships.* Geneva

1991. *One Christ – Many Religions: Towards a Revised Christology.* Maryknoll

1994. *The Pilgrim Christ – Sermons, Poems and Bible Studies.* Bangalore

1996. *Between Two Cultures: Ecumenical Ministry in a Pluralist World.* Geneva

Scott, David C. 1998. 'A Mirror to M. M. Thomas's Perspective on Inter-Religious Studies' in K. C. Abraham (ed.) *Christian Witness in Society: A Tribute to M. M. Thomas*, pp. 158–77. Bangalore

Selvanayagam, Israel. 1998. 'Components of a Tamil Shaiva Bhakti Experience' in David Emmanuel Singh (ed.) *Spiritual Traditions: Essential Visions for Living*, pp. 418–38. Bangalore

2000. *A Second Call: Ministry and Mission in a Multifaith Milieu.* Madras

Shiva, Vandana. 1988. *Staying Alive: Women, Ecology and Development.* Delhi

Shourie, Arun 1994. *Missionaries in India: Continuities, Changes, Dilemmas.* New Delhi

Smith, Donald E. 1963. *India as a Secular State.* Princeton

Sumithra, Sunand (ed.) 1992. *Doing Theology in Context.* Bangalore

Thangaraj, Thomas. 1992. 'Towards a Singable Theology' in T. Dayanandan Francis and Franklyn J. Balasundaram (eds.) *Asian Expressions of Christian Commitment*, pp. 163–72. Madras

Thangasamy, D. A. 1966. *The Theology of Chenchiah with Selections from His Writings.* Bangalore

Thanzauva, K. 1997. *Theology of Community: Tribal Theology in the Making.* Aizawl

Thomas, M. M. 1966. *The Christian Response to the Asian Revolution.* London

1970. *The Acknowledged Christ of the Indian Renaissance.* Madras

1971. *Salvation and Humanisation: Some Critical Issues of the Theology of Mission in Contemporary India*. Madras

1990. 'The Holy Spirit and the Spirituality for Political Struggles', *Ecumenical Review* 42/3–4, 216–24

1992. *Theologiegeschichte der dritten Welt: Indien*. Munich

1997. 'Indian Theology' in Karl Müller, Theo Sundermeier, Stephen B. Bevans and Richard H. Bliese (eds.) *Dictionary of Mission: Theology, History, Perspectives*, pp. 202–12. Maryknoll

Vandana, 1989. *Waters of Fire*. Bangalore

1982. *Social Justice and Ashrams*. Bangalore

1991. *And the Mother of Jesus was There: Mary – in the Light of Indian Spirituality*. Garhwal

1992. 'The Word as '*Vac*' and the Silence of Joy: A Feminine Interpretation', *Journal of Dharma* 17/3, 220–2

(ed.) 1993. *Christian Ashrams – a Movement with a Future?* Delhi

1995. *Shabda Shakti Sangam*. Bangalore

Webster, John C. B. 1992. *The Dalit Christians: A History*. Delhi

Wilfred, Felix (ed.) 1992. *Leave the Temple: Indian Paths to Human Liberation*. Maryknoll

1998. 'Towards a Better Understanding of Asian Theology: Some Basic Issues', *Vidyajyoti Journal of Theological Reflection* 62/12, 890–915

4

East Asia

Edmond Tang

For anyone attempting to give an account of the development of theology in East Asia a problem immediately arises: when and where to begin? Should it begin with the arrival of Christianity in China, Japan and Korea, or only with the emergence of alternative theologies which have made a radical break with the West and are truly responding to Asia's ancient cultural traditions as well as contemporary political contexts? It is evident from any survey of local theologies that they would often go through a period of imitation and adaptation before embarking on a creative phase. Many factors enter into the picture, one of which is the sense of gratitude and respect for tradition – the Western tradition in this case which brought Christianity to Asia – and the feeling of belonging to a historical church that often leads one to emphasise more the value of continuity and authority than that of critique and invention. It is interesting to note that up until the 1970s, before contextual theology became the order of the day, the dream of many East Asian theologians was to become an Asian Aquinas or Luther, and even today many would still be content to be followers and interpreters of Rahner, Barth or Moltmann. This conservatism is sometimes reinforced by church institutions; witness the not uncommon disciplinary actions that were taken against wayward theologians when they dared to move beyond the narrow confines of evangelical or Catholic theologies.

For the purpose of this volume, the obvious choice is to give attention to the more distinctive theological themes that arose directly from the socio-political context, and to theological styles – rather than technical methodology – which are influenced by East Asian ways of thinking, even though we may be accused of concentrating on the periphery and ignoring the mainstream of theological productions in these Asian churches. In other words, instead of attempting a general history of the development of theology in East Asia, we have opted for a more selective approach,[1] letting a choice of theologians and theologies speak for themselves, before trying to identify any common trends and theological styles at the end of the chapter. The choice is based on three considerations: a particular theology's critical view of Western theology, the way it dialogues with indigenous cultural or religious traditions, and the way it engages with the contemporary socio-political context. The meaning of the first two is rather obvious, but the third, namely the context, requires some further consideration.

THE POLITICS OF INCULTURATION IN EAST ASIA

In the last hundred and fifty years, Asia has seen more changes in its societies than perhaps in its millennia of history combined. The relative seclusion of Asian kingdoms was prised open by a combination of trade and military power, and traditional worldviews were made redundant by ideas and values associated with modern industrial society, particularly those of progress and the nation-state. Before the arrival of the modern West, the spiritual outlook of these Asian cultures was not conscious of time as linear development towards some eschatological goal, and history was conceived rather as a recurrent cycle operating under some mandate of heaven. The idea of time as linear development, although it originated in the Judeo-Christian world, has brought the whole of humanity under its spell. Even when non-Western cultures reacted against it, the reaction itself had brought them into the realm of historical thinking. A gap now appears between the past, which is being rejected or needs to be re-appropriated, and the future, which is still to be defined. The need to change as well as the responsibility to engineer that change, however, is not in doubt.

The idea of nationhood is also new to Asia. Even in countries like China, united for over two thousand years under a central government, the consciousness of being Chinese is more that of a people and a civilisation rather than of a polity. The idea of the nation-state is as radical as the idea of history in transforming the consciousness of Asian peoples. The traditional polity, based on the network of an extended family, is now seen to be not only oppressive but inefficient. The expansion of the West provoked a strong resistance from the local peoples; ironically, this resistance was the most effective when it imitated the West by generating a new nationalism

---

[1] Good general histories of theology in East Asia are rare. The most comprehensive treatment of authors and publications can be found in volume III of *Asian Christian Theologies – A Research Guide to Authors, Movements, Sources*, ed. John C. England et al., Delhi: ISPCK and Maryknoll: Orbis (2002).

through the creation of a modern state. On the one hand this new national-ism provides a psychological focus for resisting Western domination, while on the other hand it sets out the framework to rebel against as well as reform traditional political structures. By the turn of the nineteenth century, in all the countries we are dealing with, there were rumblings of a cultural renaissance – some form of Chinese or Japanese 'Enlightenment' with new parameters to define each people's political and cultural identities.

The three countries of East Asia under consideration in this chapter, namely China, Japan and Korea, share a common Confucian heritage in both core social values as well as a centralised form of government. A second feature common to these countries is that all of them have undergone a period of intense nationalism and struggle against imperialist domination. At the same time all of them embraced modernisation in the Western form in their pursuit of strong and wealthy nation-states.

The countries we are considering, despite their common heritage, could not have taken more different roads in their development. China went through two revolutions, the first in 1911 and the second in 1949, with continuous civil war and foreign invasion taking place at the same time. It finally accepted a form of Westernisation in 'scientific socialism'. Japan took the road of fighting the West with their own methods and the result is a fas-cinating combination of feudal loyalties and a capitalist-militaristic model. Korea, first the vassal of China, then the colony of Japan and some would say a colony of USA in the South, rebels against all three. It is not within the scope of a short study to describe and analyse in detail the processes just mentioned. Our interest is to see how the churches there responded to these radical changes and which kinds of theology were produced.

This is briefly the context which Christian missions encountered in East Asia in the nineteenth and twentieth centuries. The British, French, Dutch and American colonisers replaced the Spanish and Portuguese of earlier epochs. Unlike their predecessors, the new colonisers did not need the legitimation of religion; although Christian mission was encouraged in some cases and tolerated only in others, conversion of the local population was not part of their colonial policies. Nevertheless missionary institutions were very useful in forming a Westernised elite to serve as intermediaries between the colonial powers and the local population. Besides group con-versions at the grassroots, many of the educated elite, in receiving a Western education, also accepted the Christian faith.

The rising nationalism in Asian countries at the turn of the nineteenth century, however, called into question the identity of these Christian elites. Could they be truly Christian and truly Asian at the same time? Slowly there began a movement to break away from Western ecclesial structures and mentalities and to make Christianity more Asian. One way is to adapt Christian beliefs and practices to local cultures and initiate a dialogue with traditional religions and cultures. The second way is to join the task of nation-building. Almost every contextual theologian under consideration would have taken part in one or both of these ventures.

CHINA

Christ and Confucius

Christianity has been on Chinese soil on and off for fourteen centuries. The first Christians to arrive were Nestorians in the seventh to eighth centuries during the Tang dynasty. The Nestorians did not hesitate to borrow Chinese religious concepts in presenting the Christian faith. God the creator was described on the Nestorian Tablet erected in 781 AD as the one who set 'the original breath in motion and produced the two principles . . . he made and perfected all things'. The two principles refer to yin and yang in Taoist thought. The Nestorians, however, never gained sufficient inroad into the indigenous population and Nestorian Christianity remained mostly a religion practised by foreign traders in China and was banned, together with Buddhism, in 845.

After a short-lived Franciscan mission in the fourteenth century, Jesuit missionaries arrived in China again in the seventeenth. These men, Matteo Ricci and his companions, were steeped in the learning of the Renaissance in Europe. In China they encountered the highly developed philosophies of neo-Confucianism: sophisticated metaphysics, a spiritual discipline based on lifelong learning and cultivated taste for literature and the fine arts. This high Chinese culture was in turn interested in the learning of the West: philosophy, astronomy, geography, mathematics and the sciences. Ricci's approach was based on the assumption that the Confucian classics contained a 'natural law', and the ancient Chinese tradition was aware of a Supreme Being, and that human beings are able to reason from the nature of the universe to the existence and nature of God, and to develop a moral life accordingly. It was therefore legitimate to accommodate the gospel to Chinese culture generally. The philosophical and moral principles of Confucianism, once purified and supplemented by biblical revelation, could become an integral part of the Christian faith. Subsequent quarrels with other missionaries over ancestor worship and other quasi-religious rituals, popularly known as the Rites Controversy, led to the Papal decision against the method of accommodation, and as a result Christian missions were prohibited by the Chinese government in 1724. The controversies, however, highlighted the theological issues that Chinese Christians had to deal with in later generations up to the present.

What the Jesuits failed to achieve by friendship and dialogue, the nineteenth-century missionaries succeeded in doing with the help of gun-boats and diplomatic manipulations. The Opium Wars forced open China's door to the West, and 'unequal treaties' gave missionaries entry to the Chinese empire. The social dysfunction caused by the impact of Western economic and political domination led to a revolt of the peasantry against foreigners during the Boxer Rebellion of 1900 as well as the rise of nation-alism among the intellectuals in the early twentieth century. This hostility was directed especially at Christians. Against this background church lead-ers called for a fundamental Sinicisation of Christianity. First, leadership positions were to be turned over to Chinese nationals. Secondly, a Chinese apologetic was to be developed. The problem of indigenisation, on both the institutional and theological levels, was to be the dominant theme of Chinese theology in the twentieth century.

The problem of indigenisation, in an era of turbulent social changes, could not be an isolated academic or pastoral question. For it to succeed it had to address the related problem of national reconstruction. Indigeni-sation in the Asian context was first of all concerned with the Western character of Christianity and its ties with Western political expansion. The first efforts of Chinese theologians were to show that the Christian faith was a universal religion, not necessarily bound by any particular culture but at home in all cultures. In some cases they also endeavoured to identify Christianity with certain features of Confucianism, the dominant tradition in China. The wisdom of this approach was questionable, however, because Confucianism was also under attack. A good proportion of anti-Christian intelligentsia in China was equally anti-Confucian; they saw it as a feudal religion, an anti-democratic ideology holding China back from modernisa-tion. The question of Christian participation in nation-building was closely related to the concerns just mentioned. In a period of growing nationalism, could a Chinese Christian who had converted to a foreign religion be patri-otic at the same time? To what extent could the Christian vision contribute to China's social reconstruction, not only spiritually but also practically? Would and could Christians take part in the coming revolution? These closely related questions, posed with poignancy in early twentieth-century China, were equally relevant to Japan and Korea, as we shall see in surveying the contextual theologies developed in these countries.

In China, both Catholics and Protestant leaders were involved in the indigenisation movement, but the most representative theologian of the period under consideration was T. C. Chao (Zhao Zichen).[2] For over thirty years, from the 1920s to the establishment of the People's Republic in 1949, T. C. Chao was the leading intellectual of Protestant Christianity. He was professor of religious philosophy at Yenching University in Beijing – the Harvard of China – and later became the dean of the School of Religion there. Internationally Chao was also well known, taking an active part in international conferences and in 1948 was chosen as one of the six elected presidents of the World Council of Churches.

Chao's principal concern was the indigenisation of Christianity in China.

. . . the idea of an 'indigenized Christianity' has constantly been in the minds of the Chinese Christians. The basis of this thinking is rested on two factors: (a) The Christians (in China) have come to recognize that Christianity, though deeply buried in the rituals, creeds, and organizations of the Western church, has in fact an unperishable religious reality; (b) The Christians have also come to realize that Chinese culture, though contributing little to the area of science, does have its merits with regard to the spiritual aspect of life. With these two understandings, the Chinese Christians realize that the essence of Christianity and the spiritual heritage of Chinese culture can be united into one single whole. The religious life of Christianity can be injected into Chinese culture and becomes its new life blood, and the Chinese spiritual heritage can provide the media for the expression of Christianity. (quoted in Ng 1979: 248)

As Chao saw it, the project was to comprise two phases. The first step was to purify Christianity, to cleanse it both institutionally and doctrinally. By institution Chao referred firstly to the alien forms of worship – rituals, liturgies that were unnecessary, non-essential and utterly incomprehensible to the Chinese people. There is evidence that Chao was involved in some attempts to create Chinese styles of worship and he wrote hymns to Chinese music. Secondly, the church must also be purified of its denominationalism. Not only was this an 'unintelligible confusion' to the Chinese, the conflict and controversies that arose among churches were a source of scandal and an obstacle to the spreading of the gospel. Chao conceived the church as a spiritual fellowship rather than an institution. He accepted the fact that we needed some organisation to facilitate common worship, spiritual nurture, and in order to serve society and extend the kingdom of God. Differences

---

[2] The pinyin system of Romanisation of Chinese names is generally accepted today, but in Taiwan and in publications before the 1970s the Wade-Giles system is more common. For example, Chairman Mao can be written either as 'Mao Zedong' or 'Mao Tse-tung'. These two are used interchangeably in this chapter but both will be noted in the first use of any name.

will exist, as gifts of the spirit may vary, but they should be seen only as schools of thought existing within one fellowship rather than as separate denominations.

The other purification, that of doctrines, was more controversial. In the 1920s and 1930s science and reason were revered in China. In the spirit of his time, Chao demanded a 'reasonable' Christianity. He does not believe that science will explain religion, but it would be a mistake for religion to be unscientific. What is true in science cannot become falsehood in religion, and for this reason Chao is ready to purge Christianity of the doctrines of virgin birth, miracles or the resurrection of the body as foundations of belief. It was not clear how far Chao would go in this purification, and how he would determine which of the central doctrines were foundational, and which were products of Western culture. What of the Trinity, original sin and eternal life?

The second phase in his indigenisation project was dialogue with Confucianism. Chao believed that Jesus was the complete revelation of God, but God did not leave himself without witness in other peoples and cultures. In his paper written for the Madras Conference in 1938, he stated that God revealed his power and love equally through nature and through his relations with humanity. All the nations had seen God, some more clearly than others, but their visions were incomplete. In speaking about China, he argued that the sages of China, Confucius and Mencius, were akin to the Old Testament prophets in spirit and feeling, and who could say they were not truly inspired by the spirit of God (Chao 1938). According to Chao, the revelation through the sages and prophets of each people was not different in kind to the Christian revelation, but in degree and quantity. Just as Jesus was the fulfilment of the Old Testament, he was also the fulfilment of the aspirations of other nations. Because the way this earlier revelation came about was different from nation to nation, the meaning of Christ must be interpreted differently according to each historical context.

Confucianism in 1920s China, however, was not its true self. According to Chao, the common interpretation of Confucianism as non-religious was wrong. Heaven, in Confucius' thought, was a religious concept. It was the essence and foundation of morality as well as humanity's spiritual quest – to be in communion and united with Heaven. Chao further criticised the current interpretation of Confucianism as being distorted throughout the ages, ending in a fixated system of meaningless hierarchy and encouraging submissiveness and escape rather than dynamic engagement with life and new issues. Chao believed that besides the revelation of God through the sages akin to the prophets, Confucianism also shared common points of contact with Christian beliefs and values. The concept of *ren* (kindness, benevolence and similar virtues) was almost identical with the Christian concept of love, and the 'harmony' to be brought about through love was close to the kingdom of God.

Given the commonalities, what possible contribution could Christianity bring to China which Confucianism could not provide? It was in the affirmation of the individual by a personal loving God. When the Confucian strives to be in tune with nature or Heaven, the person often loses his or her individuality in the cosmic order of things. In striving to be a moral person through the working out of the different levels of human relations the individual could easily lose his or her personality in the collective good, leading instead to subservience and support of the status quo. The Christian, however, is affirmed in his or her individual dignity, and the harmony of society could be built on the basis of a spiritual fellowship. Confucianism had a dream but not the empowerment to achieve that dream, as witnessed by the failure of previous dynasties to create a more prosperous and equal world. This empowerment, according to Chao, could only come from the energy derived from a mystical union with the divine, the transcendent, as exemplified in Jesus the Christ. Any fruitful dialogue between Christianity and traditional philosophies must go through a critical reinterpretation of both.

Chao can easily be called a liberal theologian, with his optimistic views on culture. However, he also warns against any facile synthesis between Confucianism and Christianity. He criticised those who 'have surrendered Christianity to the corrupted culture in China, not knowing that Christianity was what China did not have, was contradictory to Chinese culture, and was to redeem the culture in China in that contradiction' (Ng 1971, 25). In the area of social reconstruction he was also wrongly identified with the Social Gospel movement. As he became less and less satisfied with the failure of the political and social changes undertaken by successive governments or the churches, he turned more and more to Jesus on the cross. He did not approve of the use of violence in domestic change and he did not see how political change could bring about improvement in society without first of all a spiritual change in individuals. He was clear on the principles of justice and equality but could not bring theory into effective practice. He saw the momentum of Jesus' ministry as a spiritual movement and not a material one. If the church had anything to offer it was the cross of Jesus – not his death on the cross as atonement for human sinfulness, but as a method – the only method of self-sacrificing love that could defeat evil and restore righteousness without itself being corrupted.

There were hints of a transformation model in Chao's theology, but its moderation was soon overtaken by events of war and rising class struggle. Chao, and many like him in the churches, suffered from a fundamental weakness in their theology: the approach to reality was from an idealist perspective, lacking a vigorous social analysis. The programmes run by the churches were not lacking in vision but in efficacy. It was right that Chao should return to the cross of Jesus as the source of power and judgement of concrete action, but in a situation of radical social change, it looked more like an escape from reality. In retrospect, he judged himself rather harshly. In 1950, after the success of the Communist revolution, he said rather bleakly: 'For the last forty years there is nothing in the Chinese Christian theology which is worthy of being called . . . The so-called Chinese theology is nothing more than Western-imported theology, spelled out by Western missionaries and completely digested by Chinese Christians. There has been no contribution by the Chinese on their own' (quoted in Ng 1979). Looking towards the future he still believed in the need to find a synthesis between Confucianism, Daoism and Buddhism. But above all he foresaw that theologians of the future need not be academics but the 'product of theory and practice'. Was he repeating the current slogans of the new Communist regime, or was it out of a deeper reflection on the failure of past efforts, including his own? He predicted that the 'Chinese Augustines, Tertullians, and Origens must come out of churches which go through hard and long suffering . . . Life, faith and experience can give interpretation to faith and life' (quoted in Covell 1986: 161).

The Cosmic Christ

Scholars today still dispute the true character of the Communist revolution in China. Some think that it was essentially a nationalist movement: they argue on the basis of the fact that the war with Japan rallied the middle class and peasant alike in the struggle against Japanese invasion. Others point to the tradition of peasant revolts in the history of China, pointing to previous peasant revolts such as the Taiping Rebellion. There is truth in both interpretations in that the Communist revolution was an expression of, as well as a response to, two deep-seated aspirations of the Chinese people: to rid China of one and a half centuries of domination by foreign powers, and to search for a political form that could bring about the social and cultural transformations that everyone thought necessary. The two aspirations together represent the search of the Chinese people for a new national identity.

From the vantage point of historical hindsight, one may say that the revolution simply by-passed the churches. It happened outside their narrow confines. If they did not take an active part in the revolution, there was little place for them in the new order of things after the revolution. Foreign missionaries were asked to leave or expelled, educational and medical institutions were taken over by the state, and the leadership of the churches was criticised for opposing social reforms.

With the new socialist government in place, theologians like T. C. Chao lost their relevance. The champion of the Christian cause shifted to a different kind of leader, such as Y. T. Wu (Wu Yaozhong). Wu was not an academic intellectual; his concern was not the cultural adaptation of Christianity. Although he believed, like T. C. Chao, that only an indigenised Christianity could meet the challenges of Chinese society, he was more concerned with how the church could retrieve its prophetic tradition in order to participate in the transformation of society. Wu put love at the centre of the Christian faith, equating God with love, and the way to God was through identification with Jesus as the person revealed in the Sermon on the Mount. Judged by the criteria of utter selflessness of the Beatitudes, he was able to see that although the Communists denied the existence of God, they were putting love into practice, while many Christians were professing their faith in Jesus without any commitment to the suffering masses. After the establishment of the People's Republic, Wu devoted all his energies to reforming the church and to setting up the Three-self Patriotic Movement (three-self meaning self-government, self-finance and self-propagation) that could unite all Protestant Christians in the task of assisting the new government in social and political reforms. His other concern was to find a bridge between the church and atheistic socialism, between belief and non-belief, the 'circumcised and uncircumcised'. He saw the realm of God extending beyond the narrow circle of believers to include all people who put Christian love into practice without even being conscious of it. He also saw the special meaning of Christ as the sustainer of the whole cosmos, a theme which his successor, K. H. Ting (Ding Guangxun) was to explore further after him. It is for history to judge whether he could be accused of a superficial liberalism and practically identifying the Communist revolution with the arrival of the kingdom of God, thus sacrificing the uniqueness of Christianity and making the Church entirely dependent on the policy of the government. On the other hand, it is without doubt that he, more than any Christian leader at the time, defined the context in which new theological questions were being asked.

Bishop K. H. Ting, as he preferred to be called in English, has been the leader of Protestant Christianity for over a half-century, the most important leader after Y. T. Wu. Since the churches were revived after the Cultural Revolution (1966–76), Ting had been the leader of both the Three-self Patriotic Committee as well as the China Christian Council up until his retirement from both organisations in 1996. Even today, when he is close to ninety years of age, he is still the president of the national protestant seminary, and since 1998 he has been directing a campaign of 'theological reconstruction', with the purpose of reforming the churches of their Evangelicalism and leading the churches to be more compatible with socialist society. Unlike Y. T. Wu, Ting is not an activist by temperament; he is first and foremost a church leader and an insightful theologian, although for a long time his political profile has overshadowed his theological one.

Ting has not written systematic theological works; the political situation of a fast changing society simply does not allow it. In a private occasion he once said something to this effect: 'In China we are so busy facing up to the many problems and new situations that we have no time to sit down to do systematic theology. But we write letters, much like the early apostles . . .' (1991, personal interview). Most of his writings are in the form of speeches, lectures and occasional articles spread over several decades. It is impracticable in this short chapter to situate his scattered writings in their varied political contexts but his theological framework is surprisingly simple, and his main concerns remain consistent throughout five decades.

From the 1940s to the beginning of the Cultural Revolution in 1966 his concerns were very similar to those of Y. T. Wu. He does not hide the influence of Wu in his youth and he shared with Wu the same concerns such as struggle against imperialism, against capitalist exploitation, dialogue with atheism, indigenisation of the Chinese church. During the Cultural Revolution all the churches in China were closed and the leadership isolated. In the 1980s, after the churches re-emerged, he turned his attention more to the issues of ecclesial reform and the training of new leaders. But the theme of the Cosmic Christ stands out in his writings as a point of departure as well as a point of culmination. As a point of departure it serves as correction to the false dichotomies prevalent in the Chinese church between believers and non-believers, opening a way to collaboration with atheistic Communists. As a point of culmination, the Cosmic Christ is looked at as the focus of a spiritual journey, the true omega of history.

At the time of liberation, according to Ting, there were two circumstances that greatly affected the church. First, some Christians were impressed by

Communist revolutionaries; these were people with idealism, a high moral standard and serious theoretical interests. Although they were non-believers they were tolerant of religion. They were no doubt the hope of the nation, and consequently these Christians began to wonder if there was still a place for Christianity in the new society. On the other hand, there were also Christians who refused to be reconciled with the new China on theological grounds, refusing to see the good that was happening before their eyes. For them belief in Christ was the pre-requisite to any validity of human action, including that of liberation and bringing justice. In short the Chinese churches were put in a double dilemma. On the one hand the pietist theology inherited from Evangelical missionaries cut the church off from the mainstream of social reconstruction. On the other hand, traditional liberal theology surrendered its argument to the practical achievements of Chinese Communists who were not only better examples of selfless commitment, but more competent in bringing about the social transformations that Jesus preached.

For Ting, a new theology had to be constructed for a new China. It must bring Jesus back into contemporary history, right within the realities of China's conflicts, liberation and national reconstruction. In 1981, in an article commemorating the passing away of Y. T. Wu, Ting gave a good summary of Y. T. Wu's religious insights, namely how can faith in and love of Christ be harmonised with the concern for the well-being of the Chinese people (2000, 72–85). Wu's insights were not necessarily well thought out and did not rise to a high theoretical level, but he pointed out the direction for future theological reflection, which Ting took on with gratitude and passion.

In a sense Ting continued where Wu left off, and his own career as church leader and theological educator elaborated on insights first developed through his contact with Wu. The central theme in Ting's theology is that of the Cosmic Christ. This was already hinted at in his summary of Wu's thinking – the selfless love for the suffering people was a quality of Jesus 'in harmony with the very constitution of the universe' (2000, 74). Ting returns to this theme time and again on many occasions (2000: 137, 266, 408). There are discernable influences of Teilhard de Chardin and process thought in Ting's writings on the subject, but the context which gave rise to the prominence of the Cosmic Christ was definitely the post-liberation society of China. To the comrades in the Party Ting preaches a Cosmic Christ whose love is not confined to the believer but to all of creation. To the fundamentalist Chinese Christian he asks for a new understanding of sin and a new relation to non-believers.

Firstly, in developing a new theology, Ting argues for a positive evaluation of atheism.

Ting distinguishes between three kinds of atheists. There are firstly the moral bankrupts who are theists in name but atheist at heart – no doubt a criticism of a prevalent form of prosperity gospel – since their belief in God and their moral commitments are in direct opposition. Then there are atheists who take the concept of God seriously but cannot come to believe out of intellectual honesty. It would be more correct to call them agnostics. Thirdly there is the atheism of the revolutionary humanists who rejected the religions which have become implicated in oppression and exploitation and play the role as guarantors of the status quo. By rejecting this kind of religion they reject also the God of these religions by implication.

Ting believes that atheism of the third kind has a positive content because it inspires men and women to become masters of their own destinies in the fight against fatalism and the existing social order. 'There is something sublime in this sort of atheism' because it motivates people in creative change and selfless dedication.

I would like to say to that revolutionary: Carry on your valuable work but gain a fuller sense of its meaning and importance by relating it to the ongoing creative, redemptive and sanctifying movement in the universe under what we call God, so that all your undertakings – in industry, agriculture, science and technology, art and music – get an even deeper grounding. Religious faith will not dampen your revolutionary spirit but will purify it, make it more sublime, more acceptable to God. (Ting 1989, 124–7)

Secondly, it is necessary to develop a new understanding of sin. The theology that divides the world into believers and non-believers is also built on a pessimistic conception of human nature – that human kind is depraved and damned. The world, according to this theology, is sinful, the realm of Satan, condemned to imminent hell fire. Salvation comes only from renouncing the world and all human hope to change it by human means. Against this, Ting affirms the primacy of creation. Sin has definitely corrupted creation, but the created world is still the object of God's love, otherwise how can we understand the Gospel of John when it says 'God so loved the world that he gave his only begotten son to the world?' (3: 16) The incarnation is therefore not to be understood as God's commando dropped into the world to deliver humankind from the hold of Satan, but to regain the world with grace through the cross. Therefore redemption is not only a 'no' to sin but above all a divine 'yes' to creation. 'If by the offence of one man all died, much more the grace of God and the gracious gift of the one man, Jesus Christ, abound for all (Rom. 5: 15).' Here, Ting emphasises the 'much more' and the 'for all'. Commenting on Paul, he says

The verse assures us that our human solidarity with Christ is more universal, more decisive and more efficacious than our solidarity with Adam. The greatest word in the New Testament is not sin – it is grace. (Whitehead 1989: 31–4)

The experience of the Chinese revolution has also brought a new perspective to the Christian concept of sin in that the emphasis on the sinner must be complemented by the perspective of the 'sinned against'.

What *is* (Ting's emphasis) new to many Chinese Christians is the awareness that people are not only sinners but are also sinned against. The task of evangelism is not only to convince persons of their sin but to stand alongside those who are sinned against in our society. To dwell on sin is not evangelism proper; it does not necessarily move a person to repentance and to the acceptance of Christ as saviour. (Whitehead 1989, 126)

Against the language of doom and damnation Ting proposes a language of compassion and salvation especially through identifying with the 'non-persons' in society. In this Ting comes very close to the liberation theologians of Latin America but through a different route.

Thirdly, and most importantly, the foundation of the new theology is built on the discovery of the 'Christ-like God'. The corollary to a theology of sin and damnation is often a God of judgement. Christians have been trained to think of God in terms of power, a power that is more ready to judge and condemn, rather than of God who triumphs through weakness. For Ting, the way we see God and Christ should be turned around. Instead of confessing that Christ is 'God-like', our Christology tells a different story. It is not one 'that lingers at the divinity and Godlikeness of Christ, but is one that tells of the Christlikeness of God' (Wickeri 2000, 141). Recalling the same emphasis of his mentor Y. T. Wu, Ting speaks of love as the first attribute of God. 'I believe that the God shown forth in Christ is a God of love. This attribute of love comes before and above all other attributes of God.'

Why was the Cosmic Christ so important?

For Chinese Christians the significance of knowing Christ as having a cosmic nature lies essentially in ascertaining two things: (1) the universal extent of Christ's domain, concern and care, and (2) the kind of love which we get a taste of in Jesus Christ as we read the Gospels being the first and supreme attribute of God and basic to the structure and dynamic of the universe, in the light of which we get an insight as to how things go in the world. I will not try to take you into the world of Chinese classics, but will only say that what it teaches about the unity of the universe and the benevolence with which it is governed does prepare the Chinese mind to treat favourably the proposition of cosmic Christ. (Wickeri 2000: 411)

Given the political context in China, Ting could be easily accused of introducing the concept of Cosmic Christ only as a means of building political bridges or as a corrective measure for fundamentalist Christianity, but his writings point towards a more personal spiritual vision, a foretaste of eschatological splendour:

. . . the ascended Christ, like sunshine, filling the universe, bringing out every latent spark of colour. Reality is one gigantic process, one in which matter and simple organisms achieve higher and higher expressions of existence, with the loving community as the ultimate human attainment of the image of God on the part of men and women, just as the triune God Himself is a community love. (Wickeri 2000, 144)

In 1991, in his major exposition on the Cosmic Christ, Ting was writing not long after the Tiananmen incident of 1989. The selfless Communist revolutionaries whom Ting has so much respect for have succumbed to the temptations of power and become a self-perpetuating authoritarian government which, when its existence was under threat, did not hesitate to turn the people's army against the people. Was Ting's optimism in the cosmic vision a different form of escape similar to that of otherworldly salvation that he so much criticised, the difference being an escape into historical nostalgia rather than a transcendental one? There will be critics who will question Ting's theology, whether it is anything more than an exercise in convenience adaptation in a politically sensitive context. In the face of such criticism two aspects of his thinking come to his defence. Firstly, he has consistently questioned the value of liberation theology in its Latin American form to the Chinese situation because of its adoption of Marxist analysis and its immanent understanding of history. By contrast Ting feels much more in tune with the process philosophy of A. N. Whitehead whom he has quoted as well as Teilhard de Chardin whom he has lectured on in the national seminary. Secondly, against the determinism of contemporary Chinese Marxism Ting has introduced an eschatological qualification and recognises that 'the way from alpha to omega is not a straight line, but many zigzags and curves'. However, the assurance of the cosmic dimension of God's love gives us 'an understanding of reality as becoming. It gives us hope for and beyond history' (Wickeri 2000, 148). And although there are zigzags and detours, catastrophes and sufferings such as the

Cultural Revolution (but not Tiananmen Square?), love accompanies the pilgrims.

The above discussion of an idea, from its emergence to becoming the central theme of a man's theological vision, encompasses more than half a century of turbulent history in China. It leads one to the observation that theology is so inevitably a product of history, and as a product of history it can become a form of slavery especially for the so-called 'young churches'. In the case of China, they must free their theology from this slavery before it can respond creatively to the changes in Chinese culture and society. On the other hand, it must be said that only as a part of history can theology actively engage in social changes: either by providing a framework of discourse or a key for interpretation. The discussion on the cosmic Christ serves to illustrate this dialectical tension.

The question that remains for us to ask is: how can this new theology be authenticated? The concept is no doubt founded biblically but its rediscovery in the Chinese political context challenges Chinese Christians to a re-formulation of the Christology as found in the dominant tradition of the West. In that sense, tradition could not be called on for its authentification. Will its authentification come, not so much from orthodoxy, as from its orthopraxis? If so, how will the authentification be realised? Perhaps in two areas. Firstly, if the cosmic principle is not only an escape from history but an active operating factor in that history, the principle must be representative of as well as a response to the developing concerns and values found in that historical context. It must lay claim to being a key hermeneutical tool for the Christian community. Secondly, for a historically active principle it cannot only provide for a perspective of understanding and discernment, but also be capable of assisting the development of a missionary strategy effective in influencing the outcome of society. In order to do it, it must be accompanied by a viable ecclesiology without which the concept would not have any anchor in the historical context. The concept of the Cosmic Christ, as an eschatological vision or as a hermeneutical key, will be judged by how well it answers the two concerns.

The answer, for the moment, is tentative. No doubt it has been accepted by some to be a useful corrective measure to combat the narrow theological views subscribed to by the majority of the Christian communities. Since 1998 Ting has launched in the Protestant churches a new campaign of theological reconstruction on the lines of his theology outlined above. It will be some time before an objective evaluation can take place, but is it possible already to ask: to what extent can a new Chinese theology be built on a corrective measure? How can the concept of the Cosmic Christ, conceived in the 1950s and developed in the early 1980s, take into account the more recent developments in Chinese history, especially the Tiananmen Incident in 1989, a defining experience for the younger generation similar to the Holocaust? How can the cosmic principle accommodate the continuing violence and power relations in present-day society? In other words, can we reach and affirm the cosmic principle without any form of mediation of suffering? How does the concept of the Cosmic Christ as an expression of God as Love stand vis-à-vis the death of Jesus on the cross? How are traditional doctrines of salvation and atonement to be interpreted in this new light? These, and some other questions, remain to be answered; without adequate answers to these questions, Ting's theology will be open to the same criticism of 'love monism' as Schleiermacher's was.

JAPAN

The 'Pain of God'

In the 1940s a different theology emerged from Japan on a theological principle almost opposite to that of K. H. Ting in China. While Ting emphasises the attribute of love in God to heal the rift between church and society, a different theology emerged seeking to understand 'God's pain', in the conflict between his love and his anger towards humankind. Mediating between Buddhist understanding of suffering and Christian theology of the cross, this theology was a radical reinterpretation of the essential nature of God. It was not a direct answer to the disastrous war that Japan had just engaged in, or the immediate suffering it brought about. In that sense, it was not a 'contextual' theology in the stricter sense of the word. At the same time, it was characteristically Japanese in style, and in dealing with the relation of human suffering and the 'pain of God' it could not help but be a theology relevant to the human predicament both generally and contextually. The theologian concerned was Kazoh Kitamori. His book, *The Theology of the Pain of God* (1946; ET 1958 and 1965) was hailed as the first truly Japanese theology.

Even in a world of instant communication, theology in Japan is still a well-kept secret. Unlike other churches in Asia, Japanese theologians have generally written only in their own language and for the Japanese context. Unlike the British who, also an island nation, have been a seafaring power since the Middle Ages and established the largest colonial empire in history, the Japanese have always been an island people more interested in themselves than in other peoples. Their only expansionist adventure ended in disaster and humiliation. The theological milieu also reflects this mentality. Even if many Japanese theologians studied in Germany and in America, and the theologies they have developed subsequently are heavily influenced by Western theology, they are doing it in a Japanese style for 'domestic consumption'. Rarely do they engage with the theological debate outside of Japan or see the need to do so. One exception would be Kosuke Koyama whose *Waterbuffalo Theology* (1974) was so well received in the West that he was considered to be a representative Japanese theologian. In Japan, however, his influence is insignificant. Koyama has been a missionary who lives outside Japan and writes in English which most Japanese do not read.

'The theology of Kazoh Kitamori is the most self-consciously Japanese', according to Carl Michelson (1960, 73). It is a theology developed against the background of Buddhism which he embraces as his own tradition, and he draws inspiration from traditional Japanese literature, especially the concept of *tsurasa* in classical drama. The word represents the emotion that occurs when someone has no choice but to kill himself or his loved one in order to save another life. That emotion is a complicated one; it is at the same time suffering, sadness and bitterness. This emotion is at its strongest when it has to be restrained at the same time, when that sense of suffering becomes one of 'pain'. Kitamori considers that the best analogy to understand what happens when God allows his only Son to suffer death on the cross.

What does it mean for God to suffer pain? In traditional theology, God does not suffer – he is impassible, and Patripassianism is a heresy in the Christian tradition. For Kitamori, God does not suffer in the ordinary sense of the word in that suffering is a condition on his nature or inflicted on him from the outside. Even the betrayal of sinners would not be the cause of his pain. It is the action of God 'swallowing' his wrath over human sinfulness that causes this pain. In a sense the pain is God in conflict with himself – overcoming his wrath by further extending his love to the object of his wrath, objects he could not have loved 'naturally'. It is God going outside of himself in Jesus Christ, letting him die on the cross, thus conquering his wrath for the benefit of those unworthy of his love. This is how Kitamori interprets Phil. 2 as God's self-emptying in Christ. In that sense, the meaning of the cross is not primarily in the act of redemption, but as a condition of God himself in between his love and his wrath. The 'pain of God' is an ontological concept. Human suffering, on the other hand, is an existential condition.

This universal predicament of human kind becomes, at the death of Christ, the basis for an analogical understanding of the nature of God, with 'pain' being his primary attribute. The *tsurasa,* the human willingness to bear pain for others, even someone who does not deserve love, is the symbolic witness to God's 'pain'. For Kitamori all suffering originates in humankind's alienation from God, yet God in his wrath still embraces the worthy and unworthy alike. The believer experiences the reconciliation with God through his pain, while the unbeliever does not realise this and further separates himself from God. The believer, therefore, has the responsibility of testifying to the unbeliever the meaning of his own pain through the reconciliation brought about by the 'pain of God'. Kitamori calls this analogical transition from human suffering to God's pain *analogia doloris*.

What distinguishes Kitamori's theology of the cross from others is that he puts it in the heart of the Trinity. For him modern liberal theology has made the cross irrelevant, making it only an 'accidental' illustration of the love of God for humankind. As for the Barthian theology which dominated Japanese theology of his time, it made God so absolutely other that the cross was put entirely outside of the essential understanding of God as Trinity. God the Father did not only generate the Son, but also let the Son die, an act going out of God. The death of Christ is therefore at the centre of the Trinity. What Kitarmori says is that the 'pain of God' not only describes the mercy and salvific action of God, but it belongs to his essence.

Kitamori's understanding of God's pain addresses the human predicament in both Christianity and the tradition of Buddhism in Japan. In a sense it is a theology doomed to failure because theology – as *logos* – can never fully understand the *pathos* of God. What is needed is not the construction of a new theology, but a new way of 'communicating God'. Nevertheless, the 'pain of God' must be maintained as the touchstone for any Christian doctrine, making it the hermeneutical principle for all theology. There are also consequences for the understanding of the church and its mission. The church cannot only be a happy community of the saved but a people called to live through a life of pain, a voluntary life of poverty, hard work, fasting, celibacy and renunciation of the self – very much in the Christian or Buddhist ideals of the monastery. It should be a community living a life of witness to the analogy of pain, leading to reconciliation with God in a corrupted and disrupted world. This community will always be a prophetic minority – Kitamori remains in the tradition of the No-church Movement – living out a life of contradictions, embracing the opposites of society as well as the opposites of love and wrath, loving and at the same time condemning those undeserving of love, in order to be a living analogy to the 'pain of God'.

Kitamori's theology is still a controversial one. It cannot completely answer the case of Patripassianism; at the same time it is being criticised for encouraging an escape from the struggles of the world by overstating the necessity of human pain as the witness to God's pain, to the neglect of the doctrine of the atonement. He was accused of giving 'the logic but not the feel of the pain of God', with little awareness of the actual suffering of his fellow Japanese (England 1981, 34). The exclusive emphasis on the pain of God, according to Teruo Kuribayashi, also neglected that the same God who hears the cry of the marginalised and took side with the poor (cf. Suggate 2000, 235–6).

Many in Japan question whether Kitamori is a representative Japanese theologian, as they would question whether Koyama can be called Japanese, nevertheless it is beyond doubt that he was the first theologian to attract lasting international attention, even though he wrote in Japanese and addresses mainly the Japanese cultural context. Of course theology in Japan is not limited to Kitamori. A lot of work has been done by Christian theologians and writers in the fields of systematic theology, biblical students, scientific study of religions, and so on. For the purpose of this chapter, however, Kitamori stands out in both style and method – language, metaphors, themes – which are typically Japanese, and yet his concerns are universal. He challenges all the key doctrines of traditional Christianity, from the doctrine of the Trinity to that of the atonement, from the existence of the church to the meaning of mission and witness. It also continues in the tradition of dialogue with Buddhism and opens new vistas in that dialogue.[3] If we search for similar contributions from Japanese Christianity, we may need to turn to novelists and artists, such as Shusaku Endo and Wanatabe. Endo's novels dealt with the question of how the non-theistic Japanese can embrace theistic Christianity with all the tension between belonging and betrayal. The themes of his novels are deeply 'theological', dealing with the questions of gospel and culture from the heart and psyche rather than from the intellect. Similarly Wanatabe is very successful in bringing together Christian themes and traditional Japanese woodcut styles, creating art works which are immediately recognisable as Japanese in form and expression.

It is also important not to neglect the struggle of Japanese Christianity with political power. The recent history of Japan cannot be understood without reference to its foundation as a modern state during the Meiji period (1868–1912) when the system of emperor worship was established. Two traditional Japanese values, namely Confucian filial piety and Shinto loyalty to the emperor's lineage were merged together into a new political

---

[3] See, for example, Seiichi Yagi's dialogue with the Kyoto School of Buddhist philosophy.

philosophy. The emperor system was based on the idea of a divine ruler who came from an unbroken lineage of sacred ancestors going back to the Sun Goddess, Amaterasu-o-mikami. She was the daughter of one of the two gods who engendered the world and one of her direct descendants, Jimmu-Tenno, became the first earthly emperor of Japan around 660 BC. Despite the doctrinal fluidity in Shintoism, there is a strong emphasis on the unbroken lineage of divine emperors. In theory the emperor is no more divine than his subjects, but for the people he is the embodiment of the divine, a combination of god, priest and ruler.

In the name of the emperor Japan began the period of military adventure in Asia. From the mid 1930s onwards the churches came under intense pressure to support the government's national doctrine. The government also required followers of Christianity, as well as other religions, to participate in Shinto ceremonies, justifying it on the ground that these ceremonies were national and not religious. In fact the distinction raised Shintoism to the level of a state religion and relegated other religions to the realm of private beliefs. In 1932 some students from the Catholic Sophia University refused to take part, but the Catholic authorities finally gave in to the government's interpretation of the Shinto rites. Most Protestant churches did the same. The leader of the United Church of Japan travelled even to Korea – colonised by Japan at that time – to convince the Christians there to accept Shinto ceremonies. The Koreans firmly resisted and many were persecuted. In 1937 the Japanese Catholic Church established the Committee of Catholics for Foreign Propaganda to send priests to the China war zone to explain Japanese motives for the war to Chinese Catholics. The Episcopalians adopted a resolution in 1938 committing themselves to help interpret the war as God's holy war. The National Christian Council made several statements supporting the government and explained that military action was necessary to protect peace in the Far East. The United Church of Japan declared that it would devote itself to the task of promoting the imperial war aims, and rejoiced at the upsurge of the fighting spirit in the country.

After the defeat of Japan in 1945, the new constitution written by the occupying powers kept the emperor system but not its worship. However, as a country, Japan has not yet resolved in its consciousness the role it played in the Pacific War – is it guilt or only shame of defeat? – or the tension between its nationalist tendency on the one hand and the pressure to be part of and accountable to the international order on the other. A new nationalism re-emerged since the 1960s leading to the government's supporting the revival of the Yasukuni Shrine as Japan's 'spiritual ground'.[4] The Shrine, situated not far from the Imperial Palace in Tokyo, was dedicated in 1879 by Emperor Meiji to the war dead or, more precisely to those who fought and died for the emperor. Two and a half million were honoured in the shrine and it has become a symbol of unconditional loyalty of Japanese people towards the nation. It was difficult for the Christian churches not to respond.

The response of the churches to the new nationalism came from almost all the churches. In sum, the response consists in: (1) repentance for their role in supporting the emperor system, (2) a commitment to the critique of the politico-religious system which is still very much alive in Japanese society, and (3) the search for new forms of Christian witness. On the ground, both Catholic and Protestant churches took up the cause of democracy in Korea, criticised the exploitation of workers by Japanese companies in Southeast Asia and the exportation of polluting industries.

The critique of political power became an urgent theological task, but traditional theologies did not provide the material or the means. An interesting example is the work of Kosuke Koyama who, in his book *Mount Fuji and Mount Sinai*, attempted an analysis of the elements in Japanese history leading to idolatry of the emperor system. This in turn led him to move towards the 'emotive region of the cross of Christ'. The cross is both God's compassion as well as his judgement on humanity; his 'embrace and confrontation' call on all the nations to critique the use of religion to justify greed and domination. For Koyama, a theology of peace must include an exposure of present day idols. Strangely, it is left to the most famous theologian in diaspora, disowned by academic theologians in Japan, to make this unique theological contribution in its name.

KOREA

Christ – Shaman of the Minjung

If a theology can be justly called a movement, it would be Minjung theology in Korea. It is both a theology of protest and a theology of popular culture based on unique Korean cultural experiences. It grew out of Korean

---

[4] Mr Nakasone said in 1968: 'We should resurrect the symbol of the Yasukuni Shrine as the Japanese spiritual ground.' Nakasone was the Minister of Transportation then. He later became the Prime Minister in 1985.

student activism in the 1970s and has been described sometimes as a socio-theological biography of the Korean people. In 1972 President Park Chung-hee declared Martial Law across the country in order to maintain power. The ideology of his regime was based on the concept of 'national security' and the promotion of economic growth. Opposition forces were systematically described as 'communists' and put down with brutal force. Many church groups stood up against the dictatorship and growing infringement of human rights, such as the Urban Industrial Mission, the Korean Student Christian Federation, the Christian Ecumenical Youth Council, the Catholic Farmers' Union and the Catholic Commission for Justice and Peace, and similar organisations. Christian 'koinonias' – mission groups – were organised to care for the people who were oppressed and marginalised, the *minjung*.

At the same time a different view of the mission of the church began to emerge, with a different way of doing theology. The term 'Minjung theology' was first used by the theologians Suh Nam-dong and Ahn Byung-mu in the mid 1970s (Suh Nam-dong 1975; Ahn 1975). For these theologians Jesus came to set people free from economic poverty, cultural alienation and political oppression. Jesus identified with the Minjung. The term was widely accepted at the Asian Theological Consultation in 1979 and became international currency.

The idea of *Minjung* is composed of two words: '*min*', which means the people, and '*jung*', the masses. In consciously using this new term, a distinction is made between *minjung*, the concept of people at the grassroots from *minjok*, which refers to people as a national entity, much abused by the regime's ideology of national security. Minjung, however, is not the same as the 'proletariat'. 'This difference between the Minjung and the proletariat entails different views of history. Minjung history has a strong transcendental or transcending dimension – a beyond-history – that is often expressed in religious form. There is a close relation between religion and the Minjung perception of history' (Kim Young-bock 1980, 184). Marx's concept was born in the industrial revolution; Minjung reaches deep into the history and mythology of the suffering people of Korea. The proletariat is a socio-economic concept; Minjung is historical-literary. In fact, the concept began its life in a new reading of history by Korean historians in the 1960s and 1970s. In trying to overcome a colonial or royal view of history, they identified the Minjung as the 'subject of history' and rewrote history from their point of view. At the same time, it was a movement in literature. Literary themes based on nationhood and national destiny, popular in the early period of post-colonialism, were replaced by themes of the people living at the bottom or on the margins of society. There was also a conscious effort to recover the cultural traditions of the people as Minjung, such as the mask dance, and produce literature in their 'vulgar' language. The resulting concept carries with it romantic, almost mystical, connotations, rooted in the suffering psyche of the Korean people. As part of this cultural and political movement, Minjung theology was born.

A theology of story-telling

The analytical themes of Minjung theology are very close to the theology of liberation developed in Latin America, which slowly made its influence felt in Asia. But what distinguishes Minjung theology is its embedding in Korea's unique political and cultural history, and the way they have chosen to do theology. The best way of introducing this theology is to listen to one of its stories:

I would like to tell you the story of the beautiful bell in the National Museum in Kyung ju, capital of the ancient Silla Kingdom. At the time of Silla, the country was peaceful, but the devout Buddhist king wanted to protect the nation from foreign invasion. The king was advised to build a huge temple bell to show the people's devotion to Buddha.

A specialist in the technology of bell-making, himself a devout Buddhist, was given the responsibility. He used great care and all the right methods to cast the bell, but he failed again and again to obtain a bell that gave a beautiful sound when struck. Finally he took his problems to the council of religious leaders who were greatly concerned over this matter of national security.

After long discussion, the council concluded that the best way to give a beautiful tone to the bell was to sacrifice a pure young maiden. Soldiers were sent out to fetch a 'pure young maiden' who would be sacrificed for this worthy cause. They came upon a poor mother in a farm village with her small daughter. They took the child from its mother while the child cried out piteously, 'Emile, Emile, Emile!' meaning 'Mother! Oh Mother!'

When the next huge pot of molten lead and iron was prepared for casting the bell, the little girl was thrown into it. At last the bell-maker was successful. The bell, called the Emile Bell, when struck with the gong made a sound so beautiful that no other bell could equal it.

When people heard the beautiful sound of the bell, some gave praise and thanks to the technology and art that was able to cast a bell with such a beautiful sound. But when the mother whose child had been sacrificed to obtain that beautiful sound heard the bell, her heart broke afresh, and her neighbours, who also know of the sacrifice and of the mother's pain, could not hear the bell's beautiful tone without pain. Only those who understand the sacrifice can feel the pain. Others simply enjoy the sound. (Lee 1985)

The story, an ancient one retold with contemporary connotations, was a clear indictment of the Korean capitalist system and the ideology which supported it. It was told by Lee Oo Chung, a former professor of theology at a prestigious university, and at one time president of the Association of Women Theologians. She was forced to resign by the martial law government, after which she went to work with poor female factory workers and experienced the living emotions of *han*, a Korean word meaning the grudge, the proud bitterness of the oppressed. *Han* comes from the recess of the heart and goes back down the ages. When martial law was lifted, Lee was offered reinstatement at the university, but she rejected the offer, preferring to work in a poor working class parish.

An autobiographical theology

Another way to approach this theology is through the spiritual journey of a representative exponent, David Kwang-sun Suh. Suh was a professor of theology and the dean of the College of Liberal Arts and Sciences at Ewha University when he was arrested in 1980. At that time he was experimenting with new pedagogical methods in bringing theology closer to the reality of the Korean people. 'I was in the middle of a faculty meeting when a man from the Joint Investigation Headquarters called and asked me to meet him at a nearby tea-house. I was supposed to be frightened by the call' (Suh Kwang-sun 1983, 9).

At the interrogation centre, the first thing Suh was asked to do was write his autobiography, a common interrogation technique. He was asked to write about his family, his parents, his school, his education, the books he read and the friends he frequented, not overlooking anything. He understood this confession he was to write as 'the story of Korean Minjung people – my socio-political and theological biography' (Suh Kwang-sun 1983, 11). Later on in the same centre he was to meet other Christian professors and pastors.

Suh was a scholar who trained first in Anglo-Saxon analytical philosophy, and later specialised in Paul Tillich in his studies in America. In 1969 he returned to South Korea and was soon caught up in student protests against the dictatorship of Park Chung-hee. Students in Korea, as in China and Japan, have a historical tradition of being the conscience of the nation. Already in the old kingdom, students in Korea were known for criticising royal policies. In more recent history, students were in the forefront of all national independence or democratic movements. They revolted against the Japanese in the 1920s, brought down the government of Syngman Rhee in 1960, and rose up against Park Chung-hee when he wanted to change the constitution to remain in power for a third term.

The students were socially involved as well, working the villages and slum areas, and applied their knowledge to study the sufferings of the people in the process of industrialisation. At Ewha University, where Suh taught, the Christian Studies Department began an industrial internship programme, the aim of which was to sensitise the students to the urban industrial situation, particularly that of the teenage women workers in the factories. The students in the programme were employed as regular workers and lived alongside the girls working in the factory. At the same time Suh created an audio-visual programme called 'One People in Two Worlds', showing how the two worlds coexisted in one country and in one city – two divided worlds – north and south, haves and have-nots, the poor and the rich. The whole campus was disturbed by the programme shown in the university chapel during a religious studies week.

An important discovery by the students and one which affected Suh greatly was the new awareness of the culture of the people, especially the shamanist mask dances. Shamanism has always been an undercurrent of Korean culture, shaped by the long history of oppression and foreign domination suffered by the people. In these mask dances, the people ridicule the rulers and mock at their own powerlessness. Through trance-like states and incantations, the village crowd was often brought through an oscillation of frenzy states and passive sadness, reflecting their inner depression and violence.

Through all this, Korean Christians like Suh became more and more conscious of their historical roots and their theological outlook changed. As Suh explained:

All the theological questions of the 1960s – indigenization of Christianity, the problem of text and context, and the issue of demythologization and the interpretation of the biblical language – all turned around to discover the language of the liberating gospel in the Korean consciousness, in its art forms, in its literature and music, and its dance and plays. Korean Christians found their own stories to tell alongside the stories of the Bible, the stories of a liberating Jesus and the Christian gospel. The theology of the Minjung was therefore born out of active participation in the struggle of the Korean people for a more humane and just society. (Suh Kwang-sun 1983, 24)

The power of the metaphor

It has been said that Korea has a three-tier culture: a Confucian head, a Buddhist heart and a Shaman stomach. As in China, religion has always been at the service of the state throughout Korean history. This was the case with Buddhism during the Koryo dynasty 918–1392, and with Confucianism during the Yi dynasty 1392–1910. Under the Confucian rulers, Korea adopted the entire culture of China – its philosophy, ethics, art and language. The local Korean language, which had developed its own alphabet, grammar and literature, was despised by the scholarly elite. Nevertheless, there has always been a strong underlying nationalism, which came to the fore especially under the Japanese occupation 1910–45. During the earlier part of the twentieth century many writers and intellectuals separated themselves from the 'high literary culture' to identify with the world and language of the lower classes. They saw in them the preservation of a genuine Korean spirit, and in their songs and stories the basis of a new culture.

The discovery of the feeling of *han*, an almost eternal bitterness, has given birth to a new contextual theology, and story-telling became a way of doing theology. As oppression became total, the press muzzled and publications forbidden, the expelled professors and court-martialled students met to tell stories of their experiences. Telling stories became their privilege form of communication and reflection. The contents of stories and the way it was communicated gave them an important clue to understand the style of doing theology by the people.

Firstly, the story is a way of comprehending reality, a different epistemology possessed by the poor and oppressed. The world of false order is turned upside down by the Minjung stories. Secondly, the story uses a language considered to be vulgar, used only by the uncultivated, but therein also lies its strength. It not only gives them a special identity, but when the stories are told with songs, and dances performed by the body, it is expressed, felt and experienced before being reflected upon. Thirdly, Suh sees a metaphorical identification between these stories and the stories of the gospel. Using the analysis of Sally McFague, Suh talks about Jesus as the 'parable of the Minjung' and Minjung as 'the parable of Jesus', a unity of the principle of identification and that of distinction: 'x is y and x is not y'. The metaphor leads to the identification and tension between Minjung and Jesus, between Jesus and God, and between Minjung and the Kingdom. The hermeneutic circle is thus established (Suh Kwang-sun 1983, 17–18).

From story-telling to the reconstruction of history from below through the self-definition by the Minjung, the distinct methodology of this new theology can be described as a theology of social biography. In these social biographies, the drama of oppression and resistance is played out by the people and the ruling powers, and history is its stage. At the same time it is also a drama where the resolution of these conflicts and contradictions can be resolved; in that sense Minjung is also an eschatological concept. The story of the Old Testament through the new can be re-read through the eyes of the 'slaves' (Kim Young-bock 2000).

As a theological and missionary movement, however, Minjung theology today is at the crossroads. Although it allied with Christian grassroots militancy for a short period of time, and some 'minjung congregations' were formed, these never flourished into a significant movement to change the conservative stance of the majority of churches. The 'minjung' pastors also discovered that a theology, built on a narrower political platform, was not sufficient to answer the many and varied pastoral situations in their congregations. The political understanding of salvation and spirituality were difficult to interiorise by the people. Moreover, since its democratisation, the movement has lost its visible enemy; in fact, many of the Minjung leaders have joined the government and may have lost the edge in its political criticisms. Moreover, the ills of globalisation are obvious, but the culprits are distant rather than local, and are more difficult to name and pin down. A more affluent society is also turning its attention more to the problems of the environment and Korea's cultural identity. The recent geo-political realignment in East Asia also means that South Korean society has shifted its attention more to the problem of the threat posed by North Korea as well as the desire for re-unification with it.

CONCLUSION

The case of Minjung theology shows both the strength and weaknesses of any contextual theology. It is limited in time and scope as a movement, and unless the major themes can be effectively turned into hermeneutical principles for a radical reformulation of Christian doctrines and spirituality, it will slowly lose its pertinence. The second and third-generation Minjung theologians are turning their attention to more methodological issues on the one hand and pastoral issues on the other.

For any contextual theology, the sweep of globalisation, both economically and culturally, has pulled the rug from under its foundations. The concepts of territory, nation and ethnicity on which many local theologies are based have become less relevant. On the other hand, even in a globalised world, local negotiations still take place. The case of China demonstrates the strength of the local, in both its political context as well as its eschatological projection. As a 'corrective' movement, the contextual theology of Ting, for example, is still the driving force behind a theological construction movement. The concept of the Cosmic Christ, once being rediscovered, takes on an identity of its own, and is not necessarily bound to a contextually formulated theology. Its eschatological character can even return to be a critical principle to judge and revitalise a narrower political theology.

The case of Kitamori, the least contextual of the theologies considered, demonstrates the recurrent need for systematic re-interpretation of Christian concepts of God, salvation and atonement in the light of psychological and philosophical categories of a specific culture. A successful contextual theology must still negotiate with the universal, not in the form of Western tradition, but the common predicament of human existence.

A final word must be said about the Protestant domination of East Asian theology in the last few decades. The case studies considered in this chapter are all from the Protestant traditions. This can be explained by the neo-Scholastic captivity of the Catholic theology until the Second Vatican Council. There are identifiable equivalents of contextual theologies in the Catholic Church in East Asia, but they are not distinct enough to be considered separately. In more recent times, however, great strides have been made in biblical studies, environmental theology, inculturation and the theology of non-Christian religions. The dialogue with Zen Buddhism has already produced interesting spiritual movements and theological encounters, which will become significant in future surveys of theology in East Asia.

REFERENCES AND FURTHER READING

It is difficult to suggest even a basic bibliography for theology in East Asia when only a small proportion of theological writings has been published in English or other European languages. Very often the little that exists in English reflects more the interest of a Western readership, or the fashion of ecumenical bodies than the national debate. For example the exclusive interest in political theology in the 1970s obscured the concurrent concerns for inculturation and dialogue with traditional religions or philosophies. Added to that difficulty is the lack of any consensus on what is truly representative of major trends in each country. The bibliography that follows cites the references used in this book, plus a few introductory texts. For the interested reader he or she should consult the major bibliographical work compiled by the team of Asian scholars coordinated by John England, especially volume III which is devoted to East Asia and should be available when this book appears in print. There is no substitute, however, for learning one or two of the East Asian languages in order to explore the rich and complex theological landscape there, but the reward will more than compensate for the effort.

GENERAL ASIA

England, John C. (ed.) 1981. *Living Theology in Asia*. London
England, John C. et al. (ed.) 2002. *Asian Christian Theologies – a Research Guide to Authors, Movements, Sources*, vol. 1 (vols. 2 and 3 forthcoming). Delhi
Sugirtharajah, R. S. (ed.) 1993. *Asian Faces of Jesus*. London
Torres, Sergio and Virginia Fabella (eds.) 1978. *The Emergent Gospel*. New York

CHINA

Chao, T. C. 1938. *The Authority of Faith*. Madras
Covell, Ralph R. 1986. *Confucius, The Buddha, and Christ*. New York
Ng, Lee-ming. 1971. 'An Evaluation of T. C. Chao's Thought' in *Cheng Feng*. Vol. XIV, nos. 1–2
   1979. 'Christianity in China' in *Christianity in Asia*. Vol. 1, ed. T. E. Thomas. Hong Kong
Thomas, T. K. (ed.) 1979. *Christianity in Asia – North-East Asia*, Hong Kong: Christian Conference of Asia
Ting, K. H. 1989. *No Longer Strangers: Selected Writings of K. H. Ting*, Raymond L. Whitehead (ed.). New York
   2000. *Love Never Ends: Papers by K. H. Ting* (English edition, Janice Wickeri (ed.)). Nanjing
Whyte, R. 1988. *Unfinished Encounter: China and Christianity*. London
Wickeri, Philip. 1989. *Seeking the Common Ground*. NewYork

JAPAN

Furuya, Yasuo (ed.) 1997. *A History of Japanese Theology*. Grand Rapids
Germany, Charles H. 1965. *Protestant Theologies in Modern Japan*. Tokyo Press
Kitamori, Kazoh. 1946. ET 1953. *Theology of the Pain of God*. Richmond
Koyama, Kosuke. 1974. *Waterbuffalo Theology*. New York
   1985. *Mount Fuji and Mount Sinai*. New York
Michalson, Carl. 1960. *Japanese Contributions to Christian Theology*. Philadelphia
Miura, Hiroshi. 1996. *The Life and Thought of Kanzo Uchimura*. Grand Rapids
Parratt, John. 2000. 'Kazoh Kitamori's Theology of the Pain of God Revisited' in *Mit dem Fremden Leben (Festschrift fuer Theo Sundermeier)* D. Becker (ed.) 151–8
Philips, James M. 1981. *From the Rising of the Sun – Christians and Society in Contemporary Japan*. New York
Suggate, Alan. 1996. *Japanese Christians and Society*. Frankfurt
   2000. 'Theology from below as a challenge to the West: Kuribayashi's Theology of the Crown of Thorns' in W. Ustorf and Toshiko Murayama (eds.) *Identity and Marginality: Rethinking Christianity in Northeast Asia*, pp. 229–242. Frankfurt
Sundermeier, Theo (ed.) 1988. *Brennpunkte in Kirche und Theologie Japans*. Neukirchen
Takazawa, Katsumi. 1987. *Das Heil im Heute*. Goettingen

KOREA

Chung, Hyun-Kung. 1990. *Struggle to be the Sun Again*. London

CTC–CCA (ed.) *Minjung Theology: People as the Subject of History*. New York

Kim, Young-bock. 1992. *Messiah and Minjung: Christ's Solidarity with the People for a New Life*. Hong Kong

Lee, Oo Chung. 1985. 'One Woman's Confession of Faith', *International Review of Mission*, April 1985.

Lee, Jung-young. 1984. *An Emerging Theology in World Perspective: Commentary on Korean Minjung Theology*. Connecticut

Suh, David Kwang-Sun. 1983. *Theology, Ideology and Culture*. Hong Kong
    1991. *The Korean Minjung in Christ*. Hong Kong

Suh, Nam-dong. 1975. 'Jesus, Church history, and the Korean Church' in *The Search of Minjung Theology*.

5

Africa, East and West

Diane Stinton

HUNGERING FOR AFRICAN THEOLOGY

A true story is told of a missionary who went to a remote area of north-ern Tanzania to proclaim the gospel among the Maasai, a famous warrior people:

> One day he was explaining to a group of adults the saving activity of Jesus Christ, the Son of God. He told how Jesus is the Saviour and Redeemer of all humankind. When he finished, a Maasai elder slowly stood up and said to the missionary: 'You have spoken well, but I want to learn more about this great person Jesus Christ. I have three questions about him: First, did he ever kill a lion? Second, how many cows did he have? Third, how many wives and children did he have?' (Healey and Sybertz 1996, 76–7)

The Maasai elder's questions pose a deep challenge that is not merely theoretical. On the contrary, this incident demonstrates a real crux in the living faith of millions of Christians across East to West Africa today: how can the gospel be proclaimed authentically and effectively in response to the questions of African people and in ways that are meaningful and relevant to them?

The challenge is not new. Indeed, ever since the Christian faith reached the continent of Africa – whether with the conversion of the Ethiopian eunuch in the biblical record (Acts 8: 26 ff.) or with St Mark founding the church in Alexandria, according to historical tradition – African believers have naturally interpreted the gospel in light of received biblical teach-ing *and* their own cultural heritage and current experience. For example, medieval icons of the Coptic Orthodox Church in Ethiopia illustrate per-ceptions of Jesus Christ 'through African eyes', with the 'Ethiopianism' of the figures distinguished by the use of very prominent eyes. In the twentieth century, hymns from the Kimbanguist church in the Congo, the largest indigenous church in Africa, reflect how certain Congolese Christians have perceived the biblical revelation of Christ within their own cultural

categories and contemporary realities. Through decades of persecution at
the hands of Belgian colonial authorities and mission churches, including
the thirty-year imprisonment of their leader, prophet Simon Kimbangu,
hymns like the following have emerged:

> Jesus is prisoner
> Jesus was beaten
> They beat us also
> We the blacks are prisoners
> The whites are not imprisoned
> The enemy has taken away our staff
> All suffering comes upon us
> We are ill, tears are flowing.
>
> We are suffering
> Because of the name of our Chief Jesus
> May he come to strengthen us
> His name is Chief.
>
> (Pobee 1992, 148–9)

Certainly these hymns provide examples of Christians formulating 'home-
grown' or authentic, indigenous faith reflections in the midst of particular
life circumstances.

In spite of the long history of local, oral expressions of Christian faith
in Africa, it is only in the past half century that theology has risen to a
prominent place in the writings of theologians from East to West Africa.
As recently as 1968, John Mbiti from Kenya, one of the pioneers of modern
African theology, lamented that the African Church was 'without a theology, without theologians, and without theological concern' (Mbiti 1972,
51). Interestingly, Mbiti then proceeded to outline aspects of the Christian
faith which do in fact correspond to African worldviews. Nonetheless, his
statement points out a fundamental concern that gained currency around
the middle of the twentieth century: namely, the lack of critical and systematic reflection on the gospel by Africans in light of their own cultural
inheritance and contemporary realities. In other words, a clarion call went
out for 'African theology'.

Although the term is variously defined, the essential aim expressed is for
African Christians to understand and appropriate the gospel in ways that
are meaningful and relevant to their own thought forms and life experience. Among the many definitions proposed, that of Tanzanian theologian Charles Nyamiti is especially lucid: 'In its broad sense, African
Christian theology can be defined as the understanding and expression of
the Christian faith in accordance with African needs and mentality. In its

narrow or strict sense, African Christian theology is the systematic and scientific presentation or elaboration of the Christian faith according to the
needs and mentality of the African peoples' (Nyamiti 1994, 63).

A few key observations follow from Nyamiti's definition, first concerning terminology. The term 'African' raises the risk of generalisations about
Africa without adequate regard for the diversity of its peoples, languages,
cultures and histories. However, African theologians generally agree that
there is enough commonality in African worldviews and experience to
justify using the term, and they guard against overgeneralisations by spec-
ifying the particular context or people group to which they refer. Nyamiti
also specifies 'African Christian theology' since other theologies, including traditional African and Islamic, exist on the continent. Yet the phrase
'African theology' is widely assumed to refer to African Christian theology,
so that the two terms are used interchangeably within the field of African
Christianity.

Further observations concern the nature and task of theology. Nyamiti's
differentiation between the narrow definition and the broad sense suggests certain features of African theology. First, African theologians tend
to expand the bounds of definition beyond the general associations of
theology with systematic discourse about God. Certainly they advocate
'critical African theology' as 'the organised faith-reflection of an authentically African Christianity' (Gibellini 1994, 6). However, they also point out
that the propositional style of analysis associated with scholastic theology
in the West is not the only way of expressing theology. Rather, it may also
be conveyed informally, for example in Christian art and worship, like the
Ethiopian icons and Kimbanguist hymns mentioned above. Kenyan Bishop
Henry Okullu highlights the informal nature of much African theology as
follows:

When we are looking for African theology we should go first to the fields, to the
village church, to Christian homes to listen to those spontaneously uttered prayers
before people go to bed . . . We must listen to the throbbing drumbeats and
the clapping of hands accompanying the impromptu singing in the independent
churches. We must look at the way in which Christianity is being planted in
Africa through music, drama, songs, dances, art, paintings. We must listen to the
preaching of a sophisticated pastor as well as to that of the simple village vicar . . .
Can it be that all this is an empty show? It is impossible. This then is African
theology. (Okullu 1974, 54)

Given the vitality of Christian experience across sub-Saharan Africa today,
these informal, oral expressions of theology require serious attention alongside the formal, written expressions.

Examining the 'lived' theologies brings to light a second feature of African theology: that is, the importance of the community of faith in theological formulation. The biblical affirmation of the priesthood of all believers (1 Pet. 2: 9–10) forms the basis for the priority of 'theology by the people', summarised as follows:

> The church as the whole people of God has a duty to proclaim the good news and, to that extent, they need faith and praxis, both of which involve levels of reflection . . . It is not only that everyone has a duty to theologize but that that is best done in community and while living together in faith. Theologizing is possible, nay, a duty even, outside the elitist group of professional theologians. (Amirtham and Pobee 1986, 5–6)

The statement does not aim to exclude professional theologians from the community, but to emphasise that 'what the theologian does is *in the context of* and *with* the people, not *for* the people gathered as a community of faith' (ibid., 7; italics original).

Cameroonian theologian Jean-Marc Ela is a prime example of theologising in community. After more than a decade of theological studies and teaching in Europe, Ela returned to his home country to minister cross-culturally as a parish priest among the Kirdi people in the mountains of northern Cameroon. Writing by lantern light from a remote village, he advocates what he calls 'shade-tree theology – a theology that, far from the libraries and the offices, develops among brothers and sisters searching shoulder to shoulder with unlettered peasants for the sense of the word of God in situations in which this word touches them' (Ela 1986a, vi). He then describes the theologian's role in this way:

> A theologian must stay within earshot of what is happening within the community so that community life can become the subject of meditation and prayer. In the end, a theologian is perhaps simply a witness and a travelling companion, alert for signs of God and willing to get dirty in the precarious conditions of village life. Reflection crystallises only if it is confined to specific questions. (Ela 1988, 11)

Ela's comment indicates a third central characteristic of African theology. By stressing that theology entails reflection upon specific issues of faith in a particular community, Ela exemplifies new ways of doing theology according to priorities emerging within the wider field of Third World theologies. Prior to the mid twentieth century, the 'era of noncontextualisation' in Protestant and Catholic missions generally assumed that theology (in the singular) was to be defined once and for all and then 'indigenised' into Third World cultures without losing any of its essence. Therefore Western theology, as the dominant theology, was regarded to have universal validity, and church confessions were exported in their 'unaltered – and unalterable – forms' to the younger churches overseas (Bosch 1991, 427).

In contrast, 'contextuality', a term coined by Shoki Coe in 1972, stresses the decisive role of a particular context in shaping the theology produced therein. A landmark in the recent development of contextual theology in Africa is the 'Final Communiqué' of the 1977 Pan-African Conference of Third World Theologians, held in Accra, Ghana. The concluding section recommends how theology is to be done in Africa: 'The African situation requires a new theological methodology that is different from the approaches of the dominant theologies of the West . . . Our task as theologians is to create a theology that arises from and is accountable to African people' (Appiah-Kubi and Torres 1979, 192). This new way is termed *'contextual'* theology, or 'accountable to the context people live in' (ibid., 193).

The priority of contextuality resounds throughout the works of African theologians. In 1986, Congolese theologian Bénézet Bujo warned that African theology to date had been too academic and therefore largely irrelevant to contemporary African society (Bujo 1992, 70). Instead, a widespread methodological presupposition is that African theology must take into account the real concrete, everyday experience of Africans in their political, economic, social and religious contexts. Consequently, these theologies generally seek to discern the questions arising in a specific context of the gospel and to develop theological formulations in response to those questions. Mercy Oduyoye from Ghana, a leading African woman theologian, underlines this fundamental priority as follows:

Theologians throughout the world who felt a call to speak more relevantly to their age and generation freed themselves from traditional dogmatic and systematic theology and focused on life issues. Instead of telling people what questions to ask and then furnishing them with the answers, theologians began to listen to the questions people were asking and then seek the answers. (Oduyoye 1986, 3)

A fourth aspect of African theology, stemming from this increased attention to particular contexts of theology, is the shift from 'theology' being used in the singular to the plural form 'theologies'. With the diversity of contexts in Africa, a corresponding plurality of theologies naturally developed. Rationale for plurality is found in biblical and historical precedence: just as the biblical and later Christian writers provide distinctive theological reflections from their own life situations, so too diverse theologies arise across Africa today. Variations stem from differences in the authors' political, cultural, linguistic and denominational backgrounds and life experiences, as well as from different sources and methodological approaches they employ.

In sum, key features of emergent African theologies include the duality of their formal and informal expressions, the importance of the community of faith in their formulation, their contextual nature, and their plurality in articulation.

Considering the present array of theologies across East to West Africa, this chapter concentrates on recent developments. A brief overview of origins and shaping factors provides the framework for exploring certain African theologies. The materials presented are derived from textual and oral theologies, the latter gleaned through extensive qualitative research conducted personally with selected theologians, church leaders and laity in East and West Africa. Concluding remarks focus on the contributions these theologies make to the ongoing development of Christian thought worldwide.

ASSEMBLING THE STONES: ORIGINS OF CONTEMPORARY AFRICAN THEOLOGIES

The age-old process of preparing traditional foods in Africa serves to illustrate the recent process of constructing local theologies. From East to West across the continent, Africans have long gathered three large flat stones, lit a fire in the centre of them, and placed upon them a clay pot in which local dishes are cooked. The initial step, then, entails assembling the stones. Like the gathering of these foundational rocks, indigenous theological reflection in modern Africa begins with the drawing together of three key movements around the mid twentieth century: political, cultural and theological.

In relation to the political scene, African theology as an intellectual discipline arose during the 1950s and 1960s when the struggle against colonialism led to several newly independent states. Due to the widely perceived collusion between Christianity and colonialism, African theologians were compelled to formulate an apologetic for maintaining their Christian faith in the face of nationalist critique and missionary domination of the church.

Along with the political 'wind of change' came the 'cultural revolution' which swept across the continent. In opposition to the widespread disdain for African cultures among colonials, Africans made intensive efforts to reaffirm their own identity and integrity in many spheres of life, including personal names, dress, music, dance forms, architecture and other indigenous expressions that necessarily influenced church life and practice. In particular, intellectuals reinforced cultural revival through an

African Renaissance in history, philosophy and literature. For example, the francophone movement known as *la négritude*, initiated by Léopold Senghor, Frantz Fanon and Aimé Césaire, together with anglophone writers like Nigerians Wole Soyinka and Chinua Achebe and Kenyan Ngugi wa Thiong'o, fuelled this revitalisation of indigenous cultures.

A parallel theological renaissance arose, internationally, when Vatican II sanctioned a radical reappraisal of Christian doctrine and practice, plus a more positive re-evaluation of non-Christian religions and cultures. Pope Paul VI further inspired Africans to cultivate local expressions of faith when in 1969 he urged the bishops gathered in Kampala, 'You may, and you must, have an African Christianity' (Ela 1988, xiii). Catholics and Protestants alike took new initiatives and fostered further growth, for example, through African participation in the wider context of Third World theology. Africa hosted the first Ecumenical Dialogue of Third World Theologians in Dar es Salaam in 1976, resulting in the foundation of the Ecumenical Association of Third World Theologians (EATWOT). In 1977 followed the corresponding foundation in Accra of the Ecumenical Association of African Theologians (EAAT). Finally, the remarkable rise in African initiated (or independent) churches (AICs) had already stimulated further theological fermentation across the continent. Indeed, fears of the exodus of African Christians from mission denominations to these indigenous churches encouraged theologians and church leaders to reformulate their faith so as to be more meaningful to their members.

Thus the academic discipline of African theology was established through accumulated events of political, cultural and theological change. As Desmond Tutu observes, it solidified attempts to rehabilitate Africa's rich cultural and religious heritage, and to acknowledge these as effective means for conveying the gospel in Africa. In Tutu's view, African theology was founded as 'the theological counterpart of what has happened in, say, the study of African history. It has helped to give the lie to the supercilious but tacit assumption that religion and history in Africa date from the advent in that continent of the white man.' Consequently, Tutu concludes, 'It means that we have a great store from which we can fashion new ways of speaking to and about God, and new styles of worship consistent with our new faith' (Tutu 1978, 366).

STRIKING THE FIRE: FACTORS FUELLING AFRICAN THEOLOGIES

What are the critical issues that sparked these new ways of speaking to and about God in Africa? And how do these issues kindle new expressions of theology? For as Ela insists, 'Our response to the God who has spoken through his Son has to be formulated from the struggles of our people, from their joys, from their pains, from their hopes and their frustrations today' (Ela 1986b, 46; my translation). A brief outline of certain pains and frustrations that African Christians experience sheds light on the joys and hopes expressed through the theologies explored in the next section.

One word that encapsulates the most pressing concerns fuelling African theologies is 'captivity'. For example, Ghanaian theologian John Pobee summarises the multi-faceted complexity of issues by describing African Christianity in terms of 'the North Atlantic Captivity of the Church'. He explains, 'Christianity in Africa starts with an assumed definition of the Christian faith which is definitely North Atlantic – intellectually, spiritually, liturgically, organisationally.' He further laments that 'some have misused the Christian faith to oppress Africans. In the name of bringing "Christian civilisation" to the so-called benighted Africans they have oppressed Africans intellectually, physically, spiritually, economically, and culturally' (Pobee 1983, 5).

Without elaborating the issues here, Pobee's statements highlight certain historical and missiological issues regarding the Western missionary transmission of the gospel in Africa. While granting due recognition to the many benefits gained through this missionary inheritance, Pobee, among other theologians, critiques the *tabula rasa* ('clean slate') approach that was all too common among Westerners. That is to say, the widespread denigration of African cultures hindered missionaries from acknowledging anything positive in these cultures through which the gospel message might be conveyed. Bujo puts it bluntly: 'It is hardly an exaggeration to say that the missionaries adopted an attitude of blanket condemnation of African culture in all its aspects. African converts were required to turn their backs on the whole of their tradition and the whole of their culture. Only then was it considered that the Christian faith had truly taken root in their souls' (Bujo 1992, 45). Consequently, many Africans perceived Christianity as an alien religion, and those who adopted it commonly straddled two seemingly disparate worlds of Christianity and African culture. Given the ensuing 'spiritual schizophrenia', the crisis of African Christian identity, or how to be truly Christian *and* authentically African, for many, lies at the very heart of African theology (Walls 1978; Bediako 1992).

Overlapping with Pobee's telling phrase about North Atlantic captivity is Ela's vehement cry for liberating African Christianity from its 'Babylonian captivity' to 'Roman structures' of European Christianity. In his scorching critique, Ela unabashedly raises questions like the following:

In our environment, our faith does not ask questions about the sex of the angels or the infallibility of the pope; instead we question the lack of any genuine application of the critical function inherent in the Christian faith. How can we show that the African church is blocked by an ecclesiastical praxis that is, in fact, a kind of museum of a narrow moralism, a ritualistic sacramentalism, a disembodied spirituality, and a withering dogmatics? (Ela 1988, 153–4)

What inflames such strong sentiments on the part of African theologians? First, the continued domination of Western theology and church polity rightfully evokes great outcry from African Christians. The problem here is not merely Western ethnocentrism and paternalism, but the deeper theological question of missionary misunderstanding of the gospel itself (Bediako 1992, 239). In other words, by associating Christianity so closely with Western civilisation, missionaries have often equated *conversion* to the Christian faith with *acculturation* into their own culture. Yet African Christians look to the Jerusalem Council recorded in Acts 15, which declared that Gentile Christians did not have to become 'honorary' Jews in order to become Christians. Nonetheless, as Kenyan theologian J. N. K. Mugambi concludes, 'Most missionaries insisted that an African must become an "honorary white", as a precondition for becoming a Christian. This was a gross theological error' (Mugambi 1989, 56). As a direct legacy of the modern missionary movement, African Christians face the ongoing challenge of appropriating the gospel as Africans despite the 'judaising' tendencies of Western missionaries to fashion the Christian faith according to their own image.

A second reason for Ela's outcry is the desperate need for credible Christianity within widespread contexts of suffering across Africa. He repeatedly cautions the church against simply passing by the beaten victims, like the priest and the Levite in the parable of the Samaritan (Lk. 10: 30–2). Instead, he urges the church to go beyond wrestling with abstract questions of faith, or even issues of African authenticity alone, to attend to the 'concrete, historical irruption of the poor into our midst' (Ela, 1994, 137). Hence he questions, 'How can the church *be* church within the structures of domination in which Africans must seek their identity?' (Ela 1988, 138). With characteristic incisiveness, Ela describes the contemporary context in sub-Saharan Africa in terms of the disillusionment with 'flag independences' across the continent, the international domination perpetuating injustice in political, economic, social and cultural spheres, and the local oppression of neo-colonial masters. He insists that 'these urgent problems of contemporary Africa become the obligatory *locus* of theological research' (Ela 1994, 140). He therefore concludes, 'It is impossible to attempt an overall interpretation of the Good News from our situation as Africans without making liberation the fundamental axis of a theology which comes from our people' (Ela, 1986b, 38; translation mine).

Besides 'North Atlantic captivity' and 'Babylonian captivity', a third major concern is 'cultural captivity'. The Final Communiqué from the 1977 conference of African theologians in Accra declares, 'Contextualization will mean that theology will deal with the liberation of our people from cultural captivity' (Appiah-Kubi and Torres 1979, 194). In view of the all-inclusive nature of culture, embracing language, customs, knowledge, values, symbols etc., 'cultural captivity' encompasses numerous issues from traditional and contemporary contexts. One prominent example within the development of African theology is that of sexism. Oduyoye traces the 'irruption within the irruption' as women, initially, challenged EATWOT to expand its borders from doing theology based on experiences of classism and racism in the socio-economic and political realms, to include sexism anchored in religio-cultural perceptions. Hence a new methodological stance emerged: 'The concerns and experiences of women as women are yet another *locus* for liberation theology' (Oduyoye 1983, 248). African feminist theologians began to articulate the sources of their oppression, including Western Christianity, African religio-cultural traditions, and contemporary socio-political contexts (Oduyoye 1992, 314–15). Subsequently, women and men theologians acknowledge that the need to address gender issues extends beyond the domain of women's concerns alone, since humanity is comprised of male and female.

So the single term 'captivity' bursts, like a glowing ember, to ignite many issues fuelling contemporary African theologies: historical and missiological issues, identity issues, theological and ecclesiological issues, and cultural issues spanning the political, economic and social realms.

STIRRING THE POT: THEOLOGIES SIMMERING ACROSS AFRICA TODAY

Introduction: inculturation and liberation theologies

From the burning issues identified above, what kinds of theologies are produced across Africa? African theology is commonly introduced according to two main trends that emerged from the 1950s to the 1980s: (1) 'African' or 'inculturation' theology, and (2) 'Black' or 'liberation' theology. The first trend of inculturation concerns how the gospel is planted and authentically rooted in a given culture. It essentially aims to integrate the Christian faith with the African religious heritage so as to ensure the integrity of African Christian identity (Bediako 1996, 1). Closely related terms, including 'adaptation', 'accommodation', and 'indigenisation', each carry certain nuances, although the latter in particular is sometimes used interchangeably with 'inculturation'. The associated concept of 'incarnation' theology specifies the theological rationale: just as Christ became incarnate to reveal God's message of salvation, so the gospel must be 'incarnated' in every culture. The distinguishing emphasis within inculturation theology is the ongoing, dynamic interaction between the Christian faith and culture so that both are mutually enriched. As Alyward Shorter explains, 'Inculturation implies that the Christian message transforms a culture. It is also the case that Christianity is transformed by culture, not in a way that falsifies the message, but in the way in which the message is formulated and interpreted anew' (Shorter 1988, 14).

The second trend of Black or liberation theology is often associated with southern Africa, arising out of the historical realities related to racism in that region. However, African liberation theology extends throughout sub-Saharan Africa north of the Limpopo River, with a broader scope identified as follows: 'Liberation theology in independent Africa endeavors to integrate the theme of liberation in the rest of the African cultural background. Liberation is not confined to modern socioeconomic and political levels but includes emancipation from other forms of oppression such as disease, poverty, hunger, ignorance, and the subjugation of women' (Nyamiti 1994, 66).

This broad, two-fold classification of inculturation and liberation theologies has served an important purpose in distinguishing the various contexts and aims of African theologies, plus the sources and methods favoured in their formulation. It therefore retains instructive value for an overview of theological development in Africa. However, despite certain qualifications made that they are not mutually exclusive, the tendency remains to erect a false dichotomy between the two trends. As a result, African theologians have increasingly objected to maintaining this dubious division. For example, Ela contends that *'liberation of the oppressed must be the primary condition for any authentic inculturation of the Christian message'* (Ela 1988, vi). Likewise, Bujo denounces any theology of inculturation that does not adequately address the ills of the post-colonial context which inculturation alone cannot remedy. He questions, 'How can a theology done in and for Africa so persistently close its eyes to the immense wretchedness and misery which is all around us? Can a nation develop culturally, while being politically oppressed and economically exploited to such a horrifying degree, while its people, faced with starvation and many other catastrophes, is struggling for its very survival?' He too concludes that theology cannot take '*such a onesided interest in culture* that is little concerned with the liberation of the People of God from their misery' (Bujo 1990, 125–6).

For this reason, inculturation and liberation are now clearly perceived to be two sides of the same coin. Consequently, a synthesis of the two approaches is advisable both in constructing and in interpreting African theologies today.

An integrated approach: symbolising African theology today

Given the importance of symbols in African cultures, African theologians have drawn upon one authentic image from the African heritage to illustrate certain aspects of contemporary theological construction. The cooking pot, set on the three-stone fireplace, remains common across rural Africa. Even urban Christians in Nairobi today speak of it lying at the heart of traditional communal life, and as representing 'warmth', 'love and laughter', 'social togetherness', 'one-ness' and 'home'. They also acknowledge it to be a prime place for preparing traditional foods, for communal discussions and celebration, and for singing, proverbs and story-telling. Thus the cooking pot symbolises the sharing of practical wisdom, as time-honoured insights are applied to contemporary situations and transmitted to the next generation. This metaphor of 'theology cooked in an African pot' has emerged recently in theological discussion in southern Africa.

In relating this image to theological construction, the three stones invite correspondences with other triads from biblical and Christian tradition: God the Father, Son and Holy Spirit, or perhaps theology, Christology and ecclesiology. As productive as these parallels might be, the approach preferred here is to build upon African categories of thought. In other words, what are the fundamental aspects of indigenous worldviews upon which rests the gospel's interaction with traditional cultures and contemporary realities?

Among the various possibilities, the following three concepts are selected for the present purpose: (1) Life, (2) Mediation and (3) Community. Certainly these basic human aspirations are well attested throughout Africa, as the discussion below indicates, and each 'stone' integrates issues from so-called traditional and modern perspectives. (In reality, the traditional cannot truly be separated from the modern since they intermingle in African life today. However, for the purpose of theological analysis, it helps to discern those beliefs, customs and values, derived from African realities prior to the coming of Europeans and Christianity, which exert enduring influence upon African worldviews.) Furthermore, just as all three stones must be in close proximity and properly balanced to hold the cooking pot, so these three concepts are intrinsically related to one another, and together they contribute to the holistic character generally identified with African thought.

Without pressing the analogy too far, the cooking pot might represent a particular theologian, or a particular community in which theology is constructed. Certainly each traditional clay pot has its own distinctive shape and local colouring, and yet the same vessel with shared purpose is clearly identifiable across the continent.

More important than the pot, however, are the contents. If the local dishes symbolise the actual theologies produced, then what is simmering across East to West Africa today? Before sampling from the variety, it is worth noting the preparation of African dishes. In terms of the ingredients, many of the staple foods are common to other parts of the world. Some of these foodstuffs (like sorghum and millet) are truly indigenous, having been domesticated along the Sahel several millennia ago. Others (like maize), were brought centuries ago and adopted into local cultures as everyday staples. Still others (like wheat bread) are recent imports that can represent luxury items or even economic imperialism in some places.

These ingredients find parallels in the sources of African theologies today. Some elements are truly indigenous to the continent, even if found elsewhere around the globe. Others came long ago and have naturally become part of local life. Still others have been imported more recently, and Africans must weigh whether they are actually essential for spiritual health, or unnecessary impositions that threaten the vitality of local church life while benefiting foreigners.

The 'Final Communiqué' of the 1977 Pan-African Conference of Third World Theologians outlines the sources these specialists recommend for contemporary African theologies. They point to the Bible and Christian heritage as the first source, insisting that 'the Bible is the basic source of African theology, because it is the primary witness of God's revelation in Jesus Christ. No theology can retain its Christian identity apart from Scripture' (Appiah-Kubi and Torres 1979, 192). While the interpretation and use of the Bible in Africa form increasingly prominent issues (see Mbiti 1986; West and Dube 2000), its immense significance throughout sub-Saharan Africa lies beyond dispute. In particular, the vital role of vernacular scriptures in African Christianity warrants close attention, as Ghanaian theologian Kwame Bediako notes:

There is probably no more important single explanation for the massive presence of Christianity on the African continent than the availability of the Scriptures in many African languages . . . The existence of vernacular Bibles not only facilitates access to the particular communities speaking those languages, but also creates the likelihood that the hearers of the Word in their own languages will make their own response to it and on their own terms. Probably nowhere else in the history of the expansion of Christianity has this occurred quite as widely as in modern Africa. (Bediako 1995, 62)

Moreover, since African theologies do not develop in isolation, Christian tradition from apostolic times to the present informs African reflections, albeit to different degrees. In general, African theologians weigh various church traditions in light of biblical faith, and favour ecumenical dialogue on contemporary issues.

Second, the Pan-African Conference theologians point to African anthropology and cosmology, underlining that in order for the gospel to truly penetrate the spiritual perceptions of Africans, it must be conveyed in accordance with their understanding of humanity and the cosmos. For example, in African thought, the salvation of the human person is inextricably bound to that of the cosmos. Hence African theologians urge that the gospel mystery be presented in terms of Christ ultimately summing up all things, humanity and the universe, to himself.

Third, African traditional religions are central to their fundamental premise: 'The God of history speaks to all peoples in particular ways. In Africa the traditional religions are a major source for the study of the African experience of God. The beliefs and practices of the traditional religions in Africa can enrich Christian theology and spirituality' (Appiah-Kubi and Torres 1979, 193). Granted, this presupposition is pivotal in differentiating the spectrum of theologies across Africa. On the one end, some African theologians like Nigerian Bolaji Idowu and Kenyan Samuel Kibicho so stress the radical continuity between the revelation of God in the Bible and in their own African religious tradition, that the two are deemed identical. On the other end of the spectrum, theologians like Nigerian Byang Kato, before his untimely death in 1975, and some evangelicals so stress the radical discontinuity between the Bible and African religions, they assert that 'Biblical revelation alone can point out the way the Christian should go' (Kato 1975, 24). Between these two extreme positions, the majority of theologians look to the African religious heritage as a necessary and fertile source for engagement with the gospel, while placing traditional religion under the purifying critique of biblical revelation. However crucial African traditional religions are for interpreting the gospel, the Bible remains the 'plumbline' for theology and 'the charter document of the church' (Pobee 1979, 33; 1983, 6).

The African Independent Churches (AICs) form the fourth recommended source. This in itself marks a shift in thinking. For those in the 'historic' or 'mission-founded' churches often considered these 'independent' or 'indigenous' or African 'instituted' churches to be 'heretical', 'syncretistic' or 'schismatic' aberrations of Christianity. Yet, following the extraordinary mushrooming of these churches throughout Africa in the nineteenth and especially the twentieth century, they now command much more serious attention and positive regard. Indeed, these AICs are often hailed as authentically African expressions of Christianity (although at times in an insufficiently critical manner). While generalisations are suspect, since the AICs vary so widely, these churches do exemplify appropriations of the gospel in keeping with African cultural thought forms and practices. For example, they place deep emphasis on the Holy Spirit, with the accompanying manifestations of joy, tongues and power, on healing and exorcism, on personal testimony, and on protest against foreign models of church and political government (Pobee and Ositelu 1998, 40–4). African theologians also highlight the AICs' contributions to extending the bounds of theological expression. Pobee appreciates that their means of communicating gospel realities 'are not statements but stories, not theological arguments but testimonies, not definitions but participatory dance, not concepts but banquets, not systematic arguments but songs, not hermeneutical analysis but healing' (ibid., ix). So the massive presence of AICs adds significant flavour to African Christianity and to the theological reflections arising therein.

The final source advocated is other African realities. This forms a broad category covering everything from cultural forms of life and arts, to family and communal life, to the struggles against racism, sexism and any other form of economic, political, social and cultural oppression.

Like the major food groups contributing to a full diet, these five sources contribute substantially to the theologies simmering across East to West Africa today. While the relative weight and proportion given to each source differs among individuals and communities, African theologians generally tap the potential for drawing upon all categories. As for how the sources are blended, no single method reigns supreme in 'stirring the pot' of theological reflections. Suffice it to say that whatever the approach, whether the method moves from the Bible to the African realities, or vice versa, the critical point is this: when the gospel and Christian tradition interact with the African heritage and current realities, local theologies arise and offer appropriate sustenance to African believers.

Of the many ways in which these theologies might be introduced, a thematic approach is conducive to illustrating how various voices contribute to developing fundamental theological issues from their respective contexts. Building upon the three stones identified above, these theologies demonstrate the interface between the gospel and aspects of African experience, both past and present.

Theologies of life

So central is life, as a cardinal value in traditional African cultures, that it becomes the starting point for some theologies. That is, African concepts of life are fundamental to the ways in which Christians interpret and appropriate the gospel. As Mbiti observes, 'It is within the traditional thought-forms and religious concerns that our peoples live and try to assimilate Christian teaching. These traditional thought-forms strongly colour much of their understanding of the Christian Message' (Mbiti 1972, 52). A brief outline of central aspects of life in African thought is foundational to exploring their shaping influence upon current theologies of life.

Bénézet Bujo is a leading example here, for he selects life as the conceptual framework for his theological and ethical investigations. He first underlines the widespread traditional African view that God is the creator and sustainer of all life, and the one who alone possesses fullness of life. Bujo then points out a second distinguishing concept of life in African thought: its hierarchical ordering. Life, also designated 'life-force' or 'vital union', is mediated through descending ranks of beings in the invisible and the visible world: from God through deceased clan and family members, through royalty, chiefs and elders, to heads of households and family members, to animate and inanimate elements of nature.

African thought specifies two additional characteristics of life, in being holistic and communal. That is, Africans tend to view life comprehensively, avoiding dichotomies between the physical and the spiritual, or 'between private, social, political and religious life' (Bujo 1990, 78). This holistic approach also means that life entails participation in the community, for the individual is thought to exist only in relation to the community. Hence the two cooking stones, 'life' and 'community', operate together in upholding emergent African theologies.

What happens when the gospel enters African contexts in which concepts of life hold this central place? African theologians, church leaders and laity alike profess that if Jesus is indeed 'the way, the truth and the life' (Jn 14: 6), then he ultimately fulfils the aspirations for life, not only of Africans but of the whole human race. Bujo therefore affirms, concerning Christ, 'He is the unique manifestation of the life of God, he is source and proto-model of all life. It is he who teaches us what . . . is the true life, what is to live. He has come that we might have life and have it in abundance (Jn 10: 10)' (Bujo 1995, 32). The convergence of the biblical witness with traditional African concepts of life then becomes more explicit. After expounding upon John 10:10 and other Johannine texts concerning Jesus and life, Bujo declares Jesus to be 'the true vital force and energy *par excellence* which flows into all his descendants' (ibid., 33). This perception of Jesus in African idiom has further implications for understanding the Holy Spirit and the church, overlapping with the next sections on theologies of mediation and community.

John Pobee also provides clear evidence of 'stirring the pot' to prepare African theologies of life. Like Bujo, he begins by reflecting upon traditional concepts of life among his people group, the Akan of Ghana. He, too, notes the holistic and communal character of life in their view. He then underlines the priority of the biblical revelation in stating his methodological approach as follows:

The traditional African concept of well-being can only be the *starting point*. In any case, as a Christian I believe Christ adds a new dimension, challenging the traditional culture. The task before us then is to attempt to construct a view which has for its elements the Gospel of Jesus Christ, the traditional African insights with regard to a wholistic view of life, at once vertical and horizontal, and the realities of today's world. (Pobee 1986, 19)

As a New Testament scholar, Pobee mines the Fourth Gospel for relevant metaphors of life, including bread, water, and light of life, all of which he affirms Africans are seeking. He also defines two Greek words translated as 'life' in this Gospel: *psuche*, referring to physical or biological life, and *zoe*, used metaphorically for religious or spiritual life, especially in relation to Christ. Having outlined the Akan view of life as going beyond biological life to encompass material prosperity and spiritual well-being, summed up in 'seven graces', he draws parallels between the biblical and Akan teachings. On this basis, he concludes:

The Akan concept of life outlined in the seven graces is a welcome starting point for evangelism. For all the coalescence Christianity goes further to make the unique claim that life is found in its fullness in Christ, e.g. John 1: 4: 'In him (i.e. Christ the *logos*) was life.' . . . Thus the biblical faith affirms the centrality of Christ to and for the life of human beings; the basic necessities of life are to be sought and found in Christ. In our context we can assert that the seven graces for which the Akan prays are met in Christ. (Pobee 1983, 7–8)

The conviction that African concepts of life are met in Christ becomes further evident in numerous informal expressions of theology. For example, a hymn from Ghana draws upon the biblical story of Jesus with the woman at the well (Jn 4), and expresses this image in the Ghanaian vernacular, Ga. Anglican minister Joseph Lamptey explains the hymn, saying, 'Jesus, "*wela bubu*" *is* the fountain of life. He provides our needs, both physical and spiritual. We see him as a *well* of life.'

More strikingly, not only do Christians ascribe biblical images to Jesus, but also African vernacular terms related to life. For instance, '*Oyēadeē*', a term traditionally referring to God in the Ghanaian language Twi, is now extended to Jesus. Methodist minister Robert Aboagey-Mensah translates it as follows: '"He makes things well", "he brings life into things". When you use it in the context of human well-being, it means "he makes them whole", like the biblical *shalom*. He brings wholeness.' For these African Christians, then, a coalescence forms between African and biblical traditions concerning life. The centrality of life is certainly manifest in their perceptions, and the source of life traditionally acknowledged in African concepts of God is now identified with Jesus.

As indicated above, however, the interaction between the gospel and African cultures rightfully entails contemporary realities as well as traditional thought in Africa. Consequently, a serious dilemma arises, which Appiah-Kubi expresses candidly as follows: 'To many, Jesus came that we might have life and have it more abundantly. But the perturbing question is, where is this abundant life, when all around us we see suffering, poverty, oppression, strife, envy, war and destruction?' (Appiah-Kubi 1987, 76). Needless to say, this pointed question raises grave challenges to African Christianity. How do African Christians respond, given the obvious, acute problems across the continent?

In constructing theologies of life, African theologians contrast the respect that was traditionally accorded to life, considered sacred, with the widespread violations of life in contemporary Africa. Together with lay Christians, they confront a host of current issues in light of the gospel, such as the massive suffering from preventable diseases, AIDS, poverty, famine, ethnic and domestic violence, human rights violations, and environmental degradation. Bujo castigates political leaders and their subjects for allowing these calamities to escalate, and sums up the present situation graphically as follows: 'We are all colonized by the new mights: money, power . . . That leads us to pooh-pooh life . . . Today there is killing in Africa like killing snakes, like removing weeds' (Bujo 1995, 32–3).

In the face of these life-threatening realities, one major theme in African Christianity is that of Jesus as healer, or one who restores life. Believers proclaim Jesus as healer in theological texts and religious rites, in preaching and prayers, in testimony and songs. Even visual statements to this effect can be noted in everyday life. For example, a signboard in Kasoa, Ghana, announces 'King Christ Medical Laboratory', with two pictures painted side by side: Jesus on the cross, and a microscope. *Trotros*, public transport vehicles in Ghana, bear colourful slogans like 'Dr Jesus'. Among their Kenyan counterparts, *matatus*, one broadcasts a Kikuyu inscription: '*Jesu ni wa ciama*', which translates, 'Jesus is a miracle worker' or a 'wonder worker'. So evidence abounds in African contexts for the paramount importance of Jesus as healer.

Africans justify their emphasis upon the life-giving power of the gospel both from biblical teaching, particularly Jesus' healing ministry, and from contemporary experience of widespread healing ministries. Here the AICs become prominent for their central emphasis upon healing. In fact, research indicates that healing forms the most important reason for people joining these churches (Pobee 1994, 248). Hence the AICs, together with Pentecostal and new charismatic renewal movements, now inspire greater attention to healing ministries among historic churches that had previously neglected traditional African concepts of illness and left healing ministries to doctors and hospitals. In so doing, these churches demonstrate the critical need to inculturate the gospel in 'the African universe of sickness', which 'is inseparable from the universe of spirits' (Ela 1988, 50–1).

The problem here is that the early missionaries tended to deny the reality of evil spirits and to dismiss belief in witchcraft as superstition and heathenism. They also tended to skew the gospel proclamation towards 'spiritual salvation' of the soul, betraying a dualistic view of body and soul that contravened holistic views of life in Africa. So, instead of the common approach of condemning African Christians for reverting to traditional religions in time of life crises, the more urgent and constructive task is to understand African perspectives on illness and to impart the gospel accordingly.

In brief, just as concepts of life extend beyond the physical dimensions, so Africans traditionally view health as being more than biological, encompassing physical, mental, spiritual, social and environmental well-being. Illness or misfortune signifies a disruption of harmony among these dimensions of health. While organic causes may well be recognised, the overriding belief is that spiritual or supernatural forces lie behind the sickness, such as offending God or ancestral spirits, possession by evil spirits, witchcraft, breaking taboos, or curses from offended family or community members. Therefore illness is considered a calamity which strikes not only the individual, but also the social fabric of the family and community.

Against this backdrop, African theologies of life have important implications for doctrine and praxis in relation to Christ, the Holy Spirit, and the church. First, according to many believers from East and West Africa, Jesus offers the fullness of life to which Africans aspire. As healer, he restores life wherever it has been diminished: in body, mind, spirit, and in relationships with family, society and God. Biblical and African traditions thus merge in interpreting Jesus' healing as the re-creation of wholeness in all aspects of life, encompassing the individual, communal and cosmic spheres.

Second, African interpretations of the gospel also highlight Jesus' supremacy over all evil powers at work in the universe, whether manifest in the physical, psychological, spiritual, social or any other realm. From the outset of modern African theology, Mbiti called attention to Africans' perceptions of Jesus as '*Christus Victor*' above all else. That is, Jesus holds special appeal as 'the Victor over the forces which have dominated African life from time immemorial', including 'the devil, spirits, sickness, hatred, fear, and death itself' (Mbiti 1972, 54). Ela looks to the example of St Paul, who did not condemn new converts from the Greek world for still granting great importance to principalities and powers. Instead, the Apostle proclaimed the paramount position of Christ (Col. 1: 15–20), from whom comes all salvation. Therefore African views regarding invisible forces operating in the universe are perhaps the best place in which to proclaim the primacy of Christ and his power to liberate Africans feeling menaced by the occult (Ela 1988, 141).

One controversial proposal, in this regard, is the image of Jesus as traditional healer. Some African Christians portray Jesus as '*nganga*', the vernacular term (or its cognates) in many Bantu languages for the medicine person anachronistically translated 'witchdoctor'. They argue that Jesus accomplishes the work of *nganga* in terms of healing, protecting from evil powers, and restoring community relations where disruption has occurred in the social fabric. However, objections stem from negative connotations surrounding the term (often influenced by colonial and missionary hostilities towards this traditional figure), and the consequent fear of syncretism in associating Jesus with *nganga*. While the controversy is not readily resolved, it does illustrate the complex issues entailed in the interface of gospel and culture in Africa.

Finally, theologies of life are highly relevant to the life of the church in Africa. From the discussion above, it is clear that the healing ministry forms a crucial role within the vocation of the church today, and that a holistic approach is vital in Africa where health encompasses physical, spiritual and social dimensions (see Mwaura 1994; Pobee 2001). Moreover, pervasive suffering in contemporary contexts raises complex health issues arising from colonialism, neo-colonialism and Western Christian mission. Thus the church is called to address the social injustice of 'class medicine', where health care is the privilege of the wealthy minority. It must also attend to the massive needs for pastoral care among the sick and dying, particularly those suffering from the AIDS pandemic. Again, the concerns of inculturation and liberation can hardly be separated in confronting these realities, and both concerns are critical for African ecclesiology. Hence Pobee concludes, 'African churches have rediscovered healing as part of Christian mission and ministry and therefore, of liberation, in a comprehensive sense. That is the wholeness to which the church of God is committed. But such an emphasis signals the ecclesiology that characterizes the African church' (Pobee 1994, 254).

Theologies of mediation

The second 'stone' foundational to African thought is that of mediation. With life as the central focus and purpose of African religions, the necessity for mediation becomes clear. Tanzanian theologian Laurenti Magesa explains the basic orientation of African religions as follows: 'Wherever and whenever there is a diminishment or a destruction of the force of life, something must be done to restore it; whenever there is a breach of order in the universe as established by God through the ancestors, humanity must see to it that harmony is restored. Failing this, humanity will suffer' (Magesa 1997, 77). So when afflictions occur within a community, such as wrong-doing, illness or witchcraft, African religions recognise the crucial role of intermediaries in discerning the reasons for the disharmony and prescribing measures to rectify it, thereby mediating reconciliation and restoring the force of life.

Mbiti explains that the traditional notion of intermediaries is also derived from common social and political custom in which people of higher status are approached indirectly through a third party. Consequently, while people definitely can and do approach God directly, they generally do so through the mediation of particular specialists or other beings. Certainly concepts of intermediaries vary across Africa, yet Mbiti identifies two main types: (1) human beings, such as priests, kings, healers and diviners, and (2) spiritual beings, believed to assist people in establishing closer contact with God (Mbiti 1969, 68–71). Recent proposals of 'ancestral theology', based upon this latter category, further illustrate the gospel's interaction with indigenous thought forms and current realities in Africa.

It is well attested that most African peoples accord tremendous significance to the spirits of those recently deceased. Coined the 'the living-dead' by Mbiti, or 'the ancestors' more generally, these spirits are often regarded as the best intermediaries since they are believed to know the needs of humans and to have enhanced spiritual powers through closer proximity to God. Despite the threats of modernisation and urbanisation, many African theologians contend that this cultural inheritance continues to exert vital influence in various ways at present. It therefore warrants critical engagement with the gospel.

Given the almost universal role of ancestral communion in traditional societies across East to West Africa, believers have naturally grappled with the relationship between the African ancestors and the Christian faith. Of the many issues that arise, three critical considerations are simply identified here. Methodologically, the diversity of ethnic societies across Africa requires caution in generalising about African beliefs concerning ancestors. Linguistically, problems emerge with the word 'ancestor' as the English translation for various African vernacular terms with different meanings and associations. Theologically, important questions arise: (1) the theological interpretation of the ancestors' identity, including the longstanding debate over whether African ancestors are actually worshipped or merely venerated; (2) the possible place of African ancestors within the Christian faith, especially with respect to certain doctrines regarding Christian saints; and (3) the role of African ancestors as mediators in relation to Christian claims of the sole mediation of Jesus Christ.

In spite of the complexity of these issues and the range of responses to them, some Africans have recently advocated the image of Jesus as ancestor. Admittedly, the notion is controversial, yet the convergence of biblical and African traditions gives rise to certain insights derived from African perspectives on the gospel.

While there is no set of uniform beliefs about ancestors across Africa, theologians affirm certain common ideas regarding their identity and role within the community. For example, Nyamiti outlines the following elements, that ancestors:

(1) Share a *natural relationship* with their earthly relatives, usually based on blood ties of parenthood or brotherhood;

(2) Acquire *supernatural or sacred status* through death, due to their nearness to God;

(3) Function as *mediators* between God and humanity;

(4) Are entitled to maintain *regular sacred communication* with earthly relatives, which explains their ambivalent character. (They are generally benevolent to their earthly kin, but can intervene in human affairs to bring harm to those who neglect them or commit some offence within the community);

(5) Are *exemplars* or models of good behaviour (Nyamiti 1984, 15–16).

Ghanaian theologian Peter Sarpong further specifies the conditions for becoming an ancestor, since not everyone attains this status. In order to qualify, one must have passed through the critical stages of life to attain adulthood, which assumes marriage and procreation; died a 'natural' death, excluding death through accident, suicide or in childbirth; and lived a life of exemplary conduct according to traditional morality (Sarpong 1974, 41).

Finally, the fundamental role of the ancestors is as invisible participants in the ongoing life of the community. One vital aspect is that they continue the ties of kinship beyond death, and hence the ancestral communion through acts of remembrance which actualise their presence for the living community. Thus the ultimate goal of ancestral communion is to maintain the life-force and harmony among all aspects of the created order: between the living and the dead, among the living, and with creation. It is this harmony that constitutes the abundant life which the ancestors received through their ethnic lineage, which they observed themselves, and which is to be transmitted from generation to generation (Magesa 1997, 79–82).

Without examining the challenges posed in portraying Jesus as ancestor, suffice it to say that an increasing number of African Christians affirm the meaning and significance of the image to them. They essentially explain how Jesus fulfils the role that was traditionally played by the ancestors, but in ways which far exceed them. For example, Jesus is the mediator between God and humanity, analogous to the ancestors. He is also the founder of a new community of believers, the church, and the one who establishes its identity. Moreover, he continues to participate in the life of that community, in terms of his ongoing presence, protection and power. Finally, just as the goal of ancestral communion in Africa is to foster abundant life, so Jesus is believed to provide the fullness of life that the ancestors sought to gain themselves and to transmit to their descendants.

Bujo is a leading example in strongly advocating Jesus as 'Ancestor Par Excellence' or 'Proto-Ancestor', to distinguish Jesus as the one who infinitely transcends the ideal of the God-fearing African ancestors. He contends,

If we look back on the historical Jesus of Nazareth, we can see in him, not only one who lived the African ancestor-ideal in the highest degree, but one who brought that ideal to an altogether new fulfilment. Jesus worked miracles, healing the sick, opening the eyes of the blind, raising the dead to life. In short, he brought life, and *life-force*, in its fullness. (Bujo 1992, 79)

Hence the interrelationship between the two foundational 'stones' of life and mediation become clear. On the basis of these fundamental African concepts, Bujo develops a comprehensive ancestral paradigm with penetrating insight and with far-reaching implications for theology, Christology, ecclesiology and ethics. For instance, he addresses wide-ranging issues, from the Eucharist as 'proto-ancestral meal' to the clericalism prevalent in African Christianity; from the status of the Pope to the celibacy of priests; and from polygamy to childlessness to euthanasia. While addressing these current issues, he maintains his fundamental stance in denying that 'true African liberation is possible without rediscovering deeply rooted traditional cultural values' (ibid., 7).

Perhaps no other issue is addressed more powerfully and poignantly by Bujo's ancestral theology than the deeply ingrained ethnocentrism which, together with other factors, fuelled the African genocides of the 1990s. His appeal is worth citing at length in view of the ongoing violence across Africa this new millennium. After reiterating that Jesus Christ is 'the true source of life', the '*new Ancestor*' who alone reunites all the ancestors into a single humanity, he concludes:

He has come to bring peace and to bring back all men to brotherhood by suppressing [not only] every ethnic difference but also racial and others. He is the ancestor of all humanity, for he is the second Adam who creates a new man. From now on there is neither black nor white, neither yellow nor red; there is neither Jew nor Greek, neither Tutsi nor Hutu, neither Luba nor Munyamwezi nor Chagga nor Agikuyu; there is neither slave nor free man, neither man nor woman, neither cultivator nor minister of states, '*for all you are only one in Christ Jesus. But if you belong to Christ, you are therefore the descendants of Abraham, heirs according to the promise*' (Gal. 3: 28–9). (Bujo 1995, 36–7)

Once again, the biblical revelation, interpreted by Africans in light of their cultural heritage, speaks forcefully to current situations in dire need of mediation and reconciliation.

Theologies of community

The third 'stone' of traditional African thought, already evident in examining the first two 'stones' of life and mediation, is that of community. However jeopardised by rapid modernisation, this fundamental aspect of African anthropology remains: individual identity is established and fulfilled only in the context of community. To be, is essentially to participate in family and community.

Although the emphasis on kinship and community is not peculiarly African, it is characteristically African to conceive of family as so-called 'extended' rather than 'nuclear'. Theologians point out that the definition of family as a nuclear social unit is not strictly biblical, but rather a product of industrialisation and urbanisation (Mugambi and Magesa 1989, 139). Another distinguishing feature is that traditional African concepts of community encompass the living, the dead and the not-yet-born.

Furthermore, African theologians contrast Descartes' dictum, at the heart of modern Western worldviews – '*Cogito ergo sum*', 'I think, therefore I am' – with African worldviews. Pobee argues instead: '*Cognatus ergo sum* – i.e. I belong by blood relationship, therefore I am' (Pobee 1979, 88). Likewise, Mbiti makes the oft-quoted statement about communal solidarity in Africa, 'The individual can only say: "I am, because we are; and since we are, therefore I am"' (Mbiti 1969, 107–8). On the basis of these observations, Kenyan Anne Nasimiyu Wasike, another important African woman theologian, concludes, 'Community participation is a very prominent value among the African people. It permeates all life; it is the matrix upon which all the human and social values, attitudes, expectations and beliefs are based, and it is the foundation of an African theology, catechesis and liturgy' (Nasimiyu Wasike 1986, 258).

So pervasive is the impact of African notions of community upon recent theologies that only a short overview is presented here by way of illustration. First, contemporary African Christologies reveal numerous ways in which Christians embrace Jesus as an intimate family member, friend and close member of their community. For example, the image of Jesus as brother is reflected in formal and informal Christologies, based on the interplay of biblical texts and African associations with brotherhood, such as provision and protection. As a result, local insights emerge regarding the humanity of Jesus, his intimacy, availability, attentiveness, solidarity and support.

Additionally, the image of Jesus as mother finds expression across East and West Africa. Nasimiyu Wasike is a leading voice in developing an analogy between Jesus' ministry and African concepts of motherhood: namely, one who nurtures life in all its dimensions, and who symbolises love, compassion and mercy. Confronting the many life-diminishing forces in contemporary Africa, Nasimiyu Wasike asserts that Jesus as mother calls all believers – women *and* men – to protect and nurture life without discrimination on the basis of ethnicity, social, economic or political ideology, or gender (Nasimiyu Wasike 1998, 23). Her colleagues in the Circle of Concerned African Women Theologians concur with this portrayal of Christ. They maintain that just as Jesus gives life physically and spiritually, so women give life physically, through conception, pregnancy, birth, and breast-feeding, and spiritually, through their many 'mothering' roles in the community, regardless of biological motherhood. They therefore claim that the image potentially enhances the dignity of African women within the Christian community.

Interestingly, this image of Jesus also appears in certain prayers, songs and sermons, particularly in vernacular languages. Since many African religions view God as mother and father, African Christians do not necessarily hesitate in extending the maternal metaphor to Jesus. These believers insist that the image is not tied to gender, but rather conveys the qualities associated with ideal motherhood. Thus the image of Jesus as mother not only illustrates indigenous perceptions of Christ in Africa, but also serves to recover certain feminine aspects of the Triune God that may not be adequately acknowledged in Western Christologies.

Second, African concepts of community influence contemporary ecclesiologies. For example, the church as extended family or clan forms a dominant model in recent theological reflections, with important consequences for church polity and practice. Key aspects include the need for true unity and special solidarity among fellow Christians as brothers and sisters; the need to enhance the active participation of laity and that of women in leadership; and the need for reformation in the organisation and administration of churches so as to be more in keeping with local cultures. Another attempt to indigenise church practices occurs when the Eucharist, as a communal meal, takes on local African forms. For instance, at St Francis Spiritual Centre in Nairobi, the tabernacle for the consecrated Host takes the shape of a traditional African round, thatched home, with a carved front displaying maize cobs and local festive drink in African gourds. It thereby symbolises how Africans prepare a local 'home' for Jesus to dwell in the midst of their community.

Then, in contexts of deep-seated denominationalism, theologians like John Mary Waliggo seek to overcome the divisions by portraying believers from other church traditions as 'true relatives' within the wider clan of Christ (Waliggo 1990, 125). He extends the analogy to conclude in a manner that reflects the integration of insights from all three 'stones' of African thought. Highlighting the need for interpersonal 'communion' which ensures human dignity and equality is granted to each church member, Waliggo contends, 'In this sense, the Church universal will be seen as the Mother of all clans, never excluding any but always all-embracing. In this model, Christ will clearly appear as the Proto-ancestor, the father of all clans and the pinnacle of all clans.'

Finally, core notions of community in Africa also uphold recent proposals for Christian mission in terms of social transformation. For example, Mugambi is among the vanguard of those currently advocating theologies of reconstruction. He situates his approach in the context of the dramatic changes in Africa's political landscape in recent decades: from decolonisation, through disillusionment with independences, to the 'New World Order' with the demise of the cold war and the colonial era, including apartheid. Reflecting upon what theological imagery would be appropriate for Africa in the new world order, he perceived the need to move beyond the longstanding paradigm of liberation. So, in a 1990 address to the Executive Committee of the All Africa Conference of Churches, he declared, 'We need to shift paradigms from the Post-Exodus to Post-Exile imagery, with *reconstruction* as the resultant theological axiom' (Mugambi 1995, 5).

Turning to African history and biblical traditions, Mugambi seeks to locate and integrate insights regarding social construction that can fortify local efforts in political, socio-economic and religious renewal. For instance, he develops various motifs from the Old Testament including the Exilic motif in Jeremiah, the Deuteronomic motif associated with Josiah, the Restorative motif in Isaiah 61: 4 and the Reconstructive motif exemplified in Haggai and Nehemiah (ibid., 39). In the ongoing process of applying wisdom from biblical and African traditions to contemporary needs, Mugambi expects that social transformation and reconstruction will characterise African theology in the twenty-first century.

So immediate are these concerns that the day after 30 December 2002, swearing-in of Mwai Kibaki, the first democratically elected President of Kenya, Mugambi writes of the euphoric new hopes for the nation. He states that the dramatic political transition, with the landslide victory of the opposition party, is 'comparable only to the attainment of national sovereignty in December 1963'. Anticipating the momentous tasks ahead and the tremendous potential for reconstruction, his concluding comment provides fitting closure to this section on theologies of community: 'In Kenya the Year 2003 begins with a message of hope, as was the case at the beginning of 1964. We pray that this hope will be sustained and substantiated' (Mugambi, personal communication, 2002).

In view of Africa's prominent place in Christian history at the turn of the third millennium, it follows that contemporary African theologies play a vital role in the ongoing development of Christian theology worldwide. Walls anticipates that African Christianity will potentially be 'the *representative* Christianity of the twenty-first century' (Walls 1998, 2). In other words, not just the new agendas for theology, but 'the characteristic doctrines, the liturgy, the ethical codes, the social applications of the faith will increasingly be those prominent in Africa' (Walls 1998, 2). What is more, assuming that theology which endures is that which affects the minds and lives of a significant number of people, Walls asserts that the theologies arising across Africa will have a determinative effect in shaping church history for centuries to come.

Perhaps the greatest significance of these emergent African theologies is what they manifest about the gospel itself. That is to say, while the Christian faith has always been universal in principle, only in recent history has it become truly universal in practice (Walls 1987, 76). It is not merely a matter of demographics, with the massive rise of Christianity in sub-Saharan Africa, but of demonstrating how the gospel can truly find a home in every cultural context. The theologies introduced in this chapter reveal that Africans understand and appropriate the gospel in accordance with biblical *and* indigenous traditions, and in relation to current realities in Africa. In so doing, they illustrate what is now widely acknowledged: namely, that theologies which truly capture the hearts and transform the lives of local Christians must be *contextual.* They must seriously address the questions arising in particular contexts, and express the gospel in meaningful and relevant ways within those contexts.

At the same time, local theologies must also have a 'universalising function', or a willingness to engage openly with other contextual theologies around the world for mutual enrichment and critique. As Robert Schreiter explains, 'Theology cannot restrict itself only to its own and immediate context; if the message of what God has done in Christ is indeed Good News for all peoples, then the occurrence of grace in any setting has relevance for the rest of humanity' (Schreiter 1997, 4).

That being the case, what nourishment do African theologies provide for believers, not just locally but globally? Only a few indications are offered here by way of example. From the preceding discussion, African theologies of life clearly encourage the recovery of holistic views of life and healing. This emphasis offers a valuable corrective to Western worldviews since Enlightenment times that tend to erect dichotomies between sacred and secular, natural and supernatural. Moreover, in their zest for fullness of life, African believers exhibit creative expressions of informal theologies. For instance, the Circle of Concerned African Women Theologians join their sisters in the Ecumenical Association of Third World Theologians 'to demonstrate that theology is not only written and spoken, but danced, prayed, mimed and cried' (Oduyoye 1992, 313).

African theologies of mediation address, and potentially redress, the need for reconciliation on the vertical and horizontal planes: with God, and with fellow humans divided by ethnicity, creed, class or gender. Theologies of community, derived from biblical and African traditions, challenge the rampant individualism within Western Christianity. They also tackle serious issues concerning the reformation of churches and the reconstruction of societies, both at home and abroad as Africans continue to suffer deep injustices at the hands of local and foreign masters.

Finally, the very dynamism of African Christianity provides invaluable resources for world Christianity. The growth of African-led churches in the United Kingdom and Europe, for example, attests to the potential for African theological expression to bring vital means of renewal to older churches. The characteristic emphasis on *lived* theologies, forged in the concrete realities of everyday life and symbolised in Ela's 'shade-tree theology', counters undue tendencies towards abstract or 'ivory tower theology'. Furthermore, in the global exchange of theological reflection, African theologies provide critical engagement with those from other continents: for instance, wrestling through issues regarding liberation praxis with Latin American theologians; grappling with the place of ancestors in the Christian faith, together with Asian theologians; and striving towards greater dignity for women, in dialogue with North American feminist theologians. Whatever the topic, the very gravity and complexity of life issues in Africa today stimulate penetrating theological insights that nurture Christians locally and globally.

Nor for the present time alone: like the traditional dishes that Africans bring to international feasts, these African theologies surely offer a foretaste of the distinctive contributions that Africans will ultimately make to the eschatological banquet in the kingdom of God.

REFERENCES AND FURTHER READING

Amirtham, Samuel and Pobee, John. S. (eds.) 1986. *Theology by the People: Reflections on Doing Theology in Community*. Geneva

Appiah-Kubi, Kofi. 1987. 'Christology' in Parratt, John (ed.) *A Reader in African Christian Theology*, pp. 69–81. London

Appiah-Kubi, Kofi and Torres, Sergio (eds.) 1979. *African Theology en Route*. Maryknoll

Baeta, C. 1955. *Christianity and African Culture*. Accra

Bediako, Kwame. 1992. *Theology and Identity: The Impact of Culture upon Christian Thought in the Second Century and in Modern Africa*. Oxford
    1995. *Christianity in Africa: The Renewal of a Non-Western Religion*. Edinburgh
    1996. 'Understanding African Theology in the 20th Century', *Bulletin for Contextual Theology* 3, 1–11

Bosch, David. 1991. *Transforming Mission: Paradigm Shifts in Theology of Mission*. Maryknoll

Boulaga, F. B. 1984. *Christianity without Fetishes*. Maryknoll

Bujo, Bénézet. 1990. *African Christian Morality at the Age of Inculturation*. Nairobi
    1992. *African Theology in its Social Context*. Nairobi
    1995. *Christmas: God Becomes Man in Black Africa*. Nairobi
    1998. *The Ethical Dimension of Community*. Nairobi

Dickson, Kwesi. 1983. *Theology in Africa*. London

Dickson, K. and Ellingworth, P. 1969. *Biblical Revelation and African Beliefs*. London

Ela, Jean-Marc. 1986a. *African Cry*. Maryknoll
    1986b. 'Le motif de la libération dans la théologie africaine', *Les nouvelles rationalités africaines* 2, 37–51
    1988. *My Faith as an African*. Maryknoll
    1994. 'Christianity and Liberation in Africa' in Gibellini, Rosino (ed.), *Paths of African Theology*, pp. 136–53. London

Gibellini, Rosino. 1994. 'Introduction: African Theologians Wonder . . . and Make Some Proposals' in Gibellini (ed.) *Paths of African Theology*, pp. 1–8

Healey, Joseph and Sybertz, Donald. 1996. *Towards an African Narrative Theology*. Nairobi

Kato, Byang H. 1975. *Theological Pitfalls in Africa*. Nairobi

Magesa, Laurenti. 1997. *African Religion: The Moral Traditions of Abundant Life*. Maryknoll

Martey, E. 1993. *African Theology: Inculturation and Liberation*. Maryknoll

Mbiti, John S. 1969. *African Religions and Philosophy*. London
    1972. 'Some African Concepts of Christology' in Vicedom, Georg F. (ed.) *Christ and the Younger Churches*, pp. 51–62. London
    1986. *Bible and Theology in African Christianity*. London

Mugambi, J. N. K. 1989. *African Christian Theology: An Introduction*. Nairobi
    1995. *From Liberation to Reconstruction: African Christian Theology After the Cold War*. Nairobi

Mugambi, J. N. K. and Magesa, Laurenti (eds.) 1989. *Jesus in African Christianity: Experimentation and Diversity in African Christology.* Nairobi

Mwaura, Philomena N. 1994. 'Healing as a Pastoral Concern' in Waruta, D. W. and Kinoti, H. W. (eds.) *Pastoral Care in African Christianity: Challenging Essays in Pastoral Theology*, pp. 62–86. Nairobi

Nasimiyu, Anne J. 1986. *Vatican II: The Problem of Inculturation*, PhD thesis, Duquesne University

Nasimiyu Wasike, Anne. 1998. 'Witnesses to Jesus Christ in the African Context', *Propositum* 3: 17–29

Nyamiti, Charles. 1984. *Christ as Our Ancestor: Christology from an African Perspective.* Harare

1994. 'Contemporary African Christologies: Assessment and Practical Suggestions' in Gibellini (ed.) *Paths of African Theology*, pp. 62–77

Oduyoye, Amba. 1983. 'Reflections from a Third World Woman's Perspective: Women's Experience and Liberation Theologies' in Fabella, Virginia and Torres, Sergio (eds.) *Irruption of the Third World: Challenge to Theology*, pp. 246–55. Maryknoll

Oduyoye, Mercy. 1986. *Hearing and Knowing: Theological Reflections on Christianity in Africa.* Maryknoll

1992. 'The Passion out of Compassion: Women of the EATWOT Third General Assembly', *International Review of Mission* 81, 313–18

Okullu, Henry. 1974. *Church and Politics in East Africa.* Nairobi

Parratt, John. 1995. *Reinventing Christianity: African Theology Today.* Grand Rapids and Cambridge

1997. *A Reader in African Christian Theology* (new edition). London

Pobee, John S. 1979. *Toward an African Theology.* Abingdon

1983. 'Jesus Christ – The Life of the World: An African Perspective', *Ministerial Formation* 21, 5–8

1986. 'Life and Peace: An African Perspective' in Pobee, John S. and Hallencreutz, Carl F. (eds.) *Variations in Christian Theology in Africa*, pp. 14–31. Nairobi

1992. 'Confessing Christ à la African Instituted Churches' in Pobee, John S. (ed.) *Exploring Afro-Christology*, pp. 145–51. Frankfurt

1994. 'Healing – An African Christian Theologian's Perspective', *International Review of Mission* 83, 247–55

2001. 'Health, Healing and Religion: An African View', *International Review of Mission* 90, 55–64

Pobee, John S. and Ositelu, Gabriel II. 1998. *African Initiatives in Christianity.* Geneva

Sawyerr, Harry. 1995. *The Practice of Presence: Shorter Writings of Harry Sawyerr* John Parratt (ed.). Grand Rapids and Edinburgh

Sarpong, Peter Kwasi. 1974. *Ghana in Retrospect: Some Aspects of Ghanaian Culture.* Accra

Schreiter, Robert J. 1992. *Faces of Jesus in Africa.* London

1997. *The New Catholicity: Theology Between the Global and the Local.* Maryknoll

Shorter, Aylward. 1988. *Toward a Theology of Inculturation.* Maryknoll

Tutu, Desmond. 1978. 'Whither African Theology?' in Fasholé-Luke, Edward et al. (eds.) *Christianity in Independent Africa*, pp. 364–69. London

Waliggo, John Mary. 1990. 'The African Clan as the True Model of the African Church' in Mugambi, J. N. K. and Magesa, Laurenti (eds.) *The Church in African Christianity: Innovative Essays in Ecclesiology*, pp. 111–27. Nairobi

Walls, Andrew F. 1976. 'Towards Understanding Africa's Place in Christian History' in Pobee, John S. (ed.) *Religion in a Pluralistic Society*, pp. 180–9. Leiden

    1978. 'Africa and Christian Identity', *Mission Focus* 6, 11–13

    1987. 'The Christian Tradition in Today's World' in Whaling, Frank (ed.) *Religion in Today's World: The Religious Situation of the World from 1945 to the Present Day*, pp. 76–109. Edinburgh

    1998. 'Africa in Christian History: Retrospect and Prospect', *Journal of African Christian Thought* 1: 2–15

West, Gerald. O. and Dube, Musa W. (eds.) 2000. *The Bible in Africa: Transactions, Trajectories, and Trends*. Leiden

6

Southern Africa

Isabel Apawo Phiri

Tinyiko Maluleke has rightly stated that:

It is impossible for one single theologian to be completely up to date with all the developments in all African Theology. Africa is a vast and diverse continent – diverse in religions, Christian confessions, language, cultures and so forth. (Maluleke 2002, 150)

This statement is true for me as I attempt to engage with the developments and contents of contextual theologies of Southern Africa. Christians in Southern Africa are asking different questions about their faith depending on how they experience their culture, politics, economy and the church. Even within one country, one notices that there are different theologies based on gender, culture, race, class, and political and economic environment. The context and the theology are not static either. There is a progression taking place all the time. The concentration of the theologians in Southern Africa is not balanced either. Not much is heard from Swaziland, Lesotho and Zambia. Mozambique is out of reach due to language barriers. Malawi, Botswana and Zimbabwe have a handful of writing African theologians. South Africa has the highest concentration of Black and African theologians.

What I am suggesting is that the theology coming out of Southern Africa is not homogenous because there are a variety of contexts that raise different theological questions. In this chapter I will therefore limit myself to a discussion of Southern African theology (with examples from South Africa, Zimbabwe, Botswana and Malawi); South African Black theology; and Southern African Women's Theology (with examples from South Africa, Zimbabwe, Botswana and Malawi).

THE CONTEXT OF SOUTHERN AFRICAN THEOLOGIES

The theological reflection and articulation of African theology by Africans in Southern Africa is based on a context of Western missionary Christianity and European colonialism. The context of Southern African theology includes a history of British colonialism for Malawi, Zambia, Zimbabwe, Botswana, Lesotho and Swaziland. Namibia has a history of German and South African Afrikaner colonialism. The history of colonialism is also connected to Western missionary Christianity in the nineteenth and twentieth centuries. In some cases, the Africans were not able to see the difference between the colonial government and the missionaries. They saw elements of close collaboration between colonial governments and missionaries to oppress the African people. One South African Black theologian, Mofokeng, puts the collaboration between colonial rule with missionaries in this way:

When the white man (sic) came to our country he had the Bible and we had the land. The white man said to us 'let us pray'. After the prayer, the white man had the land and we had the Bible. (1988, 34)

This sentiment is shared in all Southern African countries and cannot be ignored in the study of African Theology. In other cases, however, there was a clear separation between the missionary enterprise and the colonial powers.

Due to lack of knowledge, the majority of the missionaries who came to spread the Gospel in Southern Africa assumed that the African people had no knowledge of God and that the African traditional religion and culture were evil. Therefore it become a requirement that at baptism Africans were to acquire Western names and change their way of dressing from the local to the European form as a symbol of Christianity which was associated with Western civilisation.

Another element of missionary Christianity was European leadership in all missionary stations and churches. The training of African church leadership was very slow. It therefore took a long time before the African Christians were trusted with leadership positions. This was coupled with the missionary provision of an inferior type of Western education for Africans. All these factors gave way to feelings of dissatisfaction among the African people with missionary Christianity and colonial rule.

The result was overt and implied protest coming from the Africans to seek political cultural and ecclesiastical justice and freedom. Specifically the African reaction led to:

(a) some African Christians breaking away from mission churches to form African Initiated churches;[1]

---

[1] It should be noted that not all African Initiated churches in Southern Africa were formed as a result of protest against colonialism or and missionary Christianity. For those that have an element of political

(b) mission educated Africans forming political parties to voice out their protest against colonial rule and seek political independence;
(c) protest against mission domination in the leadership of the African churches and seeking autonomy in leadership from the sending mission churches;[2]
(d) the emergence of African theology to protest against demonisation of African traditional religions and African culture and to seek the identity of an African Christianity;
(e) the emergence of South African Black theology to protest against racism in South Africa and seek a theology that brings dignity to the African people through political and church liberation.

At a political level, there was the first wave of political revolution that led to some countries gaining political independence. In Southern Africa, Malawi became independent on 6 July 1964, followed by Zambia on 24 October 1964. Zimbabwe gained independence in 1980. Namibia followed in 1990 and South Africa finally attained majority rule in 1994.

The initial stages of political freedom in Malawi, Zambia, Botswana and Zimbabwe were dominated by calls for indigenisation – a recapture of African way of life and belief, which was destroyed by missionary teachings and colonial rule. It also meant giving leadership, which was previously dominated by whites, to Africans. The theology that dominated these countries was called inculturation.

Although Malawi and Zambia received their political independency quite early, by the 1980s, they started experiencing the strain of authoritarian rule as a result of one party system of government from the African politicians who had promised them freedom. A second stage of struggle against one party rule started in the late 1980s in Zambia, early 1990s in Malawi and late 1990s in Zimbabwe. This is a second wave of political revolution. In Malawi, the churches also experienced a period when even the sermons were censored for messages that criticised the government. Any theological work or theologian who suggested Liberation Theology was either detained or exiled. An example is the story of Bishop Kalilombe who introduced Christian base communities of Latin America in Malawi in the 1970s (see his *Doing Theology at the Grassroots: Theological Essays from Malawi* (Gweru 1999)).

---

protest in them, see e.g. Chakanza, J. C. *Voices of Preachers in Protest: The Ministry of Two Malawian Prophets: Eliot Kamwana and Wilfred Gudu* (Blantyre 1998).
[2] When theological institutions were established, the style of learning and the content of the theological institutions reflected what was taught in the Western sending missions. Thus the early African mission educated missionaries became replicas of the Western missionaries.

Nevertheless, the churches played prominent roles in protesting against social injustice. For example, in Zambia the three main Christian bodies, the Council of Churches in Zambia (CCZ), the Evangelical Fellowship of Zambia (EFZ), and the Episcopal Conference of Zambia (ECZ) worked together to oppose President Kaunda until he agreed to a multi-party system and general elections. President Chiluba was elected as the first president of a multi-party government in Zambia in 1991. Two months later he declared Zambia a democratic Christian nation.

Malawi too shows a history of political protest that was initiated by the Roman Catholic Pastoral letter of 1992, which outlined the injustices perpetrated by the Banda government on its own people. Soon there was support coming from the Christian Council of Malawi. The churches formed a pressure group that monitored the transition period from one party rule to multi-party rule of Bakili Muluzi in May 1994.

Although the churches went through a period of relaxation in their political involvement after the second political revolution, it did not take long before the second democracies too began showing tendencies of intolerance and undemocratic style of leadership. The church has again come in the forefront to fight against the spirit of 'third-termism' that is ushering in a third wave of revolution, first in Namibia (though the fight was unsuccessful); second in Zambia in 2002 and was successful in stopping it and currently in Malawi, where church leaders and ordinary people are being arrested for opposing the government.

This political history of Southern Africa is very important because in a way it determined what kind of African theology is considered to be appropriate for a particular country in a particular period. Thus the second political revolution promoted an African theology that is explicitly political, as especially in Malawi.[3]

CULTURAL THEOLOGY IN SOUTHERN AFRICA

Although South Africa is deeply involved in Black theology, Gabriel M. Setiloane has distinguished himself by doing cultural theology. For him, African theology that has been categorised as 'cultural theology' 'is the theology that is lived and practised by almost all African Christians in this country and further north in the continent – (though) indeed at varying

---

[3] See the Kachere series that was produced from 1995 to the present. Of particular interest are three publications: Nzunda, S. M. and Ross, R. K., 1995, *Church, Law and Political Transition in Malawi 1992–94*; Ross, K. R. (ed.) 1997, *God, People and Power In Malawi: Democratisation in Theological Perspective*; Ross, K. R. 1998, *Here comes your King! Christ, Church and the Nation in Malawi*.

levels' (1986, 1). It is the theology that is lived by the grassroots. He argues that African theology is necessary because missionary Christianity came to Africa wrapped up in 'Western swaddling-clothes'. In that form, it is difficult for the Africans to understand. Therefore he argues that African theology rejects the Western understanding of Christianity but still claims to be fully African and Christian.

Setiloane is well known for his stand on the relationship between God and MODIMO, the Sotho-Tswana name for the Supreme Being. He argues that the Western missionaries did not bring God to the Africans. The Africans already had knowledge of God and just transferred their understanding of MODIMO to the Christian God. He goes further to state that the African understanding of God is superior to the Christian understanding as found in the New Testament. He qualifies his claim by stating that the Christian God is limited to a 'Being' while MODIMO is 'IT'. MODIMO penetrates all things like an oil stain on a paper and is described as 'fearful, terrible, awful, unapproachable, weird, uncanny, numinous etc' (1986, 22). He sees the understanding of the Old Testament YAHWEH as being in line with MODIMO rather than the New Testament God who is the father of Jesus. At the same time, he says African theology has no problem with God's revelation in Jesus Christ. Africans understand the incarnation because in the African belief system there is room for Divinity to possess a human being. Such possessed human beings are special because they possess the foresight of Divinity. The issue of ancestors and Jesus is also not a problem to him because of the presence of *seriti* – vital force – part of the divinity – in both the living and the dead. The visitations of the ancestors to the living are not spoken of as in a form of a spirit or dream but as physical.

Paul Gundani of Zimbabwe (1998, 92) picks up the issue of Jesus and the ancestors in his analysis of Roman Catholic Church burial rituals among the Shona. He has demonstrated that prayers are offered to Mary, Jesus and ancestors as beings who live next to God and who all have a role to play in bringing the dead to God. He has also pointed out the process of adaptation from traditional religions to Christianity, which is still in the process of transformation and requires more refinement. In the same publication (Fiedler, Gundani and Mijoga 1996/7), the issue of Christ and ancestors working together is reflected in the papers of James Amanze (an AICs case study from Botswana), Obed Kealotswe (a case study of a healer from Botswana) and Joseph Chakanza (a case study of a healer from Malawi). All these articles reveal the fact that issues of Christ and ancestors are still very relevant for the modern African Christians. Western understanding of Christology has not succeeded in getting rid of ancestors in the African Christian beliefs and practices.

The struggle of how to be African *and* Christian is also clearly reflected in Ezra Chitando's paper (1998) in which he examines the impact of language and theology. He has studied the process of naming children from pre-Christian Zimbabwe to the post-independence period. He shows how African people gave names to their children to depict an event with social or/and religious significance. Conversion to Christianity required a change of name from indigenous ones to biblical or European ones as a symbol of the new life. He has also shown how during the liberation struggle some Zimbabweans changed their biblical and European names to indigenous ones, with protest and liberation meanings. After Zimbabwe's political independence, parents began to give their children indigenous names that expressed their Christian faith. Ezra Chitando has concluded by saying that:

Through the names they (parents) give to their children, they are reflecting on the implications of what it means to be a Christian in Africa . . . Through their naming practices, African Christians are engaged in African Theology. (1996/7, 118–19)

The African oral theology is also found in the studies of Chakanza (1998) and Kealotswe (1998), where the traditional healers are drawing on the African belief system of healing that is guided by the ancestors, but use the Bible and Christian songs in the healing liturgy.

African Initiated Churches have generally been presented as the space where African oral theology is done. This is because many of them are presented as reactionary churches to Western Christianity and colonial rule. Amanze (1998, 64) has supported this claim by stating that:

One of the most appealing and most powerful titles given to Jesus in the African Independent Churches in Botswana is that of mediator or intermediary. Here the Christology of the African Independent Churches assumes a full African mantle.

There are a number of African theologians in Southern Africa who support that claim (for example Chakanza 1998). However, Mijoga (2002) has observed that this claim may be based on an analysis of the rituals of AICs and not from their sermons. His argument is based on his study of AICs sermons analysed for their content of some characteristics of African communication, that including songs, questions, stories, retelling and proverbs. He concluded by stating that the sermons did not have enough African communication characteristics to warrant the AICs to be called the vanguard of African culture. We therefore need a further study of the rituals to see if the claim of African theologians that the AICs are in the forefront of African culture can be supported.

THE SOUTH AFRICAN CONTEXT FOR BLACK THEOLOGY

The South African context is central to this chapter because of the long Christian struggle against political and socio-economic oppression from colonialism. The history of colonialism in South Africa is traced from 1652 with the coming of European settlers up to April 1994 when the majority black people took over political power. The Afrikaner government came to power in 1944 in an election that excluded black people from voting. During the Afrikaner regime, a system of separate development (apartheid) between whites and blacks was introduced. This system granted the best jobs, education, medical care, housing, churches, and all social, political and economic privileges to the white population on the basis of the ideology of apartheid, which denigrated blacks to an inferior status. Therefore, the issue of colour of the skin of a person became the determining factor in a person's involvement in the society and the church.

Protest against apartheid came in different forms. 1960 was a critical year in mobilised protest, which led to the Sharpville massacre by the police. The then ruling government banned political parties that were vocal, like the African National Congress and The Pan African Congress. In 1960 the leaders of these parties, including Nelson Mandela, were imprisoned. Other leaders left the country and the ANC continued to operate from outside South Africa.

Despite police brutality against any person who opposed apartheid, in 1970 Basil Moore used the platform of the University Students Christian Movement to begin discussions about Black theology. He wrote a series of articles explaining what Black theology was all about. The first Black theology publication came out in 1973, entitled *Black theology: The South African Voice*, edited by Moore. As soon as the book came out, the apartheid government banned it. The few copies that were smuggled out of South Africa made it possible for the book to be republished in North America, Britain and Germany.

In 1976, student protest against Bantu education, which was an inferior education for black people, led to the Soweto massacres of the students by the police. In the words of Kaufmann:

The events of 1976, tragic as they were, gave new impetus to the many streams of resistance and struggle that had been flowing since the beginnings of white European settlement in the Cape of Good Hope from 1652 onwards. The year

1976 also saw the rise of new streams of defiance and opposition to the apartheid system. But the apartheid regime was not yet prepared to negotiate and once again it made full force of its power felt. In 1977 various Black Consciousness organisations and projects were banned. (Speckman and Kaufmann 2001, 18)

Steve Biko, the leader of the Black Consciousness Movement was detained and died in custody. There were many people who lost their lives through police brutality. Still the spirit of open resistance to apartheid did not stop. The beginning of the 1980s began to show indications of a political crisis. Any books or articles on American and South African Black theology, and Latin American liberation theology were banned. Black theologians were in and out of prison for seeking the liberation of Black people from racial, political and religious oppression.

As stated by Kaufmann:

In some church and theological circles questions began to be asked. What is the role of the church in this crisis? Does theology have any contribution to make in putting an end to the evil and oppressive system of apartheid? How can committed Christians minister to people of black townships whose daily bread is the bullets of the police? (Kaufmann 2001, 19)

The English-speaking mission churches found it difficult to develop a theology that was criticising the ruling government. At the same time, the Dutch Reformed churches had a theology that supported the apartheid government.

1980 saw the South African Black theologians such as Allan Boesak, Simon Maimela, Bonganjalo Goba and Frank Chikane joining together with some liberal white theologians, such as Albert Nolan, Beyers Naude, James and Renate Cochrane, Cedrick Mayson and François Bill to form the Institute of Contextual Theology (hereafter ICT). The aim of the institute was 'to develop methods of doing theology in the context of real life of ordinary people' (Kaufmann, 2001, 21). It was meant to be a theology done in the context of the oppressed. Some South African theologians have argued that 'South African contextual theology has been largely a white male affair' (Maluleke, 2001, 367). The list of Black theologians who were involved with the founding of Contextual theology as done at the ICT proves otherwise. The fact that the ICT had a Black theology project serves to affirm that it was not just a liberal white male theologians affair. What must be emphasised is that there were other contextual theologies prior to 1990s and that in the South African context, at this stage, academic and institutionalised theology was male dominated. The South African police threatened the work of the ICT when three quarters of its staff were arrested. Nevertheless, the spirit of desiring liberation from the apartheid regime was stronger so that the activities of the ICT continued and become very influential in putting pressure on the government.

Contextual theology also spread to the churches and theological institutions. It was not surprising then that it played a major role in the writing and the release of the *Kairos Document* of 28 September 1985. The document identified the categories of theology in South Africa as state theology, church theology, political theology and prophetic theology. A detailed discussion of the theologies followed that allowed the writers of the document to exclude all except prophetic theology as the way forward for the church in South Africa.

The Kairos Document has been described as the zenith of theological enterprise in South Africa for it provoked response from all walks of life in a variety of forms. Of significance is the fact that it mobilised most churches to protest against the apartheid rule in South Africa. Nevertheless, it should also be noted that the Kairos Document has been accused of failing to take into account all the theological resourcefulness (especially African and Black theology) that came out of South Africa. It was therefore felt that it did not take seriously the race, class and gender in its social analysis. The events that were happening in South Africa were echoed in Namibia and Zimbabwe as the churches and the political organisations were also engaged in socio-political struggle against racism.

1990s were very crucial in the history of South Africa. A new democratically elected government of the ANC under Nelson Mandela came to power on 27 April 1994. South Africa became the last African country to be fully independent. Learning from the experiences of other African countries, South Africa combined the first and second democratic revolutions with the third, where emphasis is on how to maintain democracy.

The transition period to democracy 1990 to 1993 inspired South African theologians like Charles Villa-Vicencio to talk more about reconstruction theology to replace the South African contextual theology that was focused on resisting apartheid. Another milestone in the post-apartheid South Africa is Desmond Tutu's theology of forgiveness, which was there is his writings in the 1970s and was developed as a result of the process of the Truth and Reconciliation Committee to deal with the atrocities of apartheid. This has sparked theological debates on the concept of forgiveness. There are some South African theologians who feel that the majority powerless people were let down because the powerful managed the get off the hook without telling the whole truth, which should have been the prerequisite for forgiveness and reconciliation. Some of the victims were dead and therefore not present to forgive the perpetrators. The compensation that was promised to the victims was either very little or so slow in coming that some are yet to receive it.

Tutu has admitted that because there was a lot of emphasis on fighting against apartheid, theologies of South Africa do not seem to know how to adjust to work with the new government. He observes:

> We had a common position, our stand against apartheid. I now realise what I did not previously, that it is a great deal easier to be against . . . Now that apartheid is being dismantled (1993) we are finding that it is not quite so simple to define what we are for . . . We no longer meet regularly as church leaders because the tyranny is over . . . We knew what we were against and opposed that fairly effectively. It is not nearly so easy to say what we are for and we appear to be dithering, not quite knowing where we want to go or how to get there. (Tutu 1995, 96)

Tutu's concerns will be revisited when examining the way forward for African theology.

SOUTH AFRICAN BLACK THEOLOGY

Black theology has its origin in North America among the African Americans. It rose as protest to racism on the part of white Americans directed towards African Americans. The African Americans were taken from Africa as slaves in inhuman conditions to work in America. Even after slavery was abolished, the African Americans were marginalised in everything because of their skin colour. This kind of injustice is difficult to deal with because the colour of one's skin cannot be controlled. A person is born black, blackness is not acquired. While in North America the African Americans are in a minority and were systematically abused by the majority white people, in South Africa, the reverse was the case. The white people, who were a small minority, colonised the Africans, but with the same treatment of racism based on colour. Maimela has summarised the case as follows:

> It is out of this painful context of oppression, dehumanisation and destruction of black personhood that Black theology was born as a theological protest against racial domination and human beings' inhumanity to other human beings. Black theology can thus be defined as a conscious, systematic, theological reflection on black experience, characterised by oppression, humiliation and suffering in white racist societies in North America and South Africa. (Maimela 1998, 112)

It is therefore the suffering black people who initiated Black theology with the aim of wanting to understand the message of God in the Bible in their context. It is also a rejection of white theology, which legitimised the oppression of black people as part and parcel of God's will that whites should rule and dominate, and that God also wills that black people should serve white people.

In South Africa, black theology originated from the Black Consciousness Movement. It works on the internalised negative attitude that black people have developed towards themselves as the result of racism. Black theology argues that black people are humans just like white people. God created black people in the same way that God created white people. When God said 'it is good' after God had created a human being, that goodness was also referring to black skin. Humanity was created in the image of God. Therefore blackness is part of the reflection of the image of God.

Furthermore, when God became a human being through Jesus Christ to liberate humanity from any form of oppression, it also means that 'Jesus Christ was a black liberator from white racist oppression' (Maimela 1998, 113). In Luke 4: 18–19, Jesus outlined his mission to the poor and oppressed of the society. In practice, in the ministry of Jesus, he associated himself with the poor, marginalised and oppressed people. Therefore, in Black theology, liberation from all forms of oppression is the central message of the Gospel. This understanding considers racism as a sin because God does not support one group of humanity oppressing another group.

Black theology follows the theme of liberation through to the Exodus experience in the Old Testament. God heard the cries of the oppressed children of Israel and liberated them from a situation of oppression. The Israelites were liberated not because they were righteous, but it is in the nature of God to side with the oppressed of any society. The experience of liberation is therefore not limited to the children of Israel but to all humanity which suffers from oppression. Black theology sees liberation as a theme that runs throughout the Old Testament. God intervenes in human history to liberate the oppressed people. God is on the side of the oppressed and poor. God rejects racism. 'Salvation' in Black theology is the end of racism and the establishment of a new social order that affirms black humanity. It is liberation from oppressive and unjust social and political structures of the society.

For Tutu and Boesak the new just society is not only for blacks. It embraces the white people as well as we shall see below.

Like all theologies, Black theology has many voices. The different varieties of Black theology bring richness for the cause of the oppressed and marginalised people of Africa. Maimela has identified three trends among Black theologians: firstly, the Black Solidarity trend; secondly, the Black Solidarity–Materialist trend; and finally the Non-Racist trend.

The Black Solidarity trend

This group is associated with Black theologians, who include, Bonganjalo Goba, Allan Boesak, Desmond Tutu, Ernest Bartman, Manas Buthelezi, Mokgethi Motlhabi and Sabelo Ntwasa. This group was very active in the formative stage of Black theology, which was from 1970 to 1980. Their emphasis was to promote solidarity among black people and black theologians in the struggle for liberation for the oppressed black people. Since Black theology is seen as emanating from the Black Consciousness Movement, it cannot separate itself from the Black consciousness. They argue that one has to be black and experience racism to be a Black theologian. Therefore a white person cannot be a Black theologian. They also believe that racism is the root of all the problems of black people. Therefore their social analysis of the oppression of black people is centred on racism.

The Black Solidarity–Materialist trend

The Black theologians who are associated with the Black Solidarity–Materialist trend include: Simon Maimela, Takatso Mofokeng, Itumeleng Mosala, David Mosoma, Lebamang Sebidi and Buti Tlhagale. This group emerged in the late 1970s but was more pronounced in the early 1980s. It was more associated with the Black theology project of the Institute of Contextual Theology. The Black Solidarity trend and Black Solidarity–Materialist group agree on all things except on the issue of social analysis. This group calls for a class analysis of the South African society when dealing with the root cause of the oppression of Black people. Apartheid has created a class of white people who have both economic and political power. It is this power that has made it possible for white elite class to maintain the apartheid social structures. The group also argues that one needs the right theory in order to oppose apartheid. Therefore they see the need for both theory and community involvement in the struggle against apartheid.

The non-racist trend

Some of the Black theologians who are associated with this group were part of the Solidarity trend but over the years, they have shifted in their emphasis of Black theology to become more inclusive. Those who shifted include Desmond Tutu, Allan Boesak and Manas Buthelezi. The additional Black theologians here are Shun Govender, Smangaliso Mkhatswa and Frank Chikane. The characteristic trait of this group is that they do not limit

Black theology and theologians to the principles of the Black Consciousness Movement. They work with the liberal white theologians and politicians. For them, the definition of the oppressed and liberation is inclusive of race, class and gender. They do not want to see a new society where a black bourgeoisie join hands with the white bourgeoisie to exploit other groups of people. In the words of Allan Boesak:

> In breaking away from the old oppressive structures of our society, seeking new possibilities, creating room for the realization of true humanity, Black theology seeks purpose of life for blacks as well as whites. Blacks want to share with white people the dreams and hopes for a new future, a future in which it must never again be necessary to make of Christian Theology an ideology or part of a particular aggressive cultural imperialism. Black theology, by offering a new way of theologising, desires to be helpful in discovering the truth about black and white people, about past and present, about God's will for them in their common world. (Boesak 1978, 127)

The three trends presented here point to different directions of how Black theology continues in the post-apartheid South Africa. It is the aim of the next section to explore this further.

Black theology in post-apartheid South Africa

Maluleke has described the post apartheid period in this way:

> After the euphoria of the end of apartheid, it would be accurate to say that South African theology and South African ecumenism are in some kind of recess if not a kind of disarray . . . As a young theologian in post-apartheid South Africa and post cold war Africa, I suddenly experience intense and acute spiritual and intellectual loneliness. This is both bad and good. Bad because I miss the defiant, passionate, and humorous 'image of God' *ubuntu* theology of Desmond Tutu. There is a huge gaping hole that has been left by my esteemed mentors and colleagues, Itumeleng Mosala, Takatso Mofokeng, Simon Maimela, Smangalitso Mkhatswa, Frank Chikane, and others – all of whom have 'gone secular' by becoming all manner of administrators and state functionaries . . . Fortunately, my loneliness as a theologian and committed academic theologian is not total. I hear encouraging voices from other parts of Africa and other parts of the world . . . Within South Africa itself, such bold and innovative post apartheid studies as those of Villa-Vicencio, Landman, Naude, Petersen, West and Tutu have kept me hopeful. (Maluleke 2001, 148–9)

Maluleke's observation of 'recess' and 'loneliness' as a Black theologian needs to be understood in terms of the trends of Black theology discussed above. If Maluleke belongs to the Black theologians that limit Black theology to the Black Consciousness Movement and the principle that one has to be black to do Black theology, then one understands the loneliness. However if one is on the side of the argument that Black theology post apartheid needs to be different from the issues raised before apartheid because of the changes in the context, then there is no silence in South African theologies. In another article, Maluleke admits that 'certain silences are not only understandable but may in fact be welcome' (2001, 372). Going back to the three trends of Black theology outlined above, it becomes clear that the silence of the first two trends of Black theology is understandable for they are too narrow in their analysis of liberation. The 'loneliness' can also reflect lack of mentoring of a new breed of theologians by the older generations to continue with the vision of what Boesak describes as a new future in which both whites and blacks are in solidarity with all the oppressed of our societies.

It seems to me that there is yet a method to be devised as a tool in engaging with the post-apartheid government to make it accountable to a culture of human rights. Having one of the best constitutions in the world and making sure that it is implemented are two separate issues. Although some South African theologians have suggested dropping the issue of 'solidarity with the poor', which is central in both Black and Contextual theology, and replacing it with a critical engagement with the government, I agree with Maluleke that is not the way forward. Although South Africa has a democratically elected government, the economic conditions of the majority poor have not changed. If anything, poverty is on the increase, due to high levels of unemployment. The new context of the post-apartheid era demands that solidarity with the poor is not a negotiable issue.

The notion that South African theology is in recess also contradicts what Maluleke has said in the last paragraph of the above quotation. The list of the South African theologians who are still very actively involved bears witness to changed parameters of theology in post-apartheid South Africa. New methodologies are being proposed of reading the Bible so that the ordinary readers and the academic readers empower each other. They have also shown that the Bible is never neutral. It can be used by both oppressors and oppressed to justify their position. Gender issues have also come on the scene in a more forceful way than before so that methods of biblical and theological analysis in South Africa should take race, class and gender seriously.

There have been calls coming from some quarters of Black theologians to drop Black theology and remain with African theology because Black theology has outlived its purpose. Mokgethi Motlhabi (1994) is an example of such theologians who have shown preference for African theology that has emphasis on dialoguing with culture and African religions over Black theology with its social-political analytical tools. It could be argued that there is so much scope for transformation in African theology that each can always chart his or her own way, without assuming that it is the only way for everyone. African theology in its broad sense is also transforming, and there is a wide range of variety within African theology. Already, in the writings of Tutu and Boesak 'African theology' has a role to play in Black theology. Indeed Tutu claims, that when he is doing Black theology, as far as he is concerned, he is doing African theology. Boesak talks about Black theology drawing from African tradition in the construction of the new social order after apartheid has been dismantled. He argues:

Black Theology sincerely believes that it is possible to recapture what was sacred in the African community long before white people came – solidarity, respect for life, humanity, and community. It must be possible to recapture it but to enhance it and bring it to full fruition in contemporary society. (Boesak 1978, 141)

Thus, African theology and Black theology compliment each other in Southern Africa, because the context that we find ourselves in demands it to be so.

AFRICAN WOMEN'S THEOLOGIES

African women's theologies belong to a wider family of Feminist theology and which may be further categorised as a form of Liberation Theology. Both are varieties of Christian theology and they acquired their names on the basis of context and approach. Feminist theology has its origins in the secular movement of women in the 1960s aimed at the liberation of women from all forms of sexism. The women's movement drew the attention to the fact that it was wrong to treat women as second-class citizens. They also argued that the existence of patriarchy is the root cause of oppression of women in all spheres of life. Christian women reflected on the issues raised by the women's movement from a faith perspective. Feminist theology has its origins among the middle-class white American and European women. Christian women of other racial and cultural groups brought to the attention of the theological world that racial, cultural, religious and social, historical and political situations contributed to the formation of their experiences of gender discrimination. Therefore, Christian women from different regions of the world began the process of localising Feminist theology so that it can speak to the particular experiences of a variety of Christian women. This gave rise to specific theologies, which bear different names. On the African continent, Christian women called reflection of their context and the Christian faith 'African women theologies'.

Why theologies and not just theology? The word theologies is used in its plural form because African women theologians want to acknowledge the fact that even within Africa there is diversity of women's experiences due to differences in race, culture, politics, economy and religions. Despite the differences in terminology, all women would like to see the end of sexism in their lives and the establishment of a more just society of men and women who seek the well-being of the other. Women go further to seek justice for all the oppressed, and also for an abused environment.

The development of African women's theologies in Southern Africa

While some theologians have been mourning about lack of serious theologies coming from Southern Africa in the 1990s and beginning of the twenty-first century, African women theologians have been mobilising to make known to Southern African Black and African theologians that the issues of women have been marginalised. Women have spoken out that they form the majority of the oppressed people. They experience colonialism, apartheid and all other atrocities differently because their oppression is coupled with denial of justice on the basis of gender. Yet such women's issues are not normally part of African and Black theologies (except for a few Black theologians, who sometimes pay lip service to them). It is for this reason that the Circle of Concerned African Women Theologians decided to promote African women's theologies, so that African women can research, write and publish about themselves and their experiences on the African continent. The purpose of this section is to follow the development and contribution of women to the African and Black theologies and the impact of the Circle in Southern Africa.

In South Africa, 1984 saw three conferences where women made a mark in the statements that came out of them. The first two conferences were organised by the Institute of Contextual Theology while the third conference was organised by the Institute for Theological Research of the University of South Africa. Of particular importance was the women's voice at the 1984 Black theology conference, which was held in Cape Town. The women delegates made it known that women feel oppressed in the communities and in church and demanded that the social analysis of Black theology ought to take this context of the oppression of women seriously. They refused to postpone solutions to women's problems to post-apartheid South Africa, because liberation of women from patriarchy is as important as national liberation. These views saw their way to the final statement of the conference. This message was repeated at another Institute of Contextual Theology feminist conference held at Hamanskraal in the same year, 1984. At this conference, women made it clear that Black theology cannot be a liberation theology if it does not take the liberation of women seriously. The women delegates emphasised the need for Black theology to create space for women to participate on an equal basis. They also argue that all meaningful liberation theologies in South Africa should be aiming for both a non-racist and non-sexist new South Africa. The Institute for Theological Research of the University of South Africa's symposium was entitled 'Sexism, and Feminism in Theological Perspective'. The proceedings that came out of this symposium were published in a book edited by W. S. Vorster, *Sexism and Feminism in Theological Perspectives*. Of particular interest to this paper is Christina Landman's observation that:

If there is any feminist theology done in South Africa, the media, popular and academic periodicals, and I myself are ignorant of it. Though I believe its roots exist orally, it does not really have a prominent spokesperson. (1984, 22)

Landman also noted that there were no theological publications coming from African women in general. This was because there were more laywomen than professional theologians. Very few women study theology because the seminaries do not employ female lecturers and few churches ordain women. The few women who had done any theological studies did not write books but worked as laypersons in the church and para-church organisations.

At one level Christina Landman's observations were true. Mercy Oduyoye started the Circle of Concerned African Women Theologians precisely to address those issues. It is also true that the theology of the majority of African women is not written down but oral. The disadvantage of oral theology is that it is local, and mostly in vernacular languages. It is communal theology and not individual. Professional theologians feel frustrated with this kind of theology because they cannot engage with it as done in the Western theologies. However, it is theology all the same and Africa, which is basically an oral society, has to take oral theology seriously.

At a second level, Christina Landman's lack of knowledge of the other two conferences organised by ICT where women delegates who were raising women's issues confirms the separation that was then visible between black and white women theologians within South Africa.

The division that was there between white and black women was acknowledged at the Rustenburg conference of 1990 and it is reflected in the women's statement. At this conference women also complained that church leaders at the conference did not take women's issues seriously. In fact an item on women was added to the agenda at the last minute and among other issues delegates were reminded of the World Council of Churches call for the decade of churches to be in solidarity with women.[4]

After the launching of the Circle of Concerned African Women Theologians in Ghana in 1989, Brigalia Bam, the then General Secretary of the South African Christian Council, attempted to form a South African National Circle in 1991. The participants were both from the black and white communities. There was a big difference in the class of the participants in that all the black women were lay church workers (except myself, who was then a PhD student at the University of Cape Town) and all the white women were from the academic world in South African theological departments at Universities and theological institutions. Although issues of research and writing on women's experiences in the church and society were raised, they did not take root. This was a disappointment because the policy of the Circle is to be inclusive of all races and religions. Its definition of an African woman theologian is inclusive of both lay and ordained women, as long as they are willing to write and reflect on their experiences of God in the context of Africa.

Despite the failure to have a South African National Circle in 1991, the Cape Town Chapter of the Circle was born coordinated by Sr Arine Matsots and myself. Since we were both theology students, we enjoyed the blessings of the Department of Religious Studies and the University of Cape Town. It was agreed that if the Circle remains at the campus, it would be too limiting in its membership. We therefore took it to the community and met in each other's home. The Cape Town Circle was unique in that it had a mixed membership of South Africans of African, white, Indian, and mixed-race origin, as well as Malawians, Swazis and Sothos: these included African traditionalists, Christians, Jews and Muslims. The Cape Town Chapter of the Circle has continued to exist over ten years and it is the longest surviving Circle in South Africa. It has achieved its purpose by researching and publishing a book edited by Denise Ackerman, Eliza Gateman, Hantie Cotze and Judy Tobler, *Claiming Our Foot Prints: South African Women Reflect*

---

[4] For more information about this conference, see Tinyiko Maluleke 'The Smoke Screen's called Black and African Theologies: The Challenges of African Women Theology', *Journal for Constructive Theology*, 3/2 (1997) and Louw Alberts and Frank Chikane (eds.) *The Road to Rusternburg: The Church Looking Forward to a New South Africa* (Cape Town 1991).

on Context, Identity and Spirituality (2000). Two years later another publication from a member of the Cape Town chapter of the Circle appeared, when Reisenberger Azila edited *Women's Spirituality in the Transformation of South Africa* (2002). The publication of *Women Hold Up Half The Sky* edited by Denise Ackerman, Jonathan Draper and Emma Mashinini (1991) deserves mention. This publication was important because it reflected on the position of women in the Anglican Church. It examined the historical background of women's roles in the Anglican Church in the context of a discussion on feminist theology from the experiences of white and black women in the church. It had both male and female contributors. The significance of this publication was that it showed a definite progress in South African feminist church history and theology. Christina Landman has pointed out that the weakness of this publication was that it left out the experiences of Afrikaaner women. Hence she felt the need to include the experiences of those women by publishing *The Piety of Afrikaans Women* (1994) and in 1995 she edited *Digging Up Our Foremothers: Stories of Women in Africa*. There was a further attempt in 1996 to hold ecumenical church-women's national conferences organised by the South African Council of Churches. The first was entitled 'Churchwomen United Conference', held in June 1996 in Johannesburg, the second 'Women in Ministry and Theologians Conference' held in November 1996 at Kempton Park. While the first conference was more of church women getting abreast issues of women and human rights, the second was more theological and praxis oriented. There were more attempts made to encourage the establishment of Circle chapters in the different towns and cities of South Africa.

The Durban Chapter of the Circle was launched in 1997 and the Pietermaritzburg Chapter of the Circle was launched in 2001. The Pietermaritzburg Circle, though young, sent a delegation of nine women theologians to the Continental Circle conference (which takes place every seven years), held in Addis Ababa in August 2002. This was the largest delegation of women coming from the same town in South Africa. In 2002, Isabel Apawo Phiri, Devarakshanam Betty Goviden and Sarojini Nadar, members of the Durban and Pietermaritzburg Chapter of the Circle edited *Herstories: Hidden Histories of Women of Faith*. This book came out of the Commission on Biographies of Women of Faith of the Circle of Concerned African Women Theologians. Its purpose was to document the contribution of African Women of Faith to the church and society. Above all it depicts a spirit of solidarity and resistance to injustice in the church and society and documents acts of transformation. The authors of the articles were women theologians from all over Africa.

The three existing chapters of the Circle in South Africa have contin-
ued with their research and writing projects. Two publications from these
Circles are underway following the Continental Conference theme of 'Sex,
Stigma and HIV/AIDS: African Women Theologians challenging Religion,
Culture and Social Practices'.

If the development of the Circle seems to be a mixed one of success
and failure in South Africa, the story is the same in the rest of Southern
Africa. The major handicap for Southern Africa, in comparison with West
and East Africa, is that it has produced few African women theologians
with doctorates, though the situation is improving. The Circle is therefore
encouraging more women to study theology at the highest level.

The theologies of African women theologians in Southern Africa

What is the content and methodology of African women's theologies in
Southern Africa? African women's theologies are a critical, academic study
of the causes of women oppression: particularly a struggle against societal,
cultural and religious patriarchy. They are committed to the eradication
of all forms of oppression against women through a critique of the social
and religious dimensions both in African culture and Christianity. African
women's theologies take women's experiences as its starting point, focusing
on the oppressive areas of life caused by injustices such as patriarchy, colonialism, neo-colonialism, racism, capitalism, globalisation and sexism. It
sees a need to include the voices of all women, not just theologians, because
it acknowledges that the majority of African women are engaging in oral
theology. Story telling is one of the powerful methodologies that African
women have revived. Musa Dube has developed a unique methodology
of reading a biblical story in the context of globalisation through story-
telling technique. Through story-telling, African women are bringing to
the attention of the world their spiritual, emotional and physical suffering
and the potential they have to transform their situation of oppression. It
includes men in its vision and struggle for African liberation from all forms
of oppression. It is seeking a partnership and mutuality with men to the
exclusion of all forms of violence against women. In various voices, it men-
tions the dangers that the institution of marriage brings to women through
its cultural and biblical teaching. For example, Madipoane Masenya has
read the book of Proverbs to challenge the cultural teachings on the relationship between husband and wife that promotes the infidelity of men and
yet treats women as pollutant. She does not go all the way to condemn the

practice of *lobola* (bride-wealth), but points to the danger of abusing the practice to bring the notion of buying wives, which opens them to abuse but no divorce (Masenya, 2001, 198–201). The tension is noted that African culture, which gives African women their identity and yet has elements in it that are life-denying, and which African women should reject.

Theology done by African women is committed to exposing the ideological base of Christianity that maintains and justifies the oppression of women. The tension is noted that, on the one hand Christianity is part of colonialism, racism and sexism, and on the other hand, the Christian gospel encourages the struggle for liberation and recognition of injustice in the church and society. Denise Ackerman has dealt with the issue of sexist language, the Bible, theology and church liturgies. She rightly protests against the liturgy that makes women say they are 'sons of God'. The focus is on the liberative potential of the Bible. The Bible is seen and read from a woman's perspective to enlighten their role in the struggle for human dignity and Christian womanhood: particularly important are the stories of women in the Bible and their life-giving encounters with Jesus and his response to women in the Gospels. The call is to follow and teach Jesus' actions of saving and protecting the most vulnerable in society. African Women's Christology derives from the Gospels and focuses on women's relationship in the life and teaching of Jesus, who reveals God. Jesus brought liberation for human kind from all forms of oppressions, including patriarchy. Jesus is seen as being on the side of women in their oppression. He is also the one who brings liberation to women from all that oppresses them. The theology of women being 'suffering servants' is denied because Jesus already suffered for the women. Women stand with Jesus to look beyond the cross to the community of the liberated people. African women's theology points out that the Church's silence over women's subordination, oppression is different from the Church that is called to be the body of Christ. The church is called to return to a Christ-like understanding of authority and ministry, a call for inclusiveness in church ministry and authority. It calls the church in Africa to work together with women in speaking out against patriarchy as evil.

It studies the Churchwomen organisations, notes the important positions held by the pastor's wives and the importance of church uniforms. Beverley Haddad (2000) and myself (Phiri 1997) have shown how the women's space can be used to exclude other women but also to express a theology of survival. This suggests ways in which the churchwomen organisations' space can be transformed to empower women for liberation. African women theologies examine the issues of resurrection in the context of restoration of the present life from death-promoting activities. They envisage the Jesus of the Gospels who healed the sick to bring healing in today's world. In this respect the issue of HIV/AIDS deserves a special attention and the Continental Circle has streamlined it as urgent.

HIV/AIDS as an urgent issue for theology in Southern Africa

In a recent publication Musa Dube has presented the following statistics:

Current HIV/AIDS statistical projections indicate that 28.5 million people are living with HIV/AIDS in Sub-Saharan Africa, ten million of these in the South African Development Community (SADC) region, thus highlighting this region as the hardest hit region in Africa. Indeed, the highest number of people living with HIV/AIDS is found in Southern Africa. Botswana leads the world with 36 per cent infection rate among its sexually active population, and South Africa has about 4.7 million of its citizens living with HIV/AIDS. (2002, 31)

With such statistics, it does not come as a surprise that African women theologians in Southern Africa have chosen to follow the lead of the Continental Circle to make HIV/AIDS the main issue for its theology in the next five years. It has agreed that research into religious, cultural and social practices that make women vulnerable to HIV/AIDS is not enough. African women theologians have taken upon themselves the task of engagement with the community to serve and save lives. Musa Dube has taken leave of absence from theological teaching and research with the University of Botswana to work as consultant of the World Council of Churches in designing and promoting HIV/AIDS curriculum for theological institutions in Africa. The aim is to work with churches and theological institutions in Africa to streamline HIV/AIDS.

Phumuzile Zondi and Bongi Zengele-Nzimani are working through the Institute of the Study of the Bible (University of Natal), and I am working through the Centre for Constructive Theology in Kwazulu Natal (the region with the highest HIV/AIDS statistics in South Africa) to streamline gender and HIV/AIDS in the church and society. Gender is highlighted because women and girls are the highest risk group in the society of HIV/AIDS due to power relations. As long as women continue to be put in subordinate positions through the interpretation of Bible teaching and African cultural practices, it will be difficult to control HIV/AIDS. Yet as the Western world has shown, HIV/AIDS is manageable, controllable and preventable. Women are also care-givers of those infected with HIV/AIDS and they take care of the orphans with minimum economic and social support. HIV/AIDS has brought us to a theology of praxis that sees all of us as agents of change to promote life.

The church is being educated to move away from a theology of HIV/AIDS as a punishment from God to a theology of God who is in solidarity with the HIV/AIDS affected and infected people. It is a theology that goes beyond looking at HIV pandemic as stigma and death to one of HIV/AIDS as preventable, manageable and controllable if there is solidarity at individual, family, community, national and international levels.

CONCLUSION

The way forward for the theologies of Southern Africa is to take the context arising out of the current situation into theological reflection. The following issues are especially pressing:

(1) The question of land in South Africa, Zimbabwe and Namibia needs immediate attention, for land has religious connotations in African religions. The fact that the Anglican Church in Southern Africa has began a process to intervene in the land crisis in Zimbabwe by volunteering to mediate between President Robert Mugabe and Prime Minister Tony Blair is a sign of hope.

(2) The issue of how to address poverty among the majority of the people of Southern Africa, caused by high unemployment, and made worse by acute shortages of food. Linked with the food issue is the debate over genetically modified grain that is being offered to Southern Africa from the Western world and the morality behind it.

(3) The issue of the sustainability of democratic governments in Southern Africa. Why is it that the Southern African presidents seem not to be able to rebuke each other when they fail to practise democracy? Can the church really continue to be prophetic and be the voice of the voiceless and call the governments to be accountable to its people?

(4) The question of how all the contextual theologies of Southern Africa unite in their fight against the HIV/AIDS pandemic. Can the theologians from Western countries be in solidarity with the African contextual theologians to mobilise for affordable drugs to stop unnecessary suffering and premature deaths of the African masses due to HIV/AIDS?

(5) There is an urgent need for the theologians of Southern Africa to engage with the politicians on the issues of African Renaissance and its suggested New Economic Partnership for African Development. We need

to know from a theological point of view what is good and what may
be wrong with these proposals for the majority African poor people.
The South African Council of Churches has already stated the process.
There should be a response from all the theologians of Southern Africa
as we are all going to be affected by it.

(6) Gender ought to be emphasised by all those doing theology in Southern
Africa. Some theologians, like Maluleke have argued for the importance
of encouraging constructive dialogue among the theologies of Africa on
the issue of gender. African women theologians want to see African male
theologians dialoguing with them in their writings, and to see this issue
on the theological curriculum. It is a deep injustice to African women
theologians for African male theologians to continue writing theology
as if African women theologies do not exist.

(7) The issue of the role of ancestors in the formation of an African Christian
identity has not yet been exhausted in South Africa, especially now in
the period of fragile unities between black and white churches. The fact
that the issue is threatening the unity of the Presbyterian churches in
Southern Africa indicates that there is still need for serious reflection on
the role of ancestors and Jesus Christ in the church in the new South
Africa.

REFERENCES AND FURTHER READING

Ackerman, D., Draper, A. and Mashinini, E. (eds.) 1991. *Women Hold Up Half the Sky*. Pietermaritzburg
Ackerman, D., Gateman, E., Cotze, H. and Tobler, J. (eds.) 2000. *Claiming Our Foot Prints: South African Women Reflect on Context, Identity and Spirituality*. Stellenbosch
Amanze, J. N. 1996/1997. 'Theology that has Already been Cooked in an African Pot' in Fiedler, K., Gundani, P. and Mijoga, H. (ed.), *Theology Cooked in an African Pot, ASTICA Bulletin* nos. 5 and 6
Boesak, A. A. 1978. *Black theology, Black Power*. London
Chakanza, J. C. 1998a. *Voices of Preachers in Protest: The Ministry of Two Malawian Prophets: Eliot Kamwana and Wilfred Gudu*. Blantyre
   1998b. 'Health and Healing: New Developments in Spirit Mediumship in Malawi' in Fiedler, K., Gundani, P. and Mijoga, H. (eds.), *Theology Cooked in an African Pot, ASTICA Bulletin* nos. 5 and 6
Chitando, E. 1998. 'What is in a Name? Naming Practices among African Christians in Zimbabwe' in Fiedler, K., Gundani, P. and Mijoga, H. (eds.) 1996/7. *Theology Cooked in an African Pot, ASTICA Bulletin* nos. 5 and 6
Dube, W. M. 2002. 'Fighting with God: Children and HIV/AIDS in Botswana' in *Journal of Theology for Southern Africa* 114 (November)

Gifford, P. (ed.) 1995. *The Christian Churches and Democratisation of Africa*. Leiden
  1998. *African Christianity: Its Public Role*. Bloomington
Gundani, P. H. 1998. 'Christology in the Inculturated Shona Burial in the Roman
  Catholic Church in Zimbabwe' in Fiedler, K., Gundani, P. and Mijoga, H.
  (eds.) 1996/1997. *Theology Cooked in an African Pot, ASTICA Bulletin* nos. 5
  and 6
Haddad, B. G. 2000. *African Women's Theologies of Survival: Intersecting Faith,
  Feminisms, and Development* Ph.D. thesis, University of Natal
Kairos document. 1985. *Challenge to the Church: A Theological Comment on the
  Political Crisis in South Africa*. Braamfontein
Kalilombe, A. P. 1999. *Doing Theology at the Grassroots: Theological Essays from
  Malawi*. Gweru
Katongole, Emmanuel (ed.) 2002. *African Theology Today*. Scranton
Kaufmann, L. T. 2001. 'The Good News for the Poor; the impact of Albert Nolan
  on Contextual Theology in South Africa' in Speckman and Kaufmann (eds.),
  Towards an Agenda for Contextual Theology, pp. 17–32
Kealotswe, O. 1998. 'Shadipinge Teaches Theology: Biblical Exegesis from an
  African Cultural Perspective' in Fiedler, K., Gundani, P. and Mijoga, H.
  (eds.), 1996/1997. *Theology Cooked in an African Pot, ASTICA Bulletin* nos. 5
  and 6
Landman, C. 1994. *The Piety of Afrikaans Women*. Pretoria
  1995. *Digging Up Our Foremothers: Stories of Women in Africa*. Pretoria
Louw Alberts and Frank Chikane (eds.) 1991. *The Road to Rusternburg: The Church
  Looking Forward to a New South Africa*. Cape Town
Maimela, S. and Konig, A. (eds.) 1998. *Initiation into Theology: The Rich Variety of
  Theology and Hermeneutics*. Pretoria
Maluleke, S. T. 1995. 'Black theology Lives! On a Permanent Crisis', *Journal of
  Theology in Southern Africa* 91, 1–30
  1995. 'Black and African Theologies in the New World Order. A Time to Drink
  from Our Own Wells', *Journal of Theology in Southern Africa* 96, 3–19
  1997. 'The Smoke Screen's called Black and African Theologies: The Challenges
  of African Women Theology', *Journal for Constructive Theology* 3/2
  2002. 'Rediscovery of the Agency of Africans: An Emerging Paradigm of Post
  Cold War and Post Apartheid Black and African Theology' in Speckman,
  M. T. and Kaufmann, L. T. (eds.), *Towards an Agenda for Contextual Theology*.
  Pietermaritzburg
Masenya, M. 2001. 'Polluting Your Ground? Woman as Pollutant in Yehud: A
  reading from a Globalised Africa' in Speckman, M. T. and Kaufmann, L. T.
  (eds.), *Towards an Agenda for Contextual Theology*. Pietermaritzburg
Mofokeng, T. A. 1988. 'Black Christians, the Bible and Liberation', *Journal of Black
  Theology in Southern Africa* 2, November, 21–34
Moore, B. (ed.) 1973. *Black theology: The South African Voice*. London
Mosala, I. and Thlagale, B. 1989. *The Unquestionable Right to be Free*. Grand Rapids
Nzunda, S. M. and Ross, R. K. 1995. *Church, Law and Political Transition in
  Malawi 1992–94*. Gweru

Parratt, J. 1995. *Reinventing Christianity: African Theology Today* Grand Rapids and Cambridge

(ed.) 1997 (revised edition). *A Reader in African Christian Theology*. London

Phiri, I. A. 1995. *Women, Presbyterianism and Patriarchy: Religious Experiences of Chewa Women in Central Malawi*. Blantyre

1997 'Doing Theology as African Women' in Parratt (ed.), *A Reader in African Christian Theology*, pp. 45–56. London

Reisenberger Azila (ed.) 2002. *Women's Spirituality in the Transformation of South Africa*. New York/Munchen/Berlin

Ross, K. R. 1995. *Gospel Ferment in Malawi: Theological Essays*. Gweru

(ed.) 1997. *God, People and Power In Malawi: Democratisation in Theological Perspective*. Blantyre

1998. *Here comes your King! Christ, Church and the Nation in Malawi*. Blantyre

Setiloane, M. G. 1986. *African Theology: An Introduction*. Braamfontein

Speckman, M. T. and Kaufmann, L. T. (eds.) 2001. *Towards an Agenda for Contextual Theology*. Pietermaritzburg

Toedt, E. (ed.) 1976. *Theologie in Konfliktfeld Suedafrika: Dialogue mit Manas Buthelezi*. Suttgart/Munich

Tutu, D. 1995. 'Identity Crisis' in Gifford, P. (ed.), *The Christian Churches and Democratisation of Africa*. Leiden

1982. *The Voice of One Crying in the Wilderness*. London

1991. *The Rainbow People of God*. London

West, G. and Dube, M. (eds.) 2000. *The Bible in Africa: Transactions, Trajectories, and Trends*. Leiden

Villa-Vincencio, C. 1994. *A Theology of Reconstruction*. Cambridge

Villa-Vincencio, C. and de Gruchy, J. 1985. *Resistance and Hope*. Cape Town

The Caribbean

George Mulrain

Geographically, the Caribbean is the region that lies between North and South America. It is the area often referred to as the 'West Indies', a name given to it after the mistake of Christopher Columbus, the fifteenth and sixteenth-century European explorer. When Columbus landed on one of the islands in the archipelago, he thought that he had reached India. Historically, the region is where firstly the Spaniards and later on other European powers had placed the slaves whom they had seized from the West African coast. Today, the Caribbean is populated mainly by descendants of Africans, Asians and Europeans. Four European languages are spoken, viz. English, Spanish, French and Dutch, but there are some languages that have been developed locally and orally due to the intermixing of the various idioms. There is, for example a Créole spoken in Haiti whose vocabulary includes words from French, English and some African languages. In Curaçao the Papiementu which is spoken has Dutch, French, Spanish and English words. There are variations of dialects (or patois) in some of the English speaking territories. The Caribbean also includes Guyana, on the South American mainland, mainly because that country shares a common history with the rest of the neighbouring islands.

This chapter acknowledges the road along which theology in the Caribbean has travelled. It examines past movements, current trends and forecasts the likely theological emphases that should arise as the twenty-first century unfolds itself. It adopts the stance that theology is about the understanding of God in relation to ourselves as human beings, as well as the understanding of ourselves in relation to God and to others. Theology is dynamic, not static. People have continuously been thinking about God, reflecting upon God and engaging in activities that are motivated by their faith in God. If this process is not taking place, then we find ourselves in a 'God is dead' situation.

ORAL THEOLOGY

One serious question that has been posed about Caribbean theology is whether it has seen its heyday. The query has come particularly from North American and European scholars who are interested in reading the different individual regional theologies, but have not been seeing on the world market many substantial contributions from Caribbean writers. Theological books from that part of the world seem to be few and far between. One can appreciate this concern about the absence of actual written texts and the fact that from Caribbean theologians, not much has emerged from their pens, typewriters, word processors and computers, the acid test of theological enterprise in a world context.

The truth is that Caribbean scholars and theological thinkers have been producing material. Indeed, Caribbean theology, heavily berthed in the oral tradition, has continued to be. Belief in the Supreme Being is widespread. Men, women and children across the region meet together, according to their preferred faith traditions, to offer prayers and praises to God. As Caribbean historian Dale Bisnauth once remarked: 'The Caribbean is a laboratory of world religions.' The theological enterprise within the Caribbean is not confined to Christians, but is inclusive of Muslims, Hindus, Jews, Rastafarians and others who meet for worship in their appointed places at their appointed times. In Christian churches, sermons have been preached from Sunday to Sunday across the region. In Muslim mosques, worshippers gather every Friday to acknowledge that their lives as well as the lives of their loved ones are being lived in submission to Allah, God Almighty. Mothers have spoken daily of God to their children, assuring them that God is worthy of all their trust. Men and women have been acting out their faith in various spheres of existence, in the home, in the work place, in their shopping, in recreational activities. The theologising, though, is not limited to activities that are carried out in 'holy' places. To quote from a book entitled *Emancipation Still Comin'* by Kortright Davis, a Caribbean theologian to whom reference will be made further in this chapter:

the real theologizing among Caribbean people is done orally, narratively, and informally . . . the real theological workshops in the Caribbean are the homes, the fields, and the street corners, rather than the seminaries or the churches. In other words, while written theology struggles, oral theology flourishes. (Davis, 1990, 93, 94).

Caribbean culture is indeed an oral one. Apart from the oral languages mentioned earlier, there is oral literature comprising the numerous proverbs, riddles and folk tales that are used to instruct persons about life issues. There is the oral music with which the region is familiar. Its rhythms are not easily reproduced on the traditional musical score. To appreciate what a Caribbean composer intends, one must hear the piece performed *live*. There is oral medical science within the region, since most herbal and other folk remedies known within the Caribbean have not been codified and written up in books, but continue to be transmitted from parent to child to grandchild by word of mouth.

Folk religion is yet another expression of the oral culture. Preference in this religious context is for narrative styles in communicating truths about the faith, as opposed to dogmatic, didactic, philosophical teaching styles. One has to remember that the biblical cosmos did resemble to a great extent the cosmos of the Caribbean. In the Old Testament world, for example, it was well known that God communicated to the prophets through dreams and visions. In Caribbean folk religion these media are still employed as tools of communication between the physical and spirit worlds.

THEOLOGY AND COLONIALISM

The 1960s saw the virtual end of the colonial era within the Caribbean. This was the time when Fidel Castro's Cuba was allied to the Soviet Union. Castro said a firm 'no' to attempts at American control. During this time there was an experiment in the formation of a federation among the ten English speaking territories. This had officially started in 1958. However the experiment collapsed and in August 1962, Jamaica and then Trinidad and Tobago proclaimed themselves to be independent territories.

The Caribbean Conference of Churches (CCC) was inaugurated in 1973. It was through the CCC people understood that 'being Church' meant engagement with and involvement in local communities. The *Caribbean Contact*, a journal supported by the CCC, not only contained news about what was taking place, but it featured articles by editors and columnists like Rickey Singh who were not afraid to question the *status quo* in the name of Christ. Until that time, the dominant feeling among Christians had been that you did not openly question those in political authority. If you did it as private citizens, that was acceptable, but you should not do it as members of the Church. However, theological thinking was able to move on to a more radical level through such new trends in Christian literature.

The period of the 1970s witnessed a wealth of theological writings, evidence that the people of the Caribbean were intentionally engaged in theological reflection. The name of Idris Hamid will long be remembered as one of the pioneers in this field. His provocative essay, *In Search of New*

Perspectives, published in 1973, was a much needed stimulus for Christian theologians to begin to think of themselves as products of the Caribbean region and not as carbon copies of Christians from European churches. From then on, there was a noticeable shift in emphasis in so far as religious pronouncements, verbal and written, were concerned. Hamid not only reflected theologically and wrote books, but he assembled and published several articles from thinkers across the region. Among these were *Troubling of the Waters* which appeared in 1973 and *Out of the Depths* in 1977. Many of the theological treatises that surfaced had to do with development, liberation and mission, and the role of the Church in such enterprises.

The 1970s and well into the next decade saw a body of Caribbean theologians who dealt with issues of colonialism and neo-colonialism. The book *With Eyes Wide Open* edited by David I. Mitchell (1973), brought together some stimulating articles by renowned Caribbean theologians including Roy G. Neehall, Michel de Verteuil, Alain Rocourt, Arthur J. Seymour, Robert Cuthbert and Fitzroy Allan Kirton, all of whom helped to provide an education on what it meant to be both Christian and Caribbean. Philip Potter's observation in the book's Foreword is worth quoting: 'When Christopher Columbus landed in the Caribbean he planted the cross as one of his first acts. But it was the Arawaks and Caribs, and the blacks and later white, Indian and Chinese indentured labourers who bore that Cross for centuries' (Mitchell, 1973, 5).

DECOLONISING THEOLOGY

Decolonising theology was treated in Noel Erskine's book of the same name (Erskine 1981) and William Watty's book *From Shore to Shore* (Watty 1981). To decolonise theology meant stripping it of its westernised mould, its Eurocentric character and incarnating it in a Caribbean context. Theologians of the region would therefore be free to think of God, to engage in God-talk and to interpret the Scriptures, in full awareness of the cultural context in which they lived and moved and had their being. The writings of African American and Latin American theologians on the theme of liberation meshed in well with concerns that were held by Caribbean people who were products of a history that included slavery. The decolonising of theology meant that Caribbean people were free to theologise and talk about those things that were not simply churchy matters, but to concentrate upon politics, economics, development, justice, peace, indeed worldly things. These became theological concerns, because they had to do with how persons interacted with one another in God's world.

Kortright Davis furthered reflections on the idea of Christian involvement in development through his book *Mission for Change: Caribbean Development in Theological Enterprise* (Davis 1982). George Mulrain's book on *Theology in Folk Culture* (Mulrain 1984) was an attempt to highlight how folk religion having its roots in Africa could cause persons to reflect upon God in unique ways. The concept, for example, of a God who can be encountered in individuals' wrestlings with spirits and the Spirit cannot lightly be dismissed. In fact, in the Haitian historical experience, God is indeed interested in the political liberation of people. Of equal interest to Mulrain was the use of calypso, a distinctive Caribbean cultural facet, in the work of biblical exegesis and hermeneutics. In practice this was to involve taking the spiritual realm seriously. Calypsonians, for example, sang about encounters that mortal beings had with spirits. This has implications for pastoral theology. Do we dismiss every manifestation of 'spirit' as being the product of some psychiatric disorder? Must every report of demon possession be subsumed under the name of neurosis? A full treatment of this issue appears in *Voices from the Margin* (Sugirtharajah 1995, 37–47).

The emphasis on liberation as a theme in Caribbean theology continued well into the start of the nineteen-nineties. Kortright Davis' book on *Emancipation Still Comin'* that came off the press in 1990 was for long to be the almost lone authority on theology within the region. In the meantime, there had been efforts by other theologians to flag up related themes.

What is noticeable about the early development of liberation consciousness within the Caribbean region is that a number of artistes, chiefly singers, tended to include lyrics that pointed in the direction of freedom. The celebrated calypsonian, Slinger Francisco, known as the Mighty Sparrow, held up the education system to ridicule with his rendition of 'Dan is De Man in De Van'. The calypsonian is someone who is politically alert. The subtle challenge that he or she gives to the authorities is similar to that of Jesus to the rulers of his day. The calypso is more than just a song. It has a subversive role to perform, often giving a profound analysis of the society, hence exercising a critical role, which is theological. Sparrow's argument was that unless the education is relevant to the needs of the people, then it is worth little or nothing. The great reggae superstar, Robert Marley who was influenced by Marcus Mosiah Garvey, is remembered for the words: 'Emancipate yourselves from mental slavery, none but ourselves can free our minds.' Almost everywhere in Caribbean song, there seemed to be an expressed interest in liberation theology.

The people of Francophone Caribbean had been well ahead of their Anglophone counterparts. The French Revolution that took place in 1789 had highlighted the cause for *liberté*, as proclaimed by the Jacobins. They emphasised the value of land ownership. In Haiti, it was *The Black Jacobins* (C. L. R. James' book was so named) that issued a reminder of the importance of property. On 14 August 1791 at the ceremony of Bois Caiman in Haiti, there began some twelve years of struggle that culminated in the country's independence from France in 1804. If the people of the French Caribbean were enthusiastic about political freedom in the eighteenth and nineteenth centuries, it so happened that in the twentieth they were very much in the forefront of mental freedom. Jean Price-Mars' book 'Ainsi Parla l'Oncle' appeared in 1928. Aimé Césaire of Martinique, in his writings of the 1930s made a distinctive contribution to the growth of *Négritude* (Black Consciousness). Frantz Fanon's book of 1952 *Black Skin, White Masks (Peau Noire, Masques Blancs)* could be classified as a document to fight against racism and fascism worldwide. True liberation of the mind was deemed important for total liberation.

EMANCIPATION STILL COMIN'

The dying stages of the twentieth century saw the Caribbean building up an interest in liberation as a theological theme. As spelt out by one Caribbean theologian (J. Emmette Weir 1991) the main principles of Caribbean liberation theology are as follows:

(i) It should be clearly identified with the struggle of the poor and oppressed

(ii) It must take into account the reality of the Caribbean society

(iii) It must begin with a careful analysis of its socio-economic context and not with the delineation of biblical and philosophical verities

(iv) It must be a political theology involved in the transformation of society.

If Weir spoke about 'liberation', it was Kortright Davis who spoke about 'emancipation' which he described as the Caribbean word for liberation. In his writings, Davis articulated effectively the essence of 'emancipation':

Emancipation is for Caribbean people a strong emotive word, connoting that spirituality of freedom which they are pursuing. The word 'liberation' does not offer as much. 'Emancipation' links us existentially with the struggle of our slave ancestors, since we are the inheritors of that struggle; it also keeps before us the strongest warning away from the bondage to which God wills that we should never return. In Caribbean terms, 'emancipation' is the word that tells us and the world that 'Massa day done'. Slavemasters are no more, nor are there to be slaves anymore. (Davis 1990, 102–3)

Davis' contention is that emancipation is still an event to be fleshed out, structured, refined and reinforced in the Caribbean system. Emancipation includes the ability to forge political links with whomever the people of the Caribbean want. One of the features of the Grenada revolution in 1979 was that Maurice Bishop had allied with Fidel Castro, an alliance that was frowned upon by the United States. Jamaica's Michael Manley in the 1980s established diplomatic ties with Cuba and was equally despised by the USA for so doing. As long as Caribbean foreign policy is dictated from outside, the region cannot claim to be free.

The people of Haiti were among the first set of Caribbean folk who tried to 'flesh out' their emancipation. Haiti's Roman Catholic Churches placed great emphasis upon Liberation Theology as evidenced, for example, in the *ti légliz*, their equivalent to Latin American base Christian communities. From the pulpits of Protestant churches, there were sermons preached on the need for the people to enjoy true freedom, something that the majority of preachers felt could not easily be done as long as the Duvaliers kept the power. Local radio stations, some of them sponsored by churches, were equally critical of the regime. During a historic visit to Haiti, the Pope John Paul II was recorded as saying 'things must change here'. The Catholic priest, Jean-Bertrand Aristide assumed the leadership of the country, but spent most of his legitimately elected period of time in exile. It is ironical that at the time of writing this chapter (December 2002) Aristide is now in power, but the masses are crying out that true freedom has not yet been attained. The exodus from Haiti continues as those who try to escape from the harsh realities of life there sneak out of the country in tiny little boats, bound particularly for the United States. Many such Haitians have turned up as illegal immigrants in the Bahamas and Jamaica and have been sent back home without being considered for refugee status. There are sad stories of the hundreds whose corpses are found floating in the sea, evidence that yet another crowded boat overturned and went under. There are thousands of Haitians who have nevertheless made their homes in the United States. Until the entire region is free, emancipation will not be a Caribbean reality. Hence emancipation is, according to Davis, *still comin'*.

NEW EMPHASES IN THE NEW CENTURY

The experience of newness is not always a sudden event. It is a gradual process, one that grows out of the old. It is a creation out of what has already been in existence. The new is the result of building upon knowledge

of the present, and creatively implementing relevant structures and features
for the future. One of the old practices that ought to continue is the singing
of calypso and reggae, but with the understanding that fewer songs should
be created on love, sex and violence. Enough of those are already in existence in the region. Caribbean artistes should also be discouraged from
performing songs that degrade women. The government of the republic
of Trinidad and Tobago was applauded when it took the decision during
the 1990s that North American artistes who use swear words during public
performances were to be prosecuted and eventually banned. Herein lay
signs of a desire for *clean* entertainment to be a characteristic of the new
century. In this way, artistes will have the challenge of being prophetic
and speaking to the people, through their songs, about things that continue to enslave Caribbean people – drugs, crime, violence and classism.
The fact that Caribbean youth in particular tend to hero-worship pop
singers would emphasise how important it is for artistes to be proper role
models.

The composition of hymns in calypso and reggae style should be encouraged as this is an important exercise in contextual theology. The names
of Barry Chevannes, Noel Dexter, Richard Holung (Jamaica), Paschal
Jordan (Guyana), Patrick Prescod (St Vincent) and Pearl Mulrain (Trinidad
and Tobago) are among those whose musical contributions have helped
Caribbean persons to appreciate that in the offering of worship, that which
is produced locally is acceptable to God.

One area that needs exploring more fully is the use of artistic expressions
in worship. There is a wealth of artistic talent in the Caribbean as evidenced,
for example, when one visits the craft markets in places like Kingston
(Jamaica) or Port-au-Prince (Haiti). Working from the premise that all of
one's gifts should be utilised in the service of God, then certainly paintings
and sculpture ought to feature more prominently as authentic tools for
doing theology. The Episcopal Cathédrale Sainte Trinité in Haiti is one
of those sacred buildings that has above the altar a series of paintings that
portray different scenes from the life and ministry of Jesus. There is the
Wedding Feast of Cana in Galilee and the Baptism of Jesus by John in
the River Jordan, just to mention two of them. These scenes are definitely
reflective of the Haitian cultural context. For example, in the painting of
the wedding, there is a boy who is running to catch the rooster, quite typical
of Haitian country life. In that of the baptism, there are women doing their
washing, unconcerned about any other event that might be taking place
in the river. In churches other than Sainte Trinité, there are beautifully
sculptured wood carvings depicting the Last Supper and the Crucifixion.

These all contribute towards the creation of an atmosphere that is conducive to the worship of the God who became incarnate in Christ. Indeed, the presentation of biblical material in painting and sculpture can help more persons to appreciate that what is being communicated through the pages of the Scriptures has to be relevant to the cultural context in which they live.

GETTING RID OF SLAVERY

The Caribbean region, despite its independence, is still dependent on hand-outs from the United States. There is the phenomenon in Jamaica of 'barrel kids'. These are the children of those who have migrated and who await the arrival of barrels containing items of food, clothing and other supplies that have been shipped from their loved ones abroad. The region cannot easily boast of being self-reliant, because there is much reliance upon the generosity of others. One needs to get rid of the dependency syndrome that is plaguing the Caribbean. Naturally there are those who cherish the easy way, namely having a *fairy godmother* or a *sugar-daddy* to provide for them. There is also the lure of quick money to be had from involvement in drugs. The mentality seems to be: Why work, why exert oneself, why sweat it out if there's an easy way? Why bother to try and get an education if in the long run there are no prospects of jobs or money?

Emancipation is still to be fleshed out. Part of the fleshing out process involves Caribbean people convincing themselves that they *can* do it. The signs of the time are there. Organisations from Europe have been withdraw-ing the grants that have helped to support the region's institutions. The new day that is dawning brings with it new responsibilities. The Jamaica National Children's Home, for example, is facing the challenge as to how it can survive purely through the initiatives of people on the local scene. Churches are awaking to the fact that they must institute new ways of financing their operations quite apart from the offering plates and begging bowls. Their finance and development committees are experimenting with projects that are financially viable. Their property committees are debat-ing whether or not they can use some of their resources of property to invest and to provide the assets that are required for the continuance of their missionary efforts. Caribbean Christians have suddenly realised that what obtained in the eighteenth or nineteenth centuries, when mission was regarded as being what rich Europeans and North Americans did in the poor 'third world', no longer holds good in the twenty-first century. Mission is what the people of God do in any part of the world, including their own. As such, 'third world' people have to take full responsibility for the growth and development of mission within their own context.

Signs of mental slavery have taken their toll on the inhabitants of the region. For too long Caribbean people have been involved in belittling themselves. They see themselves as being overshadowed by the larger countries in Europe and the United States. The ordinary man or woman in the street would speak in glowing terms about foreign persons whom they read about in the newspapers, but very disparagingly about local individuals. Products that originate within the region are still looked down upon and considered to be inferior to those coming from abroad.

What about taking pride in self and in one's identity? When one listens to the talk shows on local radio stations – talk shows being no doubt something that has been copied from the United States – one hears several callers talking plainly. However the plain talking that one gets seems to reflect a feeling that Caribbean people are no good. Whereas one ought to applaud the freedom being expressed, namely freedom to speak out and to be critical of self, there must be a balance struck. After all, Caribbean people are not all that terrible. Surely there must be some good in them. It would mean that men, women and children cease to apologise for their presence, for this has been one way of saying that others from outside are better, indeed superior to those from within the region.

In countries like Jamaica and Trinidad and Tobago, there is more talk about 'bigging up' persons, which is another way of saying that the people recognise themselves as a people of worth. In common with other persons from poorer parts of the world, Caribbean people do get tired of confessing how sinful they are. There needs to be a greater effort at affirming themselves as made in God's image and likeness and that there is much pride and dignity attached to being who they are. In the Rastafarian movement, there is always reference made to 'I and I', which is virtually a self-affirmation technique wherein the Rasta declares his or her linkage with God, the great, eternal I. There is now a general tendency to reject the underdog status that characterised the region's ancestors, as more persons take pride in affirming themselves. This is not arrogance. Arrogance would be when the Caribbean man or woman acclaims that he or she alone is great, whilst everyone else from the rest of the world is of no importance.

Self-affirmation demands that pride be taken in one's environment. No longer should one be satisfied when those who have been placed in political power allow roads to deteriorate. There ought not to be so many potholes, that within weeks of driving on them, the motorist is forced to expend money on shock absorbers and front-end parts. The goal for the environment must be one in which there is no littering on the streets, but they are well swept and kept tidy. Politicians have to be called to accountability, especially those who receive fat salaries but deliver little or nothing. Justice is being called for from both public and private sectors. In the domain of trade and commerce, justice is called for in so far as the prices being paid for items in the shops are concerned. It is no wonder, for example, that Jamaicans who can afford the trip will occasionally board a US-bound flight to go and to do their shopping in Miami. Equality of opportunity for all is something that is not yet a reality about which Caribbean people can boast. Part of the answer has to do with the ability of the countries of the Caribbean to provide goods and services for all at reasonable prices.

RELEVANT EDUCATION SYSTEM

It must be admitted that the Caribbean has come a long way from the 'Dan is the man in the van' days about which calypsonian the Mighty Sparrow sang in the sixties. The education system is now more geared to respond to Caribbean realities. The setting up of a Caribbean Examinations Council (CXC) is one of the ways whereby indigenous educators started taking account of the lived environment of the people. In the past, only London and Cambridge Universities' GCE examinations were allowed. Their subject matter was geared towards candidates from the United Kingdom, thereby placing Caribbean students at a serious disadvantage. Now they have the opportunity to read the writings of Caribbean novelists such as V. S. Naipaul. The region's own local historians, such as Eric E. Williams, have taken their rightful place in academic circles with their historical accounts being read alongside those from abroad that offer the perspective of foreign authors.

The Church has itself been making useful contributions in producing for its Sabbath and Sunday Schools literature with which children can identify. The CCC series *Fashion Me A People* (Bailey 1981) written by local Christians, has been of tremendous value. However the material has not been as widely appreciated as hoped. Apart from this, more editions are needed, otherwise the material will be glaringly outdated. One thing that will constitute a tremendous boost is if the region were to have more facilities for the publication of Caribbean material. Unfortunately, the CCC's Cedar Press that used to put on the market so much of the indigenous Christian

Education and theological productions, folded up in the late 1980s. Its place has not effectively been taken, as many would-be writers do not feel encouraged as they would have been with the CCC, to make approaches to foreign publishers who might not have the Caribbean high on their priority lists.

The advent of other universities beside the University of the West Indies (with its three campuses in Jamaica, Trindad and Tobago and Barbados) has meant that more of the region's youth population now have access to education beyond the secondary level. Tertiary institutions themselves will have to play a more leading role as creative solutions are sought for some of the region's problems of development. For example, given the fact that the Caribbean enjoys sunshine almost on a daily basis, science and engineering faculties at the universities need to encourage continued experimentation with solar power, especially as oil cannot be expected to be an everlasting source of energy.

EMANCIPATION AND THE INTER-FAITH CONTEXT

One aspect of emancipation that is often overlooked is that of inter-faith cooperation. Christians still have a fear and a suspicion of persons of other religious persuasions, including Islam and Rastafarianism. It is no doubt the effect of what has happened in places like Indonesia, the Sudan and Nigeria, countries that have a history of religious intolerance. Fear and suspicion are developing in places like Guyana and Trinidad and Tobago, where Hinduism and Islam thrive alongside Christianity. The inter-faith scene is crucial especially because of its racial implications, namely the fact that the majority of persons who are Muslims and Hindus are of Indian origin whereas those who are found in the Christian denominations are mainly of African origin. The people of Trinidad and Tobago still have a fear that the same group of Muslims under the leadership of Abu Bakr, will try once more to stage a coup that would overthrow the constitutionally elected government of the nation.

Working with people of other faiths challenges one to be creative in inter-personal relationships. One interesting suggestion is that where two or more religions have celebrations linked to a common theme, there should be some form of merger. In practice, for example, Divali, the Hindu festival of lights, would merge with the idea of Christmas, the festival celebrating Christ as the light coming into the world. The idea is revolutionary and requires more corporate reflection if it is to result in action that is geared towards better relationships among people of different faith traditions.

This new brand of theologising within an inter-faith context that is being suggested is crucial to the survival of Caribbean people.

Mention might also be made of the challenge to engage in new ways of doing hermeneutics. It is being floated as an idea that the Bible, the Qu'ran and the Bhagavad Gita can all be read and revered as the sacred writings of the majority of the Caribbean's people. Caribbean people will have the advantage, in pursuing the discipline of hermeneutics, of making use of the various scriptural and theological lenses that are available. No attempt should be made within the given situation to discredit one or more of these bodies of scripture. In fact, the republic of Trinidad and Tobago has as its expressed wish in the national anthem that 'here every creed and race find an equal place'. In practice this has meant among other things giving equal radio time or mass media time to all religions. It is also a fact that many of the nations in the region express through their watchwords and mottos the idea that unity is to be cherished as a positive feature of Caribbean life. Examples of this are 'Together we aspire, together we achieve' (Trinidad and Tobago), 'L'union fait la force' – Unity is strength (Haiti); 'Out of many, one people' (Jamaica).

AFFIRMING MANY ROOTS

One reality that Caribbean people must acknowledge is the indebtedness to the original homeland of the majority of the inhabitants. The Caribbean is a blend of several cultures, a mixture of many races, a people who speak several languages – English, French, Spanish, Dutch, Créole and Papiementu. Some Caribbean people have come from Africa, some from India, some from Europe. While not despising any, the people of the region ought to make an effort to be affirming of the mixed cultural roots in positive ways. For example in worship, in addition to the calypso and reggae hymns mentioned earlier, there can be the use of Hindi *bhajan* songs. There can be the use of some of the *parang* songs that are popular around Christmas, songs that have come about through the Spanish heritage. Dance is a cultural facet that has been a contribution of both Africa and India. Experiments in dance have been few and far between. Perhaps more pronounced in current Caribbean worship is an emphasis on the region's proximity to the United States. The 'praise in worship' slot in many churches is the time when predominantly American gospel choruses are sung. Perhaps it is good that there is something positive coming out of the USA to hold up to people, because when some Caribbean persons think of the American influence it is usually the negative effects of television violence, perverse sexual displays, and so on. On the American presence, the question being asked is how can the offerings of that culture be more creatively used.

What about affirming Caribbean culture by using, during 'praise in worship' time, not only North American and European offerings but Caribbean choruses as well? It is not the suggestion here that only Caribbean music is to be affirmed. There is such a wealth of global music from all over the world. As much use as possible should be made of what is on offer, thereby making the important point that when one comes to worship as a Church one is a member, not simply of the local congregation, but of a World Church. All are the people of God in God's world – a world of many different languages, cultures, and peoples. But even as experiments are made with the different songs, one must not forget the expressive arts that can enhance worship. In addition, there needs to be a sincere attempt to bring about a renaissance of the Carib and Arawak ancestry of the region. These tribes were virtually wiped out through European invasions from the end of the fifteenth century. It is now a justice issue. Since there are some small communities that trace their ancestry to these Amerindians, it would be helpful if attempts were made to ensure that they are not a forgotten people within the region's history.

HOPE

The people of the Caribbean region are God-fearing. They know that their destiny lies with God. One of the positive features coming out of this culture is the emphasis on hope. There was a popular political slogan that surfaced in Jamaica particularly during the 1980s around election time: 'better mus' come'. Although this was expressive of a hope that the next party elected into power would do better than the one that currently held office, it also is the articulation of a deep-seated belief among the people that somehow whenever they are faced with difficulties, God will swing things in their favour. The conviction seems always to be that better days are coming when they will be able to rise up victorious.

This hope expresses itself even in the face of disaster. The little island of Montserrat, plagued as it is by volcanic activity, is an example of the manner in which Caribbean people suffer. They are constantly reminded of their vulnerability. Yet, there is the determination on the part of the majority to submit to what is perceived to be the will of God. It is hope that causes this. It is not fatalism or resignation; it is hope. Every year, for example, one can expect hurricanes to strike somewhere in the region. The sort of hopefulness that is being referred to was seen in Jamaica in the aftermath of hurricane

Gilbert that ravaged the island during 1988. The lyrics that emerged from the mouths of the reggae singers were not expressive of despair. On the contrary, they inspired persons to be positive about the situation and in spite of adversity, to rebuild. In some cases, the lyrics inspired laughter as for example in Lloyd Lovindeer's song:

> Water come eena mih room, mih sweep out some wid a broom
> De little dog laugh to see such fun, an' de dish run away wid de spoon.
> Unno see mih dish, unno see mih dish, Anyone unno see mih satellite dish?
> Mih dish tek off like flyin' saucer, mih roof migrate without a visa
> Bedroom full up o' water, mih in a de dark, no light, no water,
> An' through mih no have no generator. Mih say one col' beer cost ten dollar,
> Mih fish an' mih meat spoil in de freezer,
> A pure bully beef full up mih structure.
> Full o' bully beef, ful o' bully beef,
> Mih cyan get fi cook so mih full o' bully beef.

The folk from the Caribbean have this ability to laugh in the face of seemingly hopeless situations. This is not merely a mechanism of defence. In actual fact, it is the reflection of a theology that spells out hope in God. Even though people walk through the valley of the shadow of death, they will not fear. They will keep their minds fixed on God because they believe, just as the psalmists, that God is on their side. God will fight on their behalf in order that the enemies might be defeated. It is the hope, too, which amplifies the people's determination not to remain as victims, but to do whatever is humanly possible to ease out of difficult situations.

From the vantage point of hope, Caribbean people are better able to cope with suffering. Of course, what one makes of the disaster of September 11, 2001 is still not clear. Like everybody else, Caribbean people also have struggles to understand evil, especially that which is inflicted upon persons seemingly at the hand of God. Although there are not thoroughly convincing answers to the plight that is faced, Caribbean people hold on to a hope that there must be some answer to the question of evil. The Christian message seems to make sense, namely that God allowed Jesus Christ, the beloved Son, to suffer. So why not those who claim to be equally God's children!

WOMEN COME OF AGE

The region has truly seen women come of age. It is not that they were incapable, but rather that their male counterparts preferred not to let them advance. The situation has changed drastically from what obtained

yesteryear. The fact is that women are making significant contributions
to the life of society within the region. They are now more high profile in
leadership positions. At least two territories – Dominica and Guyana – have
had a woman as head of state. The graduates from the tertiary institutions
including the University of the West Indies, are mostly women.

More theological insights are needed from the women of the region.
There are increasing numbers of women entering the United Theological
College of the West Indies with the intention of pursuing a full time career
within the Church. The College has more women pursuing courses in counselling. At the time of writing this chapter (December 2002), the Principal
of St Michael's, the Roman Catholic Theological College in Jamaica is a
woman – Dr Theresa Lowe-Ching, a liberation theologian. The Dean of
the United Theological College of the West Indies (UTCWI) is a woman –
Mrs Fay Rodgers-Jenkinson. The person who heads the Graduate Studies
programme at UTCWI is Dr Hyacinth Ione Boothe, a woman who constitutes a source of encouragement for women to write and to be active
in the theological enterprise. With this significant presence of women in
the ranks of theological academia, it is to be expected that more theologies from women will be forthcoming. One woman theologian, Dr Diane
Jagdeo, lecturer at the Roman Catholic Seminary of St John Vianney and
the Uganda Martyrs in Trinidad, suggested that there might be other current ways of imaging God, for example as *enchantress* or *seductress*. Her
contention is that unless we can appreciate God as the One who myste-
riously draws people towards the Supreme Being, there will be very little
credibility being attached to God as being worthy of human worship and
adoration:

A Church that is too cerebral easily becomes self-righteous and arrogant. It leaves
no room for fantasy, imagination and thus for the mystical within us to flourish. A
Church that distorts the reality of the enchantress, which women embody, cannot
conjure up the passionate love that is necessary to evoke life. Yet, the Church's
mission is to evoke and offer the fullness of life to all peoples. Our interior life
craves charm and fascination. It is a natural movement to God who is mystery.
And God lures us constantly into being and becoming. (Jagdeo 2002, 36)

Theologies produced by women in the United States have influenced
Caribbean women. However there has been the suggestion that the women
of the region are more 'womanist' than 'feminist' in orientation. Rightly or
wrongly, feminists have been accused of being so 'pro' feminine that they
give the impression of being 'anti' masculine. Womanists, on the other
hand, are viewed as persons who are not in opposition to, but are rather in

a partnership role with men. They emphasise mutual need – women need men, men need women. Caribbean women suggest that this idea has been ingrained in them from small seeing that they grew up in the homes very close to brothers and sisters. The gender roles were then emphasised – girls did this, boys did that. This was healthy, because it produced a focus that is communitarian rather than individualistic.

INFORMATION TECHNOLOGY

The twenty-first century is a time when more persons are making use of the offerings of information technology. This means that the Church has to get in on the act and be a part of the global network. Churches and other religious bodies have been establishing their own websites. Theological colleges in the region are advertising themselves in cyberspace. Possibilities are seen for communicating the Gospel via the Internet, for disseminating knowledge, for carrying out counselling sessions even on a one to one basis. This means, among other things, that there is a new type of Church emerging. It is a Church wherein the laity are being empowered particularly because the clergy have come to realise that they are not omnipotent, but that the gifts of the Spirit are imparted to all and sundry. The Church is acknowledged as being more than just a worship centre on Sundays, but an entity that is totally committed to and involved in the building up of community. The notion that the reign of God must be among us has to start with the immediate context, namely in local communities. This is why the ranging skills of the people of God are so important. Financial skills, computer skills, whatever there is, will be of value in God's employ.

CONCLUSION

The contention in this chapter has been that the process of emancipation in the Caribbean has not yet been completed. The road to be travelled is still a long, winding one with many twists and turns. There are numerous problems to be tackled before it can be claimed that the region ranks among those of the 'first' and 'second' worlds. HIV/AIDS has become a serious concern, having reached epidemic proportions in the region and having implications for the social, cultural, psychological and religious lives of the people within the region. However, it must be stated in the concluding paragraph of this chapter that being 'third' world does not mean that the theological insights of the people are third rate. In fact, whatever is shared about God from this or any other part of the world for that matter contributes significantly to the total theological picture. As human beings, we can better understand God in so far as we remain open to learn from what persons in other cultural contexts have to share out of their own experiences of God.

REFERENCES AND FURTHER READING

Bailey, Joyce (ed.) 1981. *Fashion Me A People*, A Curriculum for Church Schools Series, Caribbean Conference of Churches
Bisnauth, Dale. 1989. *History of Religions in the Caribbean*. Kingston
Boothe, Hyacinth I. (2001). *Breaking the Silence: A Woman's Voice*. Kingston
Davis, Edmund. 2002. *Beyond Boundaries: Identity, Faith and Hope Amidst Fear and Insecurity*. Jamaica
Davis, Kortright. 1982. *Mission for Change: Caribbean Development in Theological Enterprise*. Bern
    1990. *Emancipation Still Comin': Explorations in Caribbean Theology*. Maryknoll
Dick, Devon. 2002. *Rebellion to Riot: The Jamaican Church in Nation Building*. Kingston
Erskine, Noel Leo. 1981. *Decolonizing Theology: A Caribbean Perspective*. New York
Fanon, Frantz. 1967. *Black Skin, White Masks*. New York
Gregory, Howard (ed.) 1995. *Caribbean Theology: Preparing for the Challenges Ahead*. Kingston
    1973. *In Search of New Perspectives*. Barbados
    (ed.) 1973. *Troubling of the Waters*. Trinidad
    (ed.) 1977. *Out of the Depths*. Trinidad
Ibekwe, Patrick. 1998. *Wit and Wisdom of Africa: Proverbs from Africa and the Caribbean*. London
Jagdeo, Diane. 2002. 'Women's Contribution in Transforming the Caribbean Church' in *Groundings*, Special Issue. Jamaica, St Michael's Theological College Publication
James, C. L. R. 1963. *The Black Jacobins*. New York
Manuel, Peter, with Bilby, Kenneth and Largey, Michael. 1995. *Caribbean Currents: Caribbean Music from Rumba to Reggae*. Philadelphia
Mitchell, David I. 1973. *With Eyes Wide Open*. Barbados
Mulrain, George M. 1984. *Theology in Folk Culture: The Theological Significance of Haitian Folk Religion*. Frankfurt
Mulrain, George. 1995a. 'Is there a calypso exegesis?' in Sugirtharajah, R. S. (ed.) *Voices from the Margin*, pp. 37–47. Maryknoll
    1995b. 'African Cosmology and Caribbean Christianity in Sankeralli, Burton *At the Crossroads: African Caribbean Religion and Christianity*, pp. 46–65. Trinidad and Tobago
    1999. 'Hermeneutics within a Caribbean Context' in Sugirtharajah, R. S. (ed.) *Vernacular Hermeneutics*, pp. 116–132. Sheffield

2000. 'Religion and Plurality in the New Millennium: A Caribbean Perspective' in Wickeri, Philip L., Wickeri, Janice K., Niles, Damayanthi M. A. (eds.) *Plurality, Power and Mission: Intercontextual Theological Explorations on the Role of Religion in the New Millennium*. London

Mulrain, George, Kimbrough, S. T., Jr, Young, Carlton R. 2000. *Caribbean Praise*. New York

Price-Mars, Jean. 1973. *Ainsi Parla l'Oncle*. Quebec

Smith, Ashley. 1984. *Real Roots and Potted Plants: Reflections on the Caribbean Church*. Jamaica

Taylor, Godfrey, Campbell, Claudette, Flemming, Dolores. 2002. *Let Us Sing: Hymns, Songs and Choruses for Caribbean Schools*. Kingston

Watty, William. 1981. *From Shore to Shore*. Kingston

Watty, William W. and Gayle, Clement H. L. 1983. *The Caribbean Pulpit*. Barbados

Weir, J. Emmette. 1991. 'Towards a Caribbean Liberation Theology', *Caribbean Journal of Religious Studies* 12, no. 1 (April)

Williams, Lewin L. 1994. *Caribbean Theology*. New York

Postscript
The challenge of third world theologies
John Parratt

What then is the challenge of the new approaches to Christian theology which have arisen from the Third World? Primarily, of course, as all the contributors to this volume have emphasised, they are theologies which take the context extremely seriously as a source for theology. What is new here, as Bonino points out, is that context is made quite explicit as a ground for theologising, and plays a major role in setting the theological agenda. They are also a sharp reminder that theology should essentially be communication, both to those within the Christian circle but also to those outside. This should perhaps cause us to question whether much modern theology, with its obsessive intellectualism and its over use of elitist language, has not become so introverted as to be unable to communicate itself effectively outside the circle of professionally trained theologians. One of the most remarkable things about the course of Christian theology in India was that, in its initial stages, its leaders were laymen who had no formal theological training. This did not prevent men like Chakkarai and Chenchiah producing some profound theological innovations which utilised the framework of the Hindu worldview familiar to their readers. Sundar Singh (who had very minimal seminary training, which he found of little value to him) expressed his theology in the even more popular form of parable and story. The Dalit reaction, when it came, saw even the use of Hindu forms as oppressive and alien to the experience of most Indian Christians. Its language (like that of Korean Minjung theology) is direct (if at times somewhat repetitious) and draws on oral story and testimony. What we have here (and in contrast to the dense abstruseness, not to say unintelligibility, of too much academic theological writing) is a serious attempt at directness and communication with those who are outside the boundaries of technical theological discourse.[1]

---

[1] In respect of the language of theology an important issue is that much written theology in Africa and Asia (though by no means all) is written in English or French, and in South America in Spanish and

In Africa and the Caribbean, and in marginalised communities elsewhere, as our authors point out, theology is essentially oral, expressed in song, prayer, group discussion and story. And indeed there is no alternative to this in countries where literacy rates are often very limited. Art forms and dance may also be utilised to express Christian insights and experiences. These may be no less profound than those found in a weighty tome of systematic theology, for theological insight is not the prerogative of the literate only. This is perhaps the rediscovery of 'popular Christianity', which barely gets a look in in most theological discussion, but is indeed today challenging Christianity in Europe and America in the astonishing growth of both the Pentecostal and Black churches. While such oral theology may be difficult to pin down and sysematise, it has increasingly become a rich source for the literate and 'academic' theologian. Seen in this way written theology becomes (as Liberation theologians have pointed out) in part a second order activity, which is intimately related to the life and experience of ordinary Christians.

The best of Third World theology, however, does not restrict itself only to the church. It also takes account of the concerns of society as a whole, making them central to doing theology. In India M. M. Thomas (a scientist by training) was a pioneer in seeking to relate the Gospel to the secular and political issues in wider Indian society. Liberation Theology has argued that the proper concern of theology is the poor, and some would claim that it is the poor (rather than the church) who are the proper people of God, and that their experiences, fears and hopes are the proper agenda for theology today. Thus the concern of Christian theology is not simply Christians but the world.[2] That the theological task is about the basic human condition has perhaps nowhere more movingly been portrayed than by Manas Buthelezi, for whom a cardinal concept was that of 'true humanity'. Writing under an oppressive apartheid system, Buthelezi's question was how Africans could attain the true humanity given to them both in creation and redemption

---

Portuguese. This might suggest that it too is elitist. While there is some force in this argument, two points need to be kept in mind. Firstly, in countries with multiple indigenous languages one or other of these European languages is often the language of secondary (and sometimes primary) education, and therefore acts as a means of communication which transcends tribal and ethnic differences. Secondly, published works in the vernaculars are increasingly being produced, though (except for the chapter on East Asia) it has not been possible to give any detailed coverage of this in the present book. Significantly study groups, often predominantly lay, read the Bible in the vernacular languages, and their grass roots theologising finds its way into the more academic published work of Third World theologians. The Base Ecclesial Communities are perhaps the best, though by no means the only, examples of this.

[2] See Rowan Williams' comment on Bonhoeffer's secular Christianity *On Modern Theology* (Oxford 2000), 104 note 20.

under a political system which seemed to deny them this very possibility.[3] An equally burning issue now, both in Southern Africa and the Caribbean (as Isabel Phiri and George Mulrain argue) is how one may speak of God and his love to societies crippled by HIV/AIDS. Here the task of theology is to reconcile heaven and earth, to make the Gospel of life relevant to and transformative of the situation in which all men and women find themselves. The raw materials for theology are thus to be discovered as much in sociological analysis as in the more traditional sources of Bible and Christian history. Culture, society, politics and economics become central to the theological task.

Not that the traditional sources are ignored. It is evident, however, that these sources are seen with new eyes and used in a new way. This is nowhere more apparent than in the use of the Bible. Group discussion of the Bible, predominantly lay, was pioneered in the Base Ecclesial Communities, and there are numerous examples of the way this method worked in new ways of reading and understanding the scriptures.[4] Modern hermeneutical trends which emerged in the West – feminist readings, reader-response approaches – similarly have in general not simply been taken over in the Third World, but rather have been adapted, often with quite drastic modifications, to suit the appropriate contexts. This radical re-reading of the Bible is the more remarkable in that in many Third World countries a basically conservative attitude to the Bible remains widespread.

There is, of course, a plurality within Third World theologies, as there is (whether acknowledged or not) in all theology.[5] The many and varied clothes (to use Brahmabandhav Upadhyaya's imagery) in which the Christian faith is apparelled in its various geographical contexts, does indeed raise the question of what kind of 'naked body' of Christian truth there is beneath these changing clothes and of how it may be defined. This task is made all the more difficult (and perhaps impossible) since we each perceive this body of Christian truth through the lenses of our heritage and thus cannot avoid dressing it up in our own particular cultural clothing. There is no neutral position, and in this respect theologians in Europe and America have no advantage over those anywhere else in the world. All our theological efforts are culturally and contextually conditioned, whether we

---

[3] *Ansaetze Afrikanischer Theologie im Kontext von Kirche in Suedafrika* in Else Toedt (ed.) *Theologie im Konfliktfeld Suedafrika* (Stuttgart 1976), 33–132.
[4] A classic study is Carlos Mestos, *Defenseless Flower* (Maryknoll 1989); also R. S. Sugirtharajah (ed.) *Voices from the Margins* (London 1991).
[5] David Tracy, in his *Blessed Rage for Order* (rev edn. Chicago 1996), remarks that the ever increasing pluralism in theology is now 'a truism'; his understanding of pluralism though is entirely Western.

choose to acknowledge this explicitly (as most Third World theologians do) or not. The global nature of Christian theology today should then lead us to question – with a large dose of the hermeneutic of suspicion – the approach to Christian theology which has largely been accepted in the Western world since the Enlightenment, and which is to a large extent still claimed, implicitly or explicitly, to be universal. The irruption of Third World theologies in our own day has opened up a new theological epistemology, an alternative way of seeing the world as the context within which theology is to be done. It has brought theology back to its original purpose, as not simply reflection in detachment, but as reflection from within commitment. It has raised questions which force the theologian out of his or her philosophical and linguistic ghettos and into the public places where faith has to interact with culture and religions, with society and politics.

In his *Atoms and Icons* Michael Fuller writes as follows:

The scientific quest is not for fact, for complete knowledge of what is 'out there' – that is something we can never know. It is rather a quest for an ever more accurate *model* of what is out there; for a greater verisimilitude in our understanding of reality.[6]

The theologian is engaged in a similar task. God, as all theologians acknowledge, is ultimately unknowable. We perceive him only through the lenses of our experience, shaped as it is by the genealogy, tradition and context within which we stand. What Third World theologies have given to us is a richer variety of models with which to understand God and the world, models which grow out of the experiences of others with different genealogies, traditions and contexts. The global spread of Christian theology gives us deeper and more varied insights into the meaning of God and the world drawn, as the visionary writer of the Book of Revelation has it, from 'every tribe, tongue and people'.

[6] Michael Fuller, *Atoms and Icons* (London 1995).

Index

7